NATURAL
DOG CARE

NATURAL DOG CARE

Dr. Bruce Fogle

A DK PUBLISHING BOOK
www.dk.com

A DK PUBLISHING BOOK
www.dk.com

Project Editor Tracie Lee Davis
Art Editor Anna Benjamin
Managing Editor Francis Ritter
Managing Art Editor Derek Coombes
DTP Designer Sonia Charbonnier
Picture Researcher Angela Anderson
Production Gavin Bradshaw, Wendy Penn
US Editor Chuck Wills

First American Edition, 1999

2 4 6 8 10 9 7 5 3 1

DK Publishing, Inc.
95 Madison Avenue
New York, NY 10016

Library of Congress Cataloging-in-Publication Data
Fogle, Bruce.
    Natural dog care / by Bruce Fogle. — 1st American ed.
        p.   cm.
    Includes index.
    ISBN 0-7894-4124-1
    1. Dogs. 2. Dogs — Health. 3. Dogs — Diseases —
Alternative treatment. I. Title.
SF427.F6155   1999
636.7—dc21   98-31210
                                                      CIP

Reproduced by Bright Arts, Hong Kong
Printed and bound in China by
L. Rex Printing Co., Ltd.

Contents

INTRODUCTION

THE EVIDENCE IS IRREFUTABLE. Dogs are living longer than ever before. Changing social attitudes towards dogs, a better understanding of their behavior, and the successes of modern veterinary medicine have reduced unnecessary accidents, virtually eliminated some parasitic and infectious diseases, and created treatments for conditions that in the past were almost always fatal. Yet, paradoxically, our interest in less orthodox, less scientific therapies has never been greater.

CONVENTIONAL VS. COMPLEMENTARY

Conventional vets have always recommended preventative as well as illness-oriented care but today, as pet owners pursue personalized approaches to their own well-being, there is a rapidly maturing interest and understanding of complementary forms of therapy, treatments that attempt to stimulate the body's self-healing and self-regulating mechanisms. Both conventional and complementary forms of veterinary medicine have the same objective – to enhance a dog's ability to heal itself. Their approaches, however, have been different. Conventional or orthodox medicine tends to treat a specific system or organ, while complementary vets deal with the dog as a whole, considering illness to be a disruption of physical and mental well-being. They will often treat the whole body rather than targeting one specific part of it.

AN OPEN MIND

In this book I've used American veterinarian Carvel Tiekart's definition of medicine. He says it is "anything that works." In human medicine, the placebo effect – genuine improvements that occur for non-physical reasons – benefits about 40 percent of patients in any individual study. This evidence suggests that it is important to keep an open mind about therapies that we have not previously tried. Just because we can find no logical reason for a therapy to work, it does not follow that it will not have a beneficial effect.

THE PLACEBO EFFECT

Can dogs experience a placebo effect? Drs. Brenda Bonnett and Carol Poland at the Ontario Veterinary College, University of Guelph, in Canada, discovered a possible answer in a study of different medical treatments for canine arthritis. At 10 veterinary clinics throughout southwestern Ontario, vets dispensed four different treatments for dogs they had diagnosed with arthritis. The treatments all looked similar but their contents were different. The dogs were given one of the following: aspirin, a traditional Chinese herbal

BREEDING FOR THE FUTURE
Selective breeding has unwittingly increased medical problems in virtually every breed of dog. Breeding for unnatural characteristics such as hairlessness increases disease risk.

CONVENTIONAL
SUCCESS
*Sophisticated medical
procedures save the lives
of countless dogs. Use these
facilities to create the best
circumstances for your dog's
body to repair itself. Always
consider the quality of your
dog's life when deciding
what therapy is best.*

medicine formulated for arthritis, a North
American Native herbal formula for arthritic
pain, or simply gelatin capsules containing whole
wheat and rice flour – a placebo. Neither the vets
nor the owners nor, of course, the dogs knew
what was in the capsules. When the vets and
dog owners assessed responses to treatment,
around 40 percent of both groups felt their dogs
(or patients) improved on the placebo capsules.

GOOD RESEARCH STUDIES

In human medicine, approximately 40 percent
of patients respond to any new form of therapy,
probably because, like dog owners and vets,
they want new treatments to work. We should
bear this in mind when considering the value of
any new therapy. In the Ontario study, equally
fascinating was the fact that although the response
to the Native American medicine was the same
as to the placebo, the improvement on the Chinese
herbs (and also on aspirin) was greater than the
placebo. These results suggest that, for some dogs,
Chinese herbs are an effective form of therapy.

HISTORICAL REMEDIES
*Historical therapies should not be simply replaced by modern drugs.
The World Health Organization and the American Veterinary
Medical Asssociation both recognize that acupuncture alleviates
pain associated with the most common forms of joint disease.*

HOW TO USE THIS BOOK

When reading this book, remember that your
dog is a dog. It is not a human in disguise. What
works for you may not be appropriate for your
dog. For any therapy ask, "Will this stress my
dog? Does it work? Is it safe?" Don't ignore
successful orthodox treatments in favor of
unproven alternatives just because they fit your
personal or spiritual values. Understand the
nature of illness and how your dog responds to
it. Help your pet to avoid illness, and to be in
the best condition to confront it when it occurs.

Almost 150 years ago, the physician Dr. Albert
Schweitzer said that a good doctor awakens "the
physician within." Understanding your dog's
responses to health threats and using the best of
the many therapies available can help release the
"physician within" your canine companion.

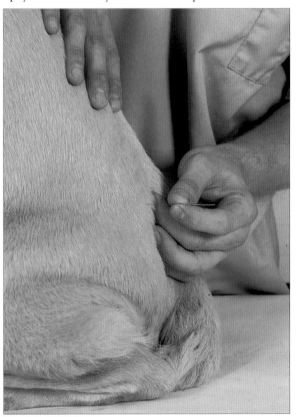

Natural Development

If you want to care for a dog in the most natural way
possible, it is important to understand its emotional
needs and development. The dog is a pack animal, just
as sociable as we are, and is self-domesticated – its
wolf ancestors actively chose to live close to human
habitation. It was the dog's choice to be relaxed in our
company, a desire we have intensified through selective
breeding. The dog remembers its early lessons best and,
like us, retains a lifelong interest in and enjoyment of
playful activities. With the right care from their
owners, dogs can now live into old age, reaching
their maximum genetic life potential.

Throughout its life, the dog retains its early love of play.

EARLY DOG DEVELOPMENT

THE DOG WAS THE FIRST ANIMAL that we "domesticated," and although its domestication was a key to our successful domestication of other species, we did not coerce it into living in servitude to man. The dog's immediate ancestors, the northern wolves, actively chose to live in close proximity to our ancestors. The relationship was once mutually beneficial, although it is not necessarily so today.

WOLF BLOODLINES
Genetically, the domestic dog is virtually identical to the wolf and probably descends mostly from Asiatic wolves. Recent genetic evidence suggests that some breeds of dog, such as the Alaskan Malamute pictured here, have bloodlines that are inherited predominantly from the timber wolf.

A NATURAL FRIENDSHIP

It has been repeated so often that it has become a cliché, but it is true that of all the animals that live on this planet, the dog is our best friend. It is in the dog's nature to enjoy living with another species that willingly provides it with food and a safe home. In return, the dog provides us with constancy, utility, and unalloyed affection.

This is a chance relationship, a very recent accident of evolution in which the best interests of both humans and wolves converged and were best served by cohabitation, both in terms of group security and food-gathering potential. For most of its history, this relationship has remained beneficial to both species, but in recent years people have imposed unnatural standards upon dogs, standards that have sometimes inadvertently promoted undesirable genetic characteristics. In aiming for breed "perfection," we have taken some breeds so far from their natural form that their viability is under threat.

THE DOG'S TRUE ORIGINS

The spontaneous relationship between dogs and people evolved when our ancestors became agrarian, dramatically altering the natural world. A new and unique ecological environment developed. Land around long-term human occupation sites was heavily exploited by the human community. Wolves were attracted to this new environment by the ready availability of human refuse and the absence of natural predators. The land provided protected breeding sites. These new environmental factors favored the survival of wolves that were relaxed when in close proximity to one of their natural competitors.

All hunter-gatherer societies that survive today show a curiosity about other animals. Wild animals are kept for the amusement of the community, and young animals in particular are enjoyed. In ancient times, some of the wolves, probably pups captured for food, were permitted to live in the human settlement. Most were used as food or fabric but some survived, perhaps because of their looks or perhaps because of the wolf pup's ability to transfer allegiance from one pack leader to another. In time, successful wolf breeding occurred within the settlements. For the first time, pups were raised from birth within the human community.

GROUP BEHAVIOR

Our willingness to develop a relationship with the wolf's descendant, the dog, comes from our shared social instincts. Although physically very different, people and dogs share a surprising variety of common social behaviors. Both species are gregarious and inquisitive, not only about others of our own kind, but about other animals too. We share common social signals, using similar body language to display our feelings. Both species have extensive facial muscles that are used to dramatic effect to portray our emotions. Like dogs, we cower when confronted by superior force and, like dogs, we snarl and show our teeth when we aggressively confront danger. We actively enjoy relaxing with our own kind, especially our extended family, and instinctively protect our family and our home.

Dogs and people are both naturally territorial. We both have resting places and hunting territories that we aggressively defend from others of our own kind. We are both omnivores, willing to taste and eat almost anything. Equally important, both species are naturally "neotenized." We retain a childlike curiosity about the world around us throughout our lives. Even when they reach adulthood, both people and dogs enjoy play virtually as an end in itself.

CONTROLLING NATURE

For thousands of years, our ancestors bred from those dogs that showed a natural inclination to perform in ways that were useful to the human community. A trait such as increased barking was valuable and these dogs became community alarm dogs. Docility and rapid weight gain made for a reliable source of food. Strength and innate protectiveness resulted in good guard dogs. Swiftness of foot and keen eyesight created superb hunting companions. Out of natural abilities developed the origins of all of today's variety of dogs.

THE BIOLOGY OF LOVE

Robert Sapolsky, Professor of Biological Sciences at Stanford University, says that, "Something roughly akin to love is needed for proper biological development." A mother's willingness to protect her young under the most adverse circumstances is a manifestation of what Professor Sapolsky calls biological love. Dogs still provide this biological love for their young but too often the type of young they have are of our choosing, not theirs. Some breeders look upon dog production as a business, but in regions of the world with a long tradition of companion-dog breeding, such as Scandinavia, northern Europe, North America, Australia, and New Zealand, it is my experience that the majority of dog breeders do what they do because they have a feeling "roughly akin to love."

URBAN LATCHKEY DOGS
Throughout the world, especially in urban communities, groups of "latchkey" dogs can be seen roaming together. Most often, these dogs spend time with their adopted pack during the day and return home to their owners for food. A group of latchkey dogs does not have a natural pack structure.

In the last millennium, humans have intervened in the dog's development even more extensively. With the advent of Kennel Clubs, variations in dogs were taken to extremes. Breed descriptions were written that unfortunately promoted these extremes; legs as short as possible, heads as big as possible, coats as fine as possible, ears as long as possible. But our desire for aesthetic perfection was at odds with nature. We produced breeds appealing to the eye but sometimes unnatural in body and spirit. We produced dogs that cannot survive without our help.

It is true that some dog breeders look upon dog production as a business, but the majority are deeply concerned about the welfare of their dogs. Unfortunately, because physical looks are so important, even loving breeders lose sight of what should be their true objectives. Unnatural features of dogs, the excesses of selective breeding, should be diminished, not enhanced. Developments such as the amputation of ears or tails, mutilations that serve only human vanities, should end. In a caring community of dog breeders, future canine developments should promote a return to a more natural range of diversity.

GENETIC DEVELOPMENT

Until recently, breed development has been "by eye," but with our increasing knowledge of canine genetics we will be able to finely tune looks and even behavior. While ethical controls will hopefully exist for human genetic manipulation, similar controls are equally necessary in canine genetics.

MATING, PREGNANCY, AND BIRTH

SELECTIVE BREEDING HAS RESULTED in dogs reaching sexual maturity earlier in life and females ovulating twice as frequently as their wolf forebears. Females can be particular and choose to mate with a third party while more dominant members of the pack vie for her favors. Even when not successfully mated, a female will still experience a full hormonal "phantom" pregnancy.

MOTHER LICKS
All mothers clean their pups at birth, stimulating them to urinate and defecate by licking their anogenital area. Some mothers, in particular Bull Terriers, sometimes carry this natural grooming to an unnatural extreme, licking, nibbling, and then actually eating their pups. Mount a watch for the first 24 hours on all Bull Terrier litters.

NATURAL MATING
The male dog is sexually active at all times and is attracted to the scent of any female in season. Females usually ovulate (come into season) twice a year. In a wild pack, when a female ovulates, a ready supply of males is available for mating. The successful male will mate with her several times and the likelihood of pregnancy is high.

Dogs have a curious adaptation to their breeding behavior. During mating, a swelling develops in the middle of the male's penis that physically prevents him from withdrawing from the female. They are "tied" together, often for 15 to 45 minutes. To protect themselves, the male swings his hind leg over the female so they remain rump to rump,

VACCINES DURING PREGNANCY
At birth, a pup inherits protection against any disease to which its mother has been exposed. Maternal antibodies against disease are passed on to the pup in the first mother's milk it receives, the colostrum. This protection, however, is only short-term: its duration varies from as short as six weeks to as long as 20 weeks. Vaccinate before pregnancy to boost maternal antibodies. Never vaccinate a bitch once she is pregnant. During pregnancy her immune system may not respond well to inoculations. Avoid vaccinating any other dogs that are kept in the same house as a pregnant female. Vaccine virus can be shed by these dogs and passed on to the mother-to-be.

physically inseparable but able to defend themselves if necessary. The evolutionary reason for this phenomenon is unknown but it is perhaps a way of the male ensuring his own progeny by preventing other males from mating with the receptive female.

Because matings are repeated and sperm can live for seven days in the female's genital tract, pregnancy almost always follows.

A NATURAL DEN
This pregnant bitch has found a secluded den in which she can deliver and raise her pups in maximum security. Her close ancestor, the wolf, would also do this. Given the opportunity, some dogs, especially terriers and other earth dogs, will "go to ground," co-opting another animal's den as its nursery.

NATURAL DEVELOPMENT

NATURAL TRAINING

NATURAL NUTRITION

NATURAL HEALTH CARE

HEALTH DISORDERS

THE FIRST TRUE PACK
Dominant/subordinate relationships are first learned when pups compete for teats, and are well developed by the time a pup leaves what is often its only true canine pack, and joins a new pack, its human family.

PREGNANCY AND FALSE PREGNANCY

Unlike that of any other domesticated species, the hormonal cycle of the bitch assumes pregnancy even when she has not mated. A female who shares your home is unlikely to mate every time she comes into season, but she will still experience the two-month "pregnancy" with attendant physical and mental changes. Her ovaries produce the pregnancy hormone progesterone even if her eggs have not been fertilized, and this causes her to produce milk and will also lead to an increase in her appetite. For some bitches this false pregnancy can even include a degree of mild labor two months later.

During false pregnancy a female can experience a dramatic variety of mood and sensory changes. My Golden Retriever has taste changes and rejects her usual food in favor of a blander diet of bread or rice. Nearing the time when she would give birth she will become restless and go off her food. Within 48 hours her behavior returns to normal and remains so until her next season.

INFLUENCES IN THE WOMB

For those bitches that are genuinely pregnant, the emotional and physical development of pups begins in the womb. Through his research at Harvard University, Dr. T. Berry Brazelton has shown that human infants are influenced in the womb by their mother's lifestyle: what the mother eats and the emotions she experiences will affect the development of the fetus. The same applies to pups, and in species such as the dog there is an additional influence of behavior — where a pup finds itself positioned in the womb, and who are its neighbors. Pups in the middle of each horn of the uterus are likely to receive the best nutrition. Female fetuses that develop between two males are believed to be bathed in tiny amounts of male hormone, which may predispose that female to develop a slightly masculinized brain and a more dominant personality.

BIRTH AND AFTERWARD

You will need to provide your pregnant bitch with a whelping box lined with newspaper, which is large enough for her and her puppies to be comfortable, and high enough to prevent the pups from escaping. A day or so before going into labor your bitch will refuse her food and seek out the whelping box. In dogs with "average" anatomy, birth is usually uncomplicated. The bitch goes into labor, produces her pups, then consumes the afterbirths and the pups' body waste in order to hide any evidence that vulnerable newborn are present.

For some breeds, selective breeding has led to complications in birth and after. This is exemplified by Bulldogs, who may give birth to pups with heads too large to pass through the birth canal. Yorkshire Terriers often give birth to pups so big they must be delivered by Caesarean section. Dalmatian litters can be so large that the mother cannot produce enough milk for all her pups. These problems have been created by our intervention in dog breeding. In a caring environment we should ensure healthy birth by breeding not for large litters and pups, but for ease of birth, and litter sizes that mothers are capable of caring for naturally.

CHECKLIST

- Do not even think of breeding from your bitch unless you know that you can find homes for the resulting litter.

- There is a popular myth that it is kind to let a bitch have just one litter before she is spayed. Dogs do not think of what might have been. Pregnancy brings with it increased medical risks.

- Only breed from females who are emotionally as well as physically mature.

- Have your vet check both the male and female for the presence of known inherited diseases.

- Offer balanced nourishment to the mother while she feeds her pups. Good nourishment is necessary for their proper development.

EARLY LEARNING

COMPARED TO US, the speed with which a dog develops mentally is phenomenal. Abilities that take us years to develop, a pup assimilates in weeks: physical dexterity, the importance of relationships, right from wrong. In the wild, early learning is essential for survival as a member of the pack. The lessons that a pup learns early in life, especially from birth until three months of age, last a lifetime.

CHECKLIST

- Ensure that mothers are "emotionally competent" to raise their pups.
- Do not expect the mother to do all the upbringing. It is your responsibility to ensure that pups are well socialized before they leave your home.
- Do not isolate young pups. Handle them frequently and expose them to mild sensory stimulations.
- Think of how the pup will live as an adult. Introduce different species early in life.
- Plan ahead. Early lessons are learned and retained. Like us, learning is more difficult in maturity.

MOTHER'S INFLUENCE

Learning is thought to begin in the womb. A mother that is stressed during pregnancy is more likely to give birth to young who grow up to be fearful, have reduced ability to learn, and suffer from extremes of behavior. Once the pups are born, the mother-pup relationship becomes one of care and dependency. The mother licks the pups and licks her own nipples, leaving a natural chemical trail for her pups to follow. For the first three weeks of life, the pups are entirely dependent upon their mother.

After three weeks, when the mother walks away from, growls at, or otherwise threatens her suckling pups, they have their first lesson in compromise, the basis of the successful pack and of the dog's relationship with us. When a mother snarls at a pup, the pup learns, not fear, but rather how to live with others' needs and desires.

A CHALLENGING ENVIRONMENT

Wolves the same size as dogs have larger brains than their domesticated cousins. One of the reasons for the dog's shrinkage in brain size is the "unchallenging" life a young pup leads. An unchanging environment is not in a pup's interest. Mild stresses early in life influence both brain development and hormonal control of emotions. In classic experiments conducted over 25 years ago, the veterinarian Michael Fox gently stimulated young pups with clicking sounds, lighting changes, frequent handling, and exercise on slight inclines. Later in life these "stressed" pups solved detour problems faster than pups raised in an unchallenging environment. Early mental stimulation accelerates body growth, reduces emotionality, and may even increase resistance to certain diseases.

CRITICAL TIMING

Until recently, early learning was divided into "critical periods," crucial time slots in the emotional development of pups. Pups develop their social manners between three and 12 weeks of age. During this time, if a pup frequently meets a member of another species it will develop a social rapport with that species. This is at the very heart of the relationship we have with dogs.

FACE LICKING
Mother introduces her pups to solid food by regurgitating a meal she has eaten previously. The pups induce her to do this by jumping up to lick her lips. Many dogs perpetuate this juvenile behavior into adulthood by jumping up and trying to licking their owners' faces.

If a dog does not learn, at this early stage, how to live in harmony with us or with other animals, natural fears or natural forms of aggression can develop. But while it is true that this is a critical learning period for a dog's social development, there is now good evidence that these are guideline figures only. Although it can be difficult, older dogs retain the ability to learn new social lessons.

RELATIONSHIPS WITH US

If you want a pup to mature into a dog that is at ease in our society, you cannot leave it to nature. If you leave all early learning to the mother and let her raise her litter on her own, the pups learn to respond to other dogs rather than to people. Some people feel that by interfering with nature in this way, we are enslaving dogs and perverting their natural inclinations to our own purposes. This may well be true of our interventions with truly wild animals but lacks any validity with dogs. The dog as a species exists to live in harmony with us. Its success depends on its ability to live in and contribute to human society.

HOW PUPPIES LEARN

Pups learn by watching what mother or littermates do, by trial and error experience, and, most important to a good relationship with us, through training. Pups between approximately five and 12 weeks of age learn reasonably well by observation, especially of their mother, but experience is always the most potent engine of brain development. It is during this sensitive stage that a puppy

must make its first visit to the vet. If I handle it roughly, stick something cold and hard in its rectum, then stab it in the back with a sharp weapon, can you blame it for learning that veterinary clinics are fearsome places? If, on the other hand, I let it sniff new odors, meet a healthy, relaxed "clinic dog," and offer it a food treat while I carry out my examination, it is more likely to learn that the clinic is at least benign. The pup is conditioned to accept visits to the vet.

NATURAL REWARDS

Food is the most potent natural reward, and one I use to help pups learn that visiting the vet can be fun. In feral conditions, a mother dog finds a meal, consumes it, and returns

"The dog as a species exists to live in harmony with us. Its success depends on its ability to live in and contribute to human society."

to her den where the pups beg by licking her mouth. In response to their begging she rewards them by regurgitating the meal. Pups and mature dogs attempt to do the same with us, trying to lick our faces when they greet us. Touch is also a potent reward and physical play, chewing, and attention from mother and other littermates all encourage early learning. Fortunately, so too do sounds. Pups learn from early experience with mother and littermates that soft sounds are positive and harsh growls are negative. Tone of voice is powerfully important when training your dog.

HIDDEN INFLUENCE

A dog's behavior is influenced by genetics as well as training, and this is true even within breeds. For example, dominance aggression develops in female English Springer Spaniels by eight months of age, but not until 35 months in males.

HARMONIOUS LIVING
If you have a cat, your pup should ideally meet cats routinely during its socialization period between three and 12 weeks of age.

LIVING WITH OTHER ANIMALS

Dogs naturally look upon small furry animals as prey. Stalking, chasing, grabbing, and shaking are natural behaviors, which is why the most common dog toys are soft and squeak when chewed. You can diminish this natural inclination by introducing a pup at an early age to its natural prey. By doing so you ensure that it treats that species as a member of its extended family.

NATURAL DEVELOPMENT

NATURAL TRAINING

NATURAL NUTRITION

NATURAL HEALTH CARE

HEALTH DISORDERS

NATURAL PLAY

YOUR DOG'S DESIRE TO PLAY is one of its most endearing qualities. Play is an essential ingredient of a dog's life and begins in the litter. During those first weeks, through play with mother and littermates, a pup learns about social relationships, develops communication skills, and practises all the physical and mental activities needed by a predator that historically had to capture its own meals.

SEX AND DOMINANCE
Mounting during play is a sign of social dominance. Pups test each other as they develop a social hierarchy. Although male pups are more likely to mount littermates, possibly because their brains were "masculinized" in the womb by male hormone, dominant female pups also play in this way.

CHECKLIST
- Play is essential for natural development.
- It stimulates physical dexterity and mental flexibility.
- Play permits experimentation under safe conditions.
- Play teaches problem solving.
- Play teaches a pup how to carry out sequences of events.
- Play is a natural lifelong activity in dogs.

YOUTHFUL PLAY

Your dog's closest relative, the wolf, is an inherently playful animal. In the wild, naturalists have watched wolves play "king of the castle" and "tug-of-war" with each other for hours at a time. Like us, both wolves and dogs continue to enjoy play throughout their adult lives. Behaviorists call animals that carry juvenile behaviors into adulthood, "neotenized." The wolf is a naturally neotenized species, and through selective breeding we have exaggerated this natural wolf behavior in the dog, creating perpetual puppies. Like us, the dog has an enjoyment of play that lasts a lifetime.

THE IMPORTANCE OF PLAY

Playful activity is fun, but it is also good schooling and molds character. Through trial and error, pups learn to communicate with each other. Playful behavior also predicts, to some extent, whether a pup is naturally dominant. Dominant playful activity in puppyhood is a firm predictor of dominant behavior later in life.

Play begins in the litter when pups are about three weeks old. The litter is a complex, but in the dog's case temporary, society. Lessons learned in this context are transferred to the pup's new human family when it is taken from its litter to live with us. We have no difficulty interpreting the puppy's invitation to play – the "play bow" – because it is an inviting call to activity. This invitation is taken up by a littermate or mother, and later us. Play is physically and mentally exhausting. Pups will play with each other then abruptly stop and snooze.

LEARNING MANNERS

During play, puppies learn manual dexterity, how to grasp with their forepaws, the effectiveness of shoulder slams, the advantage of momentum, the power of the "top dog." They also naturally learn how to inhibit their biting. Dogs use their mouths to capture and kill prey. As adults their jaw muscles are impressively powerful. During play a puppy learns how to control these powerful weapons. If, for example, a pup "jaws" its mother too hard, she reprimands it by nipping back. If the pup "jaws" another pup too severely and hurts it, the

CONSTRUCTIVE PLAY

Uncontrolled play can be worrisome for dogs. Intervene constructively and channel your pup's enjoyment of play into creative activities. With your vet's approval, arrange for your pup to meet other pups under controlled circumstances. Remember, puppies denied playful activity with other pups during the important months after leaving the litter forget their social manners. Puppy parties (*see pages 26-27*) are ideal for training pups, through play, to exercise willingly in common areas such as parks and to play with other dogs. Your dog's enjoyment of social encounters later in life increases through controlled play activities.

hurt pup squeals in pain and stops playing. To stop playing and ignore the miscreant is potent discipline and is at the root of how we can control youthful exuberance when we train dogs (*see pages 32-33*). In these natural ways puppies learn their canine social graces.

THE BEGINNINGS OF RELATIONSHIPS

Youthful play develops a puppy's physical skills and deflects natural aggression into enjoyable and benign activities. It is the way puppies develop relationships with each other. Through play, pups develop a hierarchy. They test each other through play-fighting, usually inhibiting their bites but using strength to test the limits. Natural play introduces puppies to cooperative behavior. Two pups may stalk a third. Both may chew on the same twig or play tug-of-war. Inherent differences in personalities become obvious. With experience, pups learn these differences and incorporate this understanding into their play. To perpetuate playful activity, a naturally dominant pup may learn how to "play submissive," to "accidentally" fall down, permitting the lower-ranking dog to physically dominate it. Pups learn the art of compromise.

Through natural play a puppy also learns the value of threat. Chases, ambushes, and pounces can all be fun, but watch a pup's body language carefully and you will see when play is used to threaten another pup. The dominant pup places its paw on the other's back, it stares directly with dilated pupils, its hackles may be up, and it lifts its lip, snarls, and shows its weapons. There is an intensity to this activity that is missing in relaxed play. The pups are learning the importance of power, and how to express it through body language.

LESSONS FOR LIFE

Puppies use information gained through play to position themselves in their social order. Within the pack, play establishes which dogs are confident and which are dependent individuals. If you play tug-of-war with your puppy and let it growl and win, your pup learns not only that growling wins, but that it can dominate you. Poorly thought-out play such as this, like poor schooling for us, can lead to problems later in life. Channel your dog's desire to play into constructive and safe activities for its future emotional and physical well-being.

NATURAL HUNTERS
By stalking, chasing, and pouncing on each other, puppies develop the coordination and mental flexibility for the hunt. During play-hunting and fighting all activities are slightly exaggerated, carried out with more exuberance than during the real thing.

NATURAL DEVELOPMENT

NATURAL TRAINING

NATURAL NUTRITION

NATURAL HEALTH CARE

HEALTH DISORDERS

18

NATURAL GROOMING

AS SOON AS YOU HAVE FINISHED grooming your dog, it is likely to engage in its own grooming. The reason is simple. While you groom your dog to improve its appearance, your dog keeps its coat tidy for more pragmatic reasons. The skin is the dog's first line of defence. Natural grooming stimulates and invigorates the skin's defences and reduces risks from parasites, yeasts, and bacteria.

APPLYING PERFUME

Just like us, dogs love to cover themselves in attractive smells. While we think that perfumed soaps and lotions smell pleasant, dogs are attracted to more natural perfumes such as dead fish, or the droppings of other animals. Wolves also behave this way and it may be their method of masking their scent in order to improve hunting prospects.

GROOMING TECHNIQUES

After a good meal, some dogs ritually rub one side of the face then the other against any available absorbent fabric, such as the sofa. Others spend their time chewing their nails or inserting their dewclaws in their ears then licking them. These are intelligent, self-taught grooming techniques and are simply variations of natural grooming methods. All dogs use four standard grooming techniques to care for their skin: licking and nibbling, scratching and rubbing, rolling, and shaking.

LICKS AND NIBBLES

The teeth and tongue are a dog's natural grooming utensils. From early puppyhood, dogs intuitively tackle their basic grooming needs with licks and nibbles. The action is cleansing but also soothing and comforting, which is why dogs find petting and gentle brushing comforting. Both activities have a physiological effect on a dog. With gentle strokes, a dog's state of arousal diminishes, its heart rate and blood pressure drop, and its skin temperature lowers. Sometimes, when a dog licks itself, it slips into a gentle reverie. Licking becomes slow and rhythmic. It may relax so much its tongue stops in mid-lick, glued to its leg. Nibbling is more active. The incisors are used to give a "needle massage" to the skin. The skin is

SCENT MARKERS

Dogs use scent to mark their territory and although urine is the most obvious scent marker, chemicals in the anal or scent sacs are equally important. Each time a dog passes a stool, muscles around the anus contract, anointing the droppings with scent-sac essence. Other dogs sniff this scent and information is transmitted. Such important scent-marking glands need frequent grooming. Small dogs discharge blocked anal sacs by dragging their bottoms along the grass, carpet, or floor. Larger dogs lick until the sacs unblock. If your dog persistently rubs itself along the ground or licks itself it may be unable to unblock its anal sacs. Your vet will show you how to unblock them.

stimulated and at the same time debris and surface parasites such as fleas and ticks are removed. This action may clear away skin parasites but is also the most common way dogs consume tapeworm eggs, which live in the flea's digestive system (*see pages 126-127*).

SCRATCHES AND RUBS

Scratching is really only effective with the hind paws. Although some dogs become adept at using their forepaws to groom their heads, it is really a rub rather than a scratch. One of my Retrievers, Libby, developed a delightful grooming habit of scratching inside her ear flaps with her dewclaws, but classical scratching involves vigorously rubbing the shoulders, top of the back and front legs with the hind paws' claws. The claws are extended for maximum effect.

ROLLING

Virtually all four-legged mammals body-roll to massage parts their teeth and claws cannot reach. Dogs actively choose where to roll. Some give themselves dust baths by rolling on dry, sandy soil, while others prefer to roll after rain. Both methods help keep the hair and skin surprisingly clean. Rolling to groom is quite different from rolling to anoint the skin with canine perfume.

COOL LICKS

Licking is cleansing and relaxing. Because dogs effectively do not sweat, this is also a natural way to rid the body of excess liquid. At the same time, moistening the area with saliva cools it down.

SHAKING

Some dogs shake on waking, to get their coats in order and improve circulation to resting muscles, and most will also shake after rolling. The most glorious shakes occur after getting wet. A classic shake begins at the head and builds up in amplitude as it extends in a wave down the body, finishing at the tip of the tail. This grooming technique is highly sophisticated, and requires instinctive muscle coordination.

COAT TEXTURES

All dogs inherit natural grooming methods, but because of selective breeding some have problems grooming themselves efficiently. Any dog with a coat similar to that of a standard German Shepherd will be adept at self-cleaning. The coat is firm, dense, and sheds successfully as the seasons change. The work of breeders has modified dogs' coats. Greyhounds' coats, for instance, are thin and easy to clean, but the skin is prone to injury. Poodles have hair that grows continually, so their coats become matted and prone to debris and parasites. Yorkshire Terriers' coats are so fine that self-grooming does not prevent mats and tangles. Perhaps worst of all, selective breeding has resulted in certain dogs growing hair in their ear canals. This hair traps wax and tends to provide a fertile environment for parasites and yeast. It is impossible for these dogs to groom their own ears. They need our help.

HELPING TO GROOM

When grooming your dog, use a brush that does not damage the skin and brush with gentle strokes. Frequent grooming will prevent knots building up and avoid the need for harsher grooming methods. Most important, begin early in life so that your pup thinks of your grooming simply as a continuation of its mother's grooming. Be watchful for excess grooming on your dog's part, which could indicate skin problems. In unusual circumstances, excess grooming is a dog's natural way of coping with anxiety. If this is the case, find the root of your dog's worry and eliminate that (*see pages 152-153*).

HITTING THE SPOT
Dogs appear to enjoy scratching. Puppies begin at three weeks of age when motor coordination is sufficiently developed. Old dogs may want to scratch but no longer have sufficient muscle power to do so.

CHECKLIST

Depending upon its type of coat or lifestyle, your dog may need help with any of the following natural grooming problems.

- Food debris around the lips.
- Discharge from the eyes.
- Wax buildup in the ears.
- Mats of hair from excess scratching.
- Debris caught between the toes.
- Fecal matter around the anus.
- Hair or debris lodged in the vulva.
- Blocked anal sacs.

DIFFERENT ROLLS
Scent rolling begins with a slow head or neck rub as the dog considers the scent. Rolling to groom is more spontaneous and vigorous.

NATURAL AGING

DOGS ARE LIVING LONGER than ever before, longer in fact than nature intended. Unlike people, who suffer from heart attacks and strokes, dogs have few causes of sudden death. Instead, mental and physical changes occur slowly as they age. Life expectancy is immutable. It is written in the genes. By providing an enriched environment for your dog, you can ensure that it enjoys its natural lifespan.

CHECKLIST

- Provide frequent, short walks rather than one long one.
- Groom more often. It helps circulation.
- Feed smaller meals more frequently.
- Provide your dog with soft bedding if it has calluses.
- Take your dog out after each meal, just before bedtime, and first thing each morning.
- Watch your dog's weight. It will be more healthy if it is kept trim.
- Provide warmth and comfort for sleeping and resting.
- Change the diet according to your dog's medical needs.

A NEW PHENOMENON

In the wild, a dog's life expectancy depends upon finding food and avoiding injury or illness. In the benign circumstances of living with us, there are few threats to life. As a consequence, dogs are now living very long lives, some becoming true geriatrics. Evolution did not plan for this, which is why, for example, female dogs do not undergo menopause. Under natural circumstances, quite simply, they died young. Unneutered elderly females continue to cycle, although their heat periods become more erratic and the incidence of womb infection in late life is very high (*see pages 142-143*).

THE SENSES MATURE
As your dog ages, increased reflection from its eyes is usual. It indicates connective tissue changes in the lenses. Like us as we age, near vision diminishes but distance vision remains excellent.

NATURAL AGING VERSUS ILLNESS

With natural aging, dogs slow down. In the absence of good mental stimulation, the elderly dog becomes dull and lethargic. Its appetite may change. These changes also occur when a dog is not well, so it is important to differentiate between natural aging changes and illness. The lassitude or "depression" of illness is one of the most dramatic ways in which a sick dog's body naturally responds to the stress of disease or injury (*see pages 60-61*). Do not assume that changes in your dog's behavior are just the changes of growing older. Elderly dogs benefit from twice-yearly medical examinations.

NATURAL PHYSICAL CHANGES

Professor Jacob Mosier at Kansas State University studied the natural physical changes of aging and found some of the most significant modifications in the brain. In its prime, a dog depends on the swiftness of its mental as well as physical reflexes. Messages travel along the nervous system at approximately 6,560 yds (6,000 m) per second. In the elderly dog these messages slow down to about 1,420 yds (1,300 m) per second. Other changes also affect brain function. Blood vessels in the brain lose their elasticity and the lungs become less efficient. The brain doesn't receive as much oxygen and this affects memory and learning. At the same time, tiny hemorrhages sometimes occur in brain tissue. Consequently, elderly dogs can become irritable when disturbed.

WHAT CONTROLS AGING?

With time dogs become, like us, both wiser and sillier. Aging is ultimately controlled by a genetic biological clock, located in the brain, that in turn controls the body's hormone system. Professor Ben Hart at the University of California has studied the behavior changes of aging. He found that the natural aging changes dogs experience are very similar to the changes we go through, including the changes that in humans are called senile dementia. Professor Hart found that loss of brain function was natural in most dogs by the time they were 16 years old. Typical signs of old age involve increasing disorientation, changes in social relationships with the family, alterations in housetraining, and modifications in sleep and wake times.

More specifically, by 16 years of age, about 20 percent of dogs passed urine or feces in the house, with little or no signaling, for no medical or acquired behavioral reason. Twenty-five percent of dogs this age change their sleep-wake cycles, sleeping more in the day but less at night, when they are more restless but not because they needed to eliminate. A majority of dogs this age, 60 percent, involved themselves less with their family. They greeted less, followed their owners less, and solicited less attention. (An earlier natural aging change involves following the owners more – not letting them out of sight.)

Finally, over 70 percent of 16-year-old dogs become naturally more disoriented as they aged, going to the wrong side of the door when asking to go out, getting stuck in corners, staring into space, and barking for no reason. Another curious phenomenon of aging is that while neutered females become more aggressive, neutered males get less aggressive as they grow older.

NATURAL AGING

At a chemical level, elderly dogs have more trouble turning off their stress response. Even when relaxed, elderly dogs secrete more stress-related hormones. Technically, the ultimate cause of death is an excess of these hormones, called glucocorticoids. Training your dog to relax can control its stress response and, at least in theory, could prolong life (see page 98). As aging progresses, the chemical factory in the brain and nervous system produces fewer chemicals called neuroendocrines. Specifically, production of the brain chemical called

A NATURAL DIGNITY
An aging dog shows a natural dignity in how it accepts the changes of time. While accepting its physical limitations, in the right environment it forever retains the "puppy within."

dopamine drops. This is the brain's master chemical. If dopamine production is maintained, a dog probably lives longer.

HOW YOU CAN INFLUENCE AGING

You can actively slow down natural aging by providing your dog with routine mental and gentle physical stimulation. Massaging your dog does more than help loosen up stiff joints. It improves the circulation of blood to all parts of the body. Extensive studies in the 1980s showed that with mental stimulation the brain grows in size. It does not produce more cells, but instead the cells already there grow more connections with other cells. With mental stimulation a single brain cell might develop lost connections with up to 2,000 other cells. You can slow the natural decay of memory by providing your dog with mental activities.

Feed your dog a well-balanced diet that contains the increased levels of vitamins and antioxidants that older dogs need (see pages 42-43). Until recently, veterinary nutritionists thought it was wise to reduce the protein level in diets for older dogs in order to take the strain off the kidneys. However, recent evidence suggests that, as long as the kidneys are healthy, protein helps the hemorrhage process rather than hinders it. Finally, accept the fact that your dog ages faster than you would like. Do not overexercise your companion: it does more harm than good. Let your dog set its own pace in later life but make sure that life remains stimulating.

COMPARING DOG YEARS TO HUMAN YEARS

Not long ago, one dog year was said to equal seven human years. This was based on the natural life expectancy of dogs and people at the time, of 10 and 70 years respectively. Since then both have increased, but much more for dogs than people. A more accurate comparison today is one dog year for five-and-a-half human years.

NATURAL DEVELOPMENT

NATURAL TRAINING

NATURAL NUTRITION

NATURAL HEALTH CARE

HEALTH DISORDERS

NATURAL TRAINING

The dog is naturally responsive to the needs of its
pack, to the commands of its mother and other elders,
and later the directions of the pack leader. It is an
attractively guileless animal, with an innate sense of
trust: dogs are honest. When training your canine
companion, put yourself in your dog's place.
Understand the dog's inherent desire to protect its
home, scent-mark its territory, and fill its stomach
quickly before others finish its food. You can prevent
behavioral problems by anticipating your dog's needs
and appreciating that it is unnatural for a dog to
live without mental or physical stimulation.

As well as lessons in obedience, it is important to give your dog time to play.

YOU AND YOUR DOG

FEW SPECIES LIVE NATURALLY with each other but dogs and people are a magnificent exception. The wolf evolved to live with other wolves, but its descendent the dog evolved to live harmoniously in human households. Living with us was perhaps most natural when the dog had a specific role. The modern urban environment is unnatural to the dog and this has created new stresses in its life.

CHECKLIST

- Avoid tension in relationships. Aim for stability.

- Begin your relationship as you wish to continue.

- Recognize your dog's emotional limitations. Don't ask for too much.

- Recognize your dog's intellectual capacity. Try to have realistic expectations.

- Don't use your pet as an emotional crutch.

- Never neglect your dog's needs. Benign neglect is as harmful as active neglect.

CHANGING RELATIONS

Dogs were used for centuries to help us hunt, herd, or track other animals. They guarded our livestock, pulled carts and sleds, or killed vermin for us. Historically, our relationship with the dog was practical or utilitarian, but today we live with dogs primarily for social and psychological reasons. We enjoy their company. We feel better when they are near us. And we grieve when they leave us. Over the past 20 years there have been studies revealing how and why dogs make us feel this way.

Dr. Warwick Anderson at Monash University, Australia, discovered that dog owners have less risk of heart disease than non-pet owners. Dr. James Serpell at the University of Cambridge, England, showed that dog owners suffer from fewer minor health complaints like sore throats, lower back pain, and difficulty sleeping than non-pet owners. When these studies were

themselves studied, they showed that dogs have an overall beneficial physiological effect on their owners. In the mid 1980s, the World Health Organisation (WHO) reported that, "Companion animals which are properly cared for bring immense benefits to their owners and to society and are a danger to no one." The emphasis should be on "properly cared for."

AVOIDING STRESS

There have been fewer reports on how people affect the health of dogs, but some answers are obvious. If you are a responsible owner, you train your dog carefully, protect it from disease and danger, and nurse it when it is not well. You are its "caregiver." To be an effective caregiver you need to understand the emotional as well as physical needs of your dog. If you do not, the relationship is strained and your dog may be stressed. Like us, when a dog is stressed, its hormonal biofeedback system is overworked, leading to potential medical problems. In a nutshell, uncertainty can lead to anxiety, which can lead to ill health. The body strives to maintain an equilibrium or balance called homeostasis. Stress throws the body out of balance; in an attempt to restore equilibrium, a cascade of hormones are secreted into the bloodstream, which over time can halt digestion, inhibit growth in the young, and increase sugar in the bloodstream. Stress inhibits the immune system, which is at the core of good health and all complementary therapies.

EMOTIONAL NEEDS

Dogs thrive on social integration, and they respond to consideration of their own needs. Because your dog thinks of you and your family as *its* family, emotional changes in your family can affect your dog's physical well-being. Family tension can lead to emotional conflict for the dog, a situation that on occasion can lead to self-mutilation. I have cared for a dog that viciously chewed its own leg each time its owners had a family

AT RISK
Your dog's well-being is directly affected by your relationship with it. This dog, allowed to roam freely because it is "natural", is exposed to increased risk from accidents. We have the equivalent of "parental" responsibility to reduce risk to our dogs.

ASSISTANCE DOGS

In some circumstances your relationship with your dog is reversed. You depend upon it as much as it depends upon you. Virtually all dogs willingly offer us their emotional support. Carefully trained assistance dogs offer more. Hearing dogs act as ears for deaf people, alerting them to the sound of fire alarms, the baby crying, or simply a knock on the door. Guide dogs act as eyes, guiding blind people around obstacles and making decisions for them on when it is safe to cross a road. Dogs for disabled people assist their owners who are restricted to wheelchairs by retrieving dropped items, and even pushing buttons for elevators.

MUTUAL BENEFIT
The most natural and satisfying way to enhance your relationship with your dog is through touch. Stroking your dog reduces both its stress and yours.

squabble. The dog's self-mutilation stopped when the couple separated but recurred when they tried a reconciliation that ended in further squabbles. A pet dog considers itself part of the family unit and, like our children, will be affected by family conflict.

Dogs are intensely social creatures and they will demand attention from members of their family. If a dog gains sympathy when it limps after injuring a leg, it is not unusual for it to pretend to be lame in the future, to get more care and attention. A dog may even behave badly – chewing furniture or barking incessantly – in order to gain attention. These astute individuals have learned a cause and effect, and know how to manipulate their owners. As the owner, you have a responsibility to ensure that your dog is not resorting to destructive habits in order to satisfy its needs.

INFLUENCES ON BEHAVIOR

Your relationship with your dog is even more complex than you may have realized. Studies have shown that your own temperament can affect your dog's behavior. Dr. Anthony Podberscek at the University of Cambridge studied the personalities of English Cocker Spaniels and their owners. He found that owners who were

introverted, undisciplined, and emotionally less stable than average were more likely to have aggressive Cockers than people with average scores for these characteristics. In a separate study, Dr. Valerie O'Farrell at the University of Edinburgh found that people who had high scores for neuroticism in personality tests had dogs that pestered for attention and were destructive when left alone. These studies show how dynamic the bond is between a dog and its owner. In ideal circumstances, this relationship will be mutually beneficial; your dog offering loyalty and companionship, and you providing care and a safe environment.

WHO IS PACK LEADER?

Don't assume that the relationship between you and your dog is one of pack leader and subservient follower. Through selective breeding we have made the dog a life-long dependent. The normal relationship is responsibility on our part and dependence on theirs.

EARLY LESSONS
If you hand-feed a pup, then expect it to eat from a bowl later in life, you increase its stress level. Inconsistency causes stress by creating conflict in a pup's mind. This can have a negative effect on relationships.

THINKING LIKE A DOG

THE DOG'S MIND IS SIMILAR to our own in many ways, so it is easy to understand how it thinks. Dogs enjoy social activities with their immediate family but can be wary of strangers. They respond to rewards and also to discipline. They can be selfish as well as selfless. Above all, the dog is able to learn from experience and to work with us, which is at the root of its natural trainability.

CHECKLIST

- Understand what a dog wants in life. Use those wants positively.

- Offer food and touch as rewards. Associate these with less potent rewards like words.

- Use natural discipline when necessary. Social exclusion is the most potent discipline for dogs. Use it theatrically, for seconds only, and not for retribution.

PAVLOV'S LESSON

Dogs have been trained for thousands of years, but it was not until early this century that scientists learned why dogs respond so well to training. The Russian physiologist Ivan Pavlov found that by pairing the sound of a bell with food he could train a dog to salivate when the bell rang. The new stimulus, the bell, triggered the automatic response of salivating even when food was no longer offered. I see a variation of this at the clinic, where I give vitamin treats to dogs when their medical conditions permit. On subsequent visits a dog thinks it will get another treat and as often as not starts dribbling in anticipation as it walks into the examination room.

Pavlov's observations explained how a biological response like salivating can be stimulated, but it did not explain how a dog learns to perform a complex behavior like understanding to sit when it hears a specific word or sees a certain hand signal.

SOCIAL EVENTS
Dogs do not naturally play with unrelated dogs, but if they meet other dogs before they are 12 weeks old they over-come their natural hostility.

REWARDS AND DISCIPLINES

The American psychologist B. F. Skinner explained how, by using reward and discipline, an animal can be trained to perform a desired behavior such as sitting. He called rewards positive reinforcement. Discipline could take the form either of negative reinforcement or punishment. These two forms of discipline are subtly different. A negative reinforcement is something a dog finds mildly unpleasant, but as a result of its use a dog does what you want it to. Gentle pressure with your hands on a dog's rump, to induce it to sit down, is a negative reinforcer. Punishment, though harsher sounding, is not meant to harm a dog. A punishment is used to keep a dog from doing what it should not be doing. Making a sudden noise, for example, by dropping your keys on the ground, to stop your puppy chewing the carpet is a punishment. A sharp, "No!" is just a variation of this. With learning, words are a potent punishment.

USING REWARDS AND DISCIPLINES

Dogs respond well both to rewards and to discipline because they are natural components of life with mother and litter-mates. When puppies are young, mother uses her paws in a disciplinary way. Later in life, a dominant dog puts a paw on another dog's shoulder as a symbolic gesture of dominance, a gesture instantly understood because of early learning. You pushing your dog's rump down gently to reinforce the command "sit" is a gesture your dog also instantly understands.

In the same way, a firm "No!" in your voice is simply a continuation of the natural discipline of mother barking at her pup if it inadvertently hurts her. Dogs respond to tone of voice because they naturally interpret inflections in the different sounds other dogs make. Rewarding good behavior also relates to a dog's early learning, as its mother will have rewarded calm and responsive behavior with food and licking, the equivalent to meals and stroking.

SOCIAL THINKING

Littermates form relationships with each other early in life. They too, unwittingly, use rewards and discipline to create relationships that develop into a hierarchy within the pack. A pack is blood-related, and it is unnatural for members, in adulthood, to play with unrelated dogs. Other dogs are considered potential intruders. Without our intervention, the dog's natural inclination means it is unwilling to enter into social activities with another dog – it is likely to want to expel it from its territory.

For dogs to integrate successfully into human society it is important that they get on well with each other. Fortunately, because their minds are open to early experience, we can mold a young dog's way of thinking so that it enjoys meeting other strange dogs. One of the best ways to achieve this is through early controlled socializing with other dogs, through puppy parties or playschool.

PUPPY PLAYSCHOOL

Dr. Ian Dunbar, a British-trained veterinarian in California, first developed the idea of puppy socialization classes almost 30 years ago. The concept proved so successful that today puppy playschool groups exist wherever there are large concentrations of pet dogs. The objective of playschool is to allow the type of social activity that existed within the pup's litter to continue, under our

control, after a pup leaves its litter and enters its new home. Dr. Dunbar understood that by isolating a puppy from other dogs during the sensitive weeks immediately after it leaves its litter, unwittingly we were creating behavior problems for the future.

WHAT HAPPENS AT PLAYSCHOOL

Playschool allows dogs to continue to learn about the natural behavior of other dogs, in a controlled way. Puppies continue to develop their understanding of canine body language. At the same time, their owners learn about their dogs' natural body language and needs. At puppy playschool, pups have fun with other pups, and learn at the same time. The beauty of it is that owners have fun and learn just as much.

Playschools usually offer six to eight weekly one-hour sessions at which both pups and their owners learn the value of toys, commands, and good relationships. Lessons learned at school are carried out at home. Owners learn how a dog's mind works, and come to understand, for example, that it is pointless to discipline a dog if you find it has messed in the house; discipline is only useful when you actually see it in the act. Dogs do not think in the abstract the way we do. You can be conditional with your children and say, "If you do that once more, I'll be angry with you," but you simply cannot expect your puppy to understand that type of statement. If you can transport yourself into your dog's way of thinking, then training becomes a breeze simply because you'll never be asking a dog to do more than it naturally can.

HOME ALONE
It is both boring and unnatural for a pup to be left alone for long periods of time but, realistically, being at home alone is part of life with us. Leave your pup alone for lengthening periods of time when it is young, and always provide it with mentally stimulating toys.

DISEASE RISKS
Puppy parties are an ideal way to teach dogs to meet other "new" dogs, but there is a potential health hazard because your pup may come into contact with infectious disease. You should discuss these risks with your vet. The incidence of infectious disease varies from one locality to another, and your vet should know if a particular disease is prevalent in your area.

CRATE TRAINING
Harness your dog's natural instincts by introducing it to a crate early in life. You may think that a dog crate looks like a jail, but a dog that is introduced to a crate or a pen when it is a pup will think of it as a personal, safe den. Dogs naturally feel more secure in covered enclosures. A crate, especially one that is covered on top with a towel, is psychologically satisfying to a pup, especially if it finds an attractive reward like a toy or a food treat inside. Never use a crate as a punishment, and never leave a dog in a crate for longer than two hours.

NATURAL DEVELOPMENT

NATURAL TRAINING

NATURAL NUTRITION

NATURAL HEALTH CARE

HEALTH DISORDERS

EARLY TRAINING

PUPPIES ARE NATURALLY HYGIENIC. They avoid soiling their resting sites but willingly leave their urine and feces elsewhere. Through early training, while your puppy's mind is still malleable, you can shape its toilet habits to your requirements. House training takes time, but if you use dog logic, not human logic, this training period is shorter and learning remains life-long.

CAT-FLAP TRAINING
Small dogs can be trained to use cat flaps. After eating, playing, waking up, and when your pup simply sniffs the ground, show it how to use the cat flap.

CHECKLIST

Dogs might urinate in the "wrong" place for any of the following reasons.

- Lack of early house training.
- Territory marking, both by males and females.
- Anxiety over separation from the family.
- Fear.
- Excitement.
- Over-submission.
- To gain attention.
- Predisposition of the breed.
- Disease.

AN OPEN MIND

Employing a dog's natural instincts allows us a marvelous window of opportunity when they are young, to train them to behave as we want them to. The dog's close relation, the wolf, is naturally hygienic. In the wild, approximately twice each day, wolves empty their bowels away from the den. The reason for this behavior is likely to be evolutionary. Dogs with the most fastidious sanitary habits were more likely to raise offspring successfully, because the young would not have been exposed to dangerous amounts of intestinal parasites.

Dogs have inherited this behavior and rarely soil their own beds. They need our guidance to learn that they are not to soil our homes either. House training is most successful when it begins early, certainly at less than three months of age. I can attest, from personal experience, that pups kept in cages until five months old are extremely difficult to house train. At university, my roommates "rescued" a redundant six-month-old laboratory Beagle pup. We were never fully successful at house training it. Start house training your new pup the day you bring it into your home.

DOG LOGIC

When training a puppy, use rewards — positive reinforcement — as you would with an older dog. It is pointless, even counter-productive, to use discipline when house training a puppy. Never, ever push a pup's face in its mess and scold it. It has not the faintest idea why you are doing it. Never verbally reprimand a pup for messing in the house unless you catch it in the act. Pups lack the ability to think in the abstract. An angry, "Do you see what you did?" makes you feel better, but all a pup hears is that you are angry and it will have no idea why. Just because it cringes when you come home and find a mess does not mean it understands cause and effect. It has learned simply that on previous occasions you have returned home and scolded it. You alone are responsible for interpreting your pup's needs and making your own needs clear to the pup. Plan house training logically, by understanding when a pup is most likely to empty its bladder and bowels and by placing yourself on "red alert" at those times. Pups are most likely to need to toilet when they wake up, after playing, and after eating. Plan your intervention carefully.

LITTERBOX TRAINING

Getting a puppy outside from an urban high-rise apartment to a designated toileting area can be tedious and time-consuming, too time-consuming for a puppy's bladder. Avoid puddles in the foyer by training your small dog to use a cat-litter tray. Select litter appropriate for your dog's coat texture, so that it is not trailed throughout your home. Litter trays eliminate the need to dash outdoors but outdoor socializing episodes are still an important early experience for your puppy.

PAPER TRAINING

While some pups are delightfully precocious in their bowel and bladder control, do not expect your pup to develop total waste management until it is perhaps 18 to 20 weeks old. Your aim is to teach your pup to relieve itself outdoors, but until it is old enough to control itself overnight you will need to train it to eliminate on newspaper. Even for pups with frequent access to the outdoors, paper training is useful.

The simplest way to paper-train a puppy is passively. Restrict your young canine to one room and cover the floor entirely with newspaper. Because it has no other choice, it will eliminate on the paper. Praise it when it eliminates on the paper and an early lesson has been learned. Once a pup associates newspaper with toileting, you can slowly reduce the amount of paper in the room, until just a couple of sheets will suffice. If this paper is then restricted to the area near to your back door, for instance, you will be reinforcing to the pup that outdoors is the preferred destination when it needs to go.

PAVLOV'S LESSON

Pavlov's experiment showed that it is possible to train a dog to salivate at the sound of a bell. You can use his experiment to help house train your dog to urinate or defecate when it hears certain words. Each time your dog urinates or defecates, say something specific like "Hurry up." By using this phrase repetitively, each time your dog

INDOOR PAPER TRAINING

Pups naturally sniff the ground just before toileting. Some also race about more frantically. When you see this activity you have only seconds to move your pup onto already positioned newspaper. Leaving a trace of soiled newspaper on the replacement encourages your pup to return.

toilets, through sound association your dog eventually learns to eliminate when it hears these words. Just as a dog's saliva glands can be conditioned to empty, so too can its bladder and bowels. If you train your dog to associate toileting with a specific sound, it will toilet where and when you want it to. This is particularly useful if you intend to take your dog on long car journeys.

LOSS OF TRAINING

Perhaps the most common house training mistake is to stop training too soon. Do not assume your puppy is trained when it first toilets as you want it to. Reinforce the training by continuing it further. Training can often be lost when the weather changes; some dogs need encouragement to go outside in wet or cold weather.

A refresher house training course is more difficult than primary training. Train day and night, and in all but the most extreme weather. Confine your dog to a comfortable small space, such as its crate, when you cannot supervise it. Every three hours, and after waking, eating, or playing, escort your dog to its toilet site and give it only a few minutes to do its business. Use word association. When it does perform, praise it and give it a small food treat. If it does not perform after a few minutes, bring it back in, wait 15 minutes, and repeat the exercise. This will be tedious for you but remedial training is almost always successful within a few days.

BE HYGIENIC

Canine urine and feces potentially carry health dangers for us. The disease *Leptospirosis* can be transmitted in urine. Dogs can be protected through vaccination (*see page 120*). Dog feces can also transmit the roundworm, *Toxocara canis*, infectious to us. Efficient worming eliminates this problem (*see page 138*).

NATURAL DEVELOPMENT

NATURAL TRAINING

NATURAL NUTRITION

NATURAL HEALTH CARE

HEALTH DISORDERS

BASIC OBEDIENCE

THE ESSENCE OF OUR SUCCESSFUL relationship with the dog is trust. We trust it to behave like a dog and it trusts us to behave not so much as the leader of the pack but as "mother," as the provider of food, safety, comfort, and security. We become carers and take on the responsibility to train our dogs to avoid unnecessary risk. The basis of training is obedience, a willingness to do as we command.

CHECKLIST

- The success of obedience training depends partly upon the natural personality of your dog.

- Provide mental stimulation early in life.

- Play constructively and give rewards immediately when appropriate.

- Always use social deprivation, not physical abuse, as discipline.

- Train before feeding time, when your dog is alert.

- Keep training sessions short and finish each time with a reward.

WHAT DOGS THINK OF US

How rapidly a pup learns is influenced by a variety of factors, such as whose genes it inherited, how it is treated by its littermates, and what happens, accidentally or otherwise, during its first few months of life. We tend to think that to be a successful trainer, we take on the pack leader role. This is partly true, but it is probably more accurate, although to some people a little deflating, to take on the role of mother. Throughout life, we feed it, comfort it, and give it security. The most effective way to obedience-train your dog is to use a mother's natural methods for teaching. She rewards good behavior with food, and disciplines bad behavior with a threat or social ostracism but never with severe abuse.

PERSONALITY TYPES

Genetics and early experience ultimately create different personality types (*see pages 68–69*). Some dogs are naturally confident while others are insecure. A dog's personality influences both its willingness to learn and the speed of learning. It also affects how a dog copes with the stress of illness.

Curiously, more confident dogs can take longer to learn obedience. In the wild, these dogs would become leaders and would issue commands, not receive them. A naturally dominant dog displays its authority with intimidating body language – tail held high, staring you in the eye, even baring its teeth – or by simply disregarding you. Less dominant dogs, especially those that perpetuate juvenile characteristics, such as enjoying being petted, are easier to train.

These dogs make up the vast majority of all canines. They are natural followers, perpetual pups, willing to take instruction from who they consider to be a parent or a pack leader.

STIMULUS AND RESPONSE

All learning involves a stimulus and a response. A pup learns what to eat and what not to eat by tasting it, what to chase and what not to chase according to how the chase concludes, who to obey and who not to obey according to the result of tactic. During any training, use natural puppy rewards, the most potent being food, when your pup responds positively. Use natural discipline, the most potent being social isolation, when your pup, according to your desires, misbehaves. Rewards and discipline must both be issued immediately, at the time of the behavior. To most dogs, touch is almost as important a reward as food. In nature, a mother growls or barks at her pups to discipline them. Use soothing words as rewards and a harsh "No!" or "Bad dog!" for immediate discipline.

CRATE TRAINING

Dogs naturally feel comfortable in a den under a table or chair. Train your pup from an early age to use a den you have selected: a dog crate. A comfortable crate, with a toy, bedding, food, and water, is a secure haven where your dog can be conveniently confined when necessary. Travel problems are eliminated by using the crate when your dog travels in your car.

COME, SIT, DOWN, STAY

During obedience-training sessions, act naturally. Make sure your dog has eye contact with you. Do not use threatening body language or overstimulate your dog. Keep sessions short and simple. Anticipate your dog's behavior, and avoid unplanned rewards. Use short, simple commands with obvious hand signals. Train your dog to come, sit, stay, and lie down when it is mentally most active, which means before a meal, not after it, and always finish with fun.

COME

In a quiet hallway, with your pup on its lead and food in your hand, speak your pup's name and, as it begins to walk to you, give the command "Come." Bending down and encouraging your dog with open arms can be less threatening than standing. As your pup approaches, praise it, stroke it, and give the food reward.

SIT

Command "Come." As your pup reaches you, move your right hand with the food treat over its head. As your dog bends its hindlegs to sit, keeping its eyes on the reward, give the command "Sit." Gradually reduce rewards until only the word is used.

DOWN

With your pup sitting, hold its collar with your left hand and a food treat in your right. Move the treat in an arc from the pup's nose to the floor. As it naturally lowers itself, give the command "Down."

STAY

From the "Down" position, use a hand signal and the word "Stay." Avoid food rewards as these are too exciting. Release from "Stay" by saying "OK" a few seconds later, extending eventually to minutes.

NATURAL DEVELOPMENT

NATURAL TRAINING

NATURAL NUTRITION

NATURAL HEALTH CARE

HEALTH DISORDERS

NATURAL PROBLEMS INDOORS

DOGS ENJOY THE LUXURIES of physical comfort, readily available food, and companionship, but these alone are not enough. The dog is an outdoor animal. Its energy reserves are prodigious and it needs mental and physical activity. However, most dogs today live in the confined space of our homes. Problem behaviors are bound to occur when we fail to understand that this environment is unnatural.

They bark or howl to summon others of their social group, act creatively to provide themselves with mental or physical activity, and greet us over-enthusiastically when we return. All of these behaviors are natural for a dog but unacceptable to us. These problems can be avoided through early, or, when necessary, remedial learning.

SUITABLE TOYS

Through trial and error, discover what type of toy your dog prefers. Balls are good for chasing, catching, and retrieving, while tough nylon and hard rubber are good for chewing. Tug toys are excellent for tug-of-war but avoid these with naturally dominant dogs. They want to win too much.

LUXURIOUS JAILS

Dogs are marvelous companions and we enjoy their enthusiastic greetings. We feel important, loved, and wanted. The very basis of our relationship with the modern dog is attachment, but this ideal partnership is difficult to maintain in the reality of our own lives. Dogs must, on occasions, be left at home alone. This should be part of early training so that a young dog becomes accustomed to periods without its "family."

We may assume that because our dogs are well fed, warm, and safe, they will be content to enjoy the luxurious surroundings we provide. But from a dog's perspective, a comfortable home can be an environment lacking in any form of mental or physical stimulation. In these circumstances, dogs do what comes naturally.

NATURAL GREETINGS

A profound part of human nature is that we admire people who never lose contact with the child within. In the dog, we created a species that perpetuates the excitement of youth throughout its life. In our honorary role of parents to our dogs, we are greeted as they would greet their own mother, enthusiastically jumping up to lick the face and lips, hoping for a food reward. If you are content for your dog to greet you this way, that is your business, but remember that other people might not share your views. It is your responsibility to train your dog from puppyhood not to jump up on people.

BARKING AND HOWLING

Dogs talk with whimpers and whines, growls and howls, shrieks and barks. Barking can be difficult to interpret accurately. Wolves only bark when stressed, but alarm barking may have been selectively bred for in dogs by early breeders. Howls are easier to interpret; together with barking they are often a sign of canine separation anxiety. The amount that a dog barks or howls is programmed in its genes. Some breeds, most terriers for example, are supreme barkers and only moderate howlers, while many hounds are superb howlers and only passable barkers.

Because barking and howling are such innate behaviors, overcoming "problem" barking and howling requires patience. Your first objective is to determine what causes the behavior. Separation anxiety is a common cause, as are unexpected sights or sounds. As with all behavior problems, basic obedience is at the root of retraining. Concentrating on a command takes a dog's mind off barking.

JUMPING UP

Dogs naturally jump up to greet their mothers. Avoid this problem by training your dog to sit on command. Come and go from your home quietly to avoid encouraging your dog's euphoria or anxiety. Never inadvertently reward jumping up. Disregard your dog until it sits, then calmly greet it.

EXCESS ENERGY

In the wild, the wolf uses endurance, rather than speed, to capture its prey. A hare may be faster or a deer larger but a wolf can travel over 50 miles (80 kilometers) a day following food. As long as breeding has not physically deformed your dog, with experience your dog is capable of comparable physical exercise. Think of the ground covered by a young terrier while it accompanies its owner for a walk. Although one tenth its owner's size, it probably covers three or four times the distance the owner walks. Put all that potential energy indoors and it has to be released. Some dogs pace or run from one part of the house to another. Some jump and dig at the door or adjacent wall, removing wallpaper, even plaster. Some try to chew their way out of "jail."

All of these quite natural responses can be prevented if you provide daily physical exercise before you leave your dog at home alone. Feed your pet before you leave rather than after you return. Like us, dogs are more likely to rest on a full stomach.

DESTRUCTIVE BEHAVIOR

The dog is one of the most inventive of all non-primate mammals. It uses its substantial mental abilities to investigate its surroundings. A life locked indoors is mentally stifling. In these circumstances a dog will naturally

create its own mental stimulation. It will investigate places it has never been before, such as table tops and cupboards, taste or eat some items, and chew others.

Avoid destructive behavior by providing your dog with mental stimulation in your absence. Toys are ideal but they need to be kept appealing. Store them away and only bring out one on special occasions – like your departure. Hollow, hard rubber toys with a dab of cheese spread or peanut butter inside are excellent. Many dogs are content to work away at these toys getting intermittent food rewards. Larger balls that drop bits of food when pushed around are equally rewarding for home-alone dogs.

SEX SUBSTITUTES

In my experience, most owners expect their dogs to show interest in sex only when the owners think it right for them to do so. How silly. We cannot expect a male dog to go through puberty without latching on to whatever is available. In the absence of other dogs, what is available is our arms and legs, stuffed toys, and cushions.

Because canine population control is our responsibility, very few dogs will, or should, have the opportunity to mate. As far as your dog's sex life is concerned you have a choice. You may let it do as it likes, but train it not to make advances on strangers, which is very difficult, or you can neuter him or her. It is just as easy to argue that it is unnatural for dogs to be kept as pets as it is to argue that it is unnatural to neuter them. Neutered dogs are less stressed, have lower risk of injury and disease, and live longer than unneutered dogs.

PRACTICAL PUNISHMENT

Punishment is meant to decrease the undesirable behavior of your dog. It should be theatrical or symbolic, not painful or too frightening. Punishment does not "treat" the underlying cause of a behavior problem. Rather than punish, change the circumstances that cause the undesired activity and it should wither away. When this is not practical, treat a behavior problem with ingenuity. For example, distract a barking dog with another sound. Toss an empty soft-drink can filled with a few coins on the floor. It gets your dog's attention and permits you to get back to basics.

COMFORT SEEKER

If you do not want your dog on the furniture, never allow it on, even as a pup on your lap. If it does get on the sofa, leave its leash on. Once it has jumped up, remove it by its leash and immediately isolate it in an empty room for one minute.

CHECKLIST

Consider these points when dealing with a problem behavior:

- The "problem" is either a natural dog activity or an acquired behavior.
- Prevention is always easier than cure.
- Basic obedience training is at the root of containing most behavior problems.
- You must eliminate the satisfaction your dog gets from the unwanted behavior.
- Retraining takes time. Do not expect instant miracles.

OUTDOOR TRAINING

THE OUTDOORS IS EXCITING and as invigorating to a dog as it is to most people. It is a dog's natural home but it is also dangerous. More pet dogs die from road traffic accidents than from disease in the first years of life. We have a responsibility to our dogs, to our neighbors, and to our communities to control our dogs outdoors, and to ensure that they live safely in a risky world.

CHECKLIST

- Train when your dog is most alert, twice each day for 15 to 20 minutes.
- Train in quiet locations. It is best to begin outdoor training in the quiet of indoors.
- Carry food rewards with you.
- Only permit your dog outdoors when it wears identification.
- Do not be democratic or conditional. Dogs can learn right and wrong but will only be confused if you are not consistent.

NEW EXPERIENCES

Outdoors may be the natural environment for dogs, but today few individuals are raised there. The introduction to outdoors should be carefully planned to prevent not only exposure to dangers, but unwanted early learning as well. Dogs should learn to enjoy, not to fear, meeting new people, other dogs, and other strange animals. They should be taught road sense, and to enjoy the potentially nausea-inducing and quite unnatural sensation of traveling in a car. The first and most important lesson is to teach your dog to walk obediently by your side, wearing a collar and leash. Once this lesson is learned, further training is simple.

POWER GAMES

Democracy is a human ideal but not natural to dogs. To prevent overexcitement, make sure your dog thinks of all people as leaders, not equals. Avoid physical contact games like wrestling or tug-of-war with all but the gentlest individuals. During any play, periodically emphasize the relationship by stopping the activity and commanding your dog to sit and stay. If you are playing ball with your dog and it refuses to "Drop it" on command, stop the game and walk away. Always be alert for signs that your dog is "testing" your family, especially the smaller members, to see if it can move up in rank.

SAFE CONTROL

Choke collars are unpleasant for most dogs and can be dangerous for those, such as some toy breeds, with pliable, potentially collapsible windpipes. There are less drastic restraints that utilize a dog's natural behavior to control its activities. Correctly used, a soft nylon head halter allows the leash to be attached under the

WALKING TO HEEL

1 With your dog in a sitting position to your left, hold it by its collar, speak its name, and show it a food reward. As your dog moves towards the reward, walk forward in a straight line giving the command, "Heel." Keep your left hand low, ready to grab the collar.

2 As your dog walks forward following the food, stop walking and command it to "Wait." To discourage jumping up, hold the snack down low. Reward good behavior. It may be necessary to use your left hand under your dog's waist to prevent forward movement.

jaws, not over the neck as it would to a typical collar. When a dog pulls forward on a leash attached to a head halter, its own momentum pulls its jaws shut and its head down towards the ground. This is not a position a dog enjoys, and it soon learns that it is more fun to walk, not pull, so that it can hold its head high. Head halters are not appropriate for all dogs. Body harnesses are good for flat-faced individuals and, if your dog is very boisterous, half-check collars, with nylon around the throat section, are excellent.

IDENTIFICATION

Make sure your dog is properly identified before you venture outdoors with it. Tiny microchip implants are safe, effective, and meet international standards. These are ideal for permanent identification. Tattoos are also excellent, although sometimes they can be difficult to read. In addition to these permanent forms of ID, your dog should always wear a collar and identity tag with a telephone number. When you travel away from home, make sure to add an appropriate number for the location you are visiting.

3 When your dog consistently walks to heel in a straight line, introduce turns. Begin with right turns in front of your body. Guide your dog into the turn with the food treat. Gradually introduce more difficult left turns away from your body.

ENJOYABLE WALKS

Train your dog, initially indoors, to accept a collar by putting it on, giving a reward then taking it off. Leash training is similar. Put on the leash, give a reward, then take it off.

"The first and most important lesson is to teach your dog to walk obediently by your side, wearing a collar and leash."

When your dog is familiar with the collar and leash, it is ready for outdoor training. Some people think it unnatural for a dog to walk on a leash, and it would be if there were no traffic or other dangers. We have a responsibility to train our dogs to walk to heel. Once this training is successful, your dog will walk by your side on or off the lead. When it is safe to do so, you can release it from its "heel" position and let it run, sniff, and investigate to its heart's content.

GOOD GAMES

Outdoor games provide your dog with mental and physical stimulation and, if used properly, will reinforce obedience training. Different games are suitable for different personalities.

Fetching games are useful for energetic dogs as they give more exercise to your dog than to you. Dogs love to chase and catch moving objects. Throw low to prevent accidental injuries. Chase games are excellent for building the confidence of shy dogs. Trot or run with your dog's favorite toy, then, on the run, give the toy to your dog. Do not play this game with overexcited dogs as it will stimulate them to jump at your hand for the toy. Play football with a beach ball, letting your dog have possession for only half of the time, but avoid this game with natural heel nippers. Play hide-and-seek with a favorite toy by telling your dog to "Sit-Stay" while you hide it. Shout encouragement when it gets closer to its prize. Tug-of-war should only be played with dogs willing to release a grip on command. It is a dangerous game to play with dogs that have a need to win.

PERFECT REWARDS

The best food rewards are usually the smelliest. Dehydrated bits of liver are a favorite with dog trainers, while cheese and yeast tablets are also very effective. Through trial and error, discover what really tickles your dog's nose, then use this snack as a reward only when training.

NATURAL PROBLEMS OUTDOORS

THE OUTDOORS DOES NOT necessarily provide more potential problems than indoors, but the problems that are encountered are often more serious, even life-threatening. Chasing bikes and vehicles, running into traffic, attacking animals or being attacked, and getting lost are all problems you can and should anticipate in your dog and prevent by reinforcing obedience training.

CANINE INSECURITY

Dogs that have been kept at animal shelters are much more likely to show signs of separation anxiety – barking, digging, and destruction – than dogs raised from puppyhood in a secure home. Such dogs need gentle handling. Gradually increase periods of separation from you over weeks or months.

CORRECTING BAD BEHAVIOR

The most common early warning signal of potential problems is pulling on the leash. Bad habits such as this can be cured by a simple retraining programme. Make sure your dog readily obeys the commands "Come," "Sit," "Stay," and "Down." If you are in the park and sense that your dog is about to get into trouble, you can stop your dog in its tracks and regain control of the situation by issuing the command, "Ben, stay!" If you are uncertain whether your dog will obey, do not let it off its leash. Giving a command you cannot enforce teaches your dog that there is no need to obey you.

Eliminate the satisfaction your dog gets from bad behavior. Chasing cars or bicycles is fun because they run away. The dog "wins." You need to create circumstances where the dog loses. Dog trainers have experienced all your dog problems before, so it makes sense to benefit from their creativity in order to correct your dog's unwanted behavior.

CHASING VEHICLES
Spoil the fun of chasing. Ask a friend to cycle or drive past your dog. As it begins to chase, the rider/ driver should stop suddenly and activate an air horn or squirt a water pistol, and shout, "No!"

PULLING ON THE LEASH
To remedy leash-pulling, return to walking-to-heel training. With your dog to your left, hold its leash in both hands. When your dog begins to pull, slide your left hand firmly down the lead and command your dog to sit. Once your dog does so, resume walking to the command "Heel." Repeat. Repeat. Repeat. And always reward good behavior.

PULLING ON THE LEASH

Pulling on the leash is a dog's response to boredom or to restraint. It also can be a sign of aggression or dominant behavior. For dogs not trained to walk to heel, the leash itself can incite a dog to pull. Trying to match your dog's strength by pulling back on the leash is counterproductive. Remedy this problem by reverting to basic training (*see caption above*). Always exercise your dog before beginning a retraining session.

CHASING

Chasing is a normal dog behavior that, through selective breeding, we have intensified in some breeds and diminished in others. Sight hounds and terriers are reflex chasers, while scent hounds, pointers, setters, and

MISSING DOG

You should not let your dog off its leash until you are sure it will respond to the command "Come." If you do lose your dog, carry out an immediate search, helped by others if possible. Contact the police, local dog shelters, and your microchip, tattoo, or tag registry. If this is not successful, contact local veterinary clinics to see if your dog has been taken there. Make a flyer with a photo of your dog and appropriate information to post and send to everyone called. Keep a list of everyone you have contacted. After your dog returns, call all contacts with the good news.

retrievers are a little less inclined to instant reactive pursuit. The instinct is stimulated by movement and reinforced if other dogs join in. This problem may be overcome with aversion training (*see caption, below left*), but prevention, as always, is easier than "cure."

SIGNS OF DOMINANCE

It is easy to mistake early warning signs of dominance for playful exuberance. Be concerned if your dog growls when its toys are taken away, or snatches them possessively as you approach. Grabbing at a toy or at your empty hand when you run is equally worrying. So too is an unwillingness to let go of objects. Listen to your dog's voice; a change of tone will signal a change of attitude from play to aggressive play. Norwegian veterinarians discovered that a male dog's level of the sex hormone testosterone drops after a course of obedience training. If you sense any signs of dominance, stop the game immediately and give your dog an obedience command. This is simply our variation of what a dominant wolf does when a member of the pack gets too uppity during play.

AGGRESSION TOWARD OTHER DOGS

Aggression is often directed at a dog of the same sex, and the problem is most likely to occur when a dog is on what it considers to be its own territory. If you intervene during a fight, in the heat of the moment you are as likely to be bitten by your own dog as by the other. A tight hold on the leash can actually exaggerate your dog's aggressive intent. Fortunately, the natural instinct of dogs is first to posture and growl intent, which gives us time to intervene with obedience commands. Be vigilant, and intervene with an obedience command as soon as your dog makes eye contact with a potential adversary.

CHECKLIST

- Obedience training is the best way to overcome outdoor behavior problems.
- Use a collar and leash suitable for your dog's shape and personality.
- A lack of daily mental and physical stimulation will lead to disobedience problems.
- Your dog should always be under the control of a responsible individual.
- What is "natural" in a forest-living wolf is not always acceptable behavior for an urban-living dog.
- It is our responsibility, to our neighbors and community, to train our dogs.

DIGGING THE GARDEN
Dogs dig because of boredom, to escape, or to build nests. Exercise your dog before leaving it alone in the garden and, if possible, provide a sandpit to dig or nest in.

NATURAL DEVELOPMENT

NATURAL TRAINING

NATURAL NUTRITION

NATURAL HEALTH CARE

HEALTH DISORDERS

Natural Nutrition

Hunger is the dog's natural state. It is the driving force of many of its activities. If a dog has sufficient mental and physical stimulation, it may balance its energy consumption and expenditure, but it is a rare dog that has such a natural life. Obesity is a common problem in dogs because their lives are often insufficiently active. Remember, your dog depends on you to provide it with the right quantities of nutrients necessary for maintaining a healthy body and efficient immune system. What it needs will vary according to its age, sex, size, body condition, level of activity, personality, and state of health.

Gnawing on hard bones can be beneficial to the health of your dog's teeth and gums.

YOUR DOG'S NUTRITIONAL NEEDS

PROVIDING A WHOLESOME, well-balanced diet is the best way to achieve and maintain your dog's good health. Feed a nutritious diet of what is good for dogs, which is not necessarily the same as what is good for us. All dogs thrive on a balanced basic diet. Careful selection of the ingredients may also enable you to enhance your dog's immune system and help it to avoid illness.

FOODS YOU SHOULD LIMIT
Never give any food or nutrient in excess. Avoid meat-only diets, especially with fussy eaters such as small but demanding dogs. Meat alone is deficient in a variety of essential nutrients, especially calcium. Avoid savory "human" snack foods. Use healthier snacks such as dried meat or vitamin tablets for dog training.

BENEFICIAL BACTERIA
At birth, a pup's intestines first become inhabited by good bacteria that have been passed on in its mother's milk. As the pup grows, it receives new bacteria from the different foods it is given by its mother, or from food that it finds itself. Most of these bacterial "guests" are transient and die off within a few days, but some stay longer, creating a stable environment for digesting nutrients from the food that is eaten.

Inside a pup's intestines there is a competitive ecosystem, with bacteria vying with each other for space and ultimately striking a balance among themselves. This creates the homeostatic balance necessary for optimum digestion of the nutrients needed by different parts of your dog's body. The good bacteria are also necessary for an efficient immune system that will protect your dog from harmful bacteria.

NATURAL CARNIVORE
The design of the dog's digestive system is that of an evolutionary carnivore. Small mammals are its natural diet, but this source of food, like any other, has advantages and disadvantages. All diets are compromises between benefits and risks.

WHAT IS A NATURAL DIET?
A whole rabbit – skin, bones, and intestines – is probably the most natural diet a dog can eat. Fur and intestine content provide fiber while the liver, muscle, and bones provide protein, fat, vitamins, and minerals. This "natural" diet is not necessarily safe. A freshly killed rabbit contains potentially harmful bacteria and parasites, bones that may damage the intestines, and fur that might cause vomiting or a blockage.

Any diet you choose to feed your dog, no matter how "natural" or how "synthetic," is a compromise between potential benefits and possible risks. Canine nutrition is a matter of common sense, not a religion. Common sense means striking a balance between experience and new information. Modern science helps us to understand why some foods are so good for dogs (and us). For example, certain strains of the bacteria *Lactobacillus acidophilus*, available in milk, are beneficial in a pup's diet because they enhance the immune system. These good bacteria protect the intestines from colonization by harmful bacteria. When it comes to science, remember that ideas constantly change. At any given time, it is thought that about half the information disseminated by scientists is correct. It can be difficult to know which dietary guidelines are well founded.

When considering your dog's nutritional needs, remember that the reason for eating is both to sustain life and to maintain a natural balance within the intestines. An efficient immune system, and therefore good health, depends on a healthy digestion.

IN OUR HANDS
Feeding a dog is similar to feeding a baby, in that neither has much of a say in what it eats. They depend on us to make the right decisions. This can be difficult because you cannot apply directly to dogs what you know to be nutritionally good for us.

For example, fiber from wholegrains may help prevent the buildup of carcinogens that cause colonic cancer in people, but wholegrains have never been a natural part of the dog's diet, except under conditions of extreme starvation. Chocolate lifts our spirits, but if an excessive amount is given to dogs it can poison them. It may even kill small dogs. When we are stressed, a vitamin C supplement may be beneficial because we do not have the ability to make our own vitamin C. Dogs manufacture their own vitamin C from glucose in their livers. During stress, it is likely that dogs have the same ability that rats have, to increase their own natural production of vitamin C.

Your dog's natural nutritional needs are those of a scavenging carnivore. Watch any puppy at a food bowl and it is obvious that the drive to eat is overwhelmingly potent. Like pigs at the feeding trough, puppies are competitive gorgers. From birth, each pup is in competition with its siblings for its mother's milk and then for solid food. "Eat first. Eat fast. Eat most." This is an excellent gambit when food is scarce, but for dogs fed by us, this brain-driven need to eat what is available is at the root of the most common nutritional "disease" today, obesity.

WHAT ALL DOGS NEED

The dog shares many of our nutritional needs, but its optimum levels of vitamins, minerals, essential fatty acids, carbohydrate, protein, fat, and fiber are different from ours. All dogs need protein to provide amino acids, the building blocks of all body

THE LEVIN ARCHIPELAGO

The changes that take place in the variety of intestinal bacteria were illustrated in a unique experiment carried out by the microbiologist Bruce Levin. For a year, he cultured and classified the bacteria on his toilet tissue. In scientific circles, the ebb and flow of bacterial life in Dr. Levin's intestines came to be known as the Levin Archipelago, a living environment constantly altered by external events. For example, when another member of his family was treated with antibiotics, the bacteria in Levin's intestines were also affected.

EATING GRASS
While dogs are essentially carnivores, they evolved to survive without meat by eating other foods. Grass, berries, roots, and vegetables are emergency sources of nourishment. Dogs can survive on a sub-optimum diet, but meat and animal fat remain the most efficient sources of nourishment for dogs.

tissues and the enzymes that support the body's chemical reactions. The most natural source of protein is meat, but, like us, dogs can get all the essential amino acids they need to sustain life from vegetable protein. (Cats cannot. If a cat's only source of protein is vegetarian, eventually it will die from essential amino-acid deficiencies.)

Dogs also need fat, the most energy-dense nutrient, with more than twice as many calories per gram as protein. Fat transports fat-soluble vitamins around the body. It also contains essential fatty acids that a dog cannot manufacture itself.

Carbohydrates are not a natural source of energy for dogs, but dogs are able to convert carbohydrates to the sugar glucose. This is used to produce glycogen, which is stored in muscle as a source of energy. The Greyhound, bred as an athlete, is particularly good at storing glycogen.

Vitamins and minerals are essential for energy conversion, enzyme activity, and bone growth. Fiber promotes good digestion and solid stools, while water, the most mundane of all nutrients, is an obvious essential for life. Each individual dog has its own unique requirements for each of these nutrients.

CHECKLIST
Be wary of "experts" who say that:

- Canine malnutrition is common.
- All commercial pet foods contain poisons.
- Their own brand of dog food or supplement is uniquely natural.
- There is a conspiracy to withhold information about food dangers to dogs.

These statements are myths with no foundation.

Changing Nutrition Through Life

Your dog's nutritional requirements change during life, but not all dogs change at the same time. Needs vary according to age, size, state of health, inherited metabolic rate, and level of activity. Puppies need extra nutrients to grow and to maintain themselves. During illness, extra vitamins and minerals may be beneficial. When feeding your dog, take into account all of these factors.

A Natural Diet?

Rodents would seem to be the dog's natural diet, but they have a high fat content, almost 40 percent on a dry weight basis. In feeding tests, dogs were found to be healthier if their diet contained considerably less fat than found in wildlife.

Checklist

- Food preferences are generally established early in life.
- Arbitrary diet changes as dogs age are not necessary.
- Nutritional demands during illness are different from those in good health.
- Nutrient demands are highest during lactation, not during pregnancy.
- Stable weight is an excellent guide to homeostasis.
- Any sudden weight gain or loss is a sign of imbalance.

Nourishment from Mother

Nutritionists have discovered that well-nourished mothers produce puppies that are not only healthier, they also walk, run, and play earlier, learn faster, and have fewer emotional problems than puppies from malnourished mothers. The effects of malnourishment can be perpetuated for generations. The young of poorly nourished mothers become poor mothers themselves.

Even during the hormonal changes of a false pregnancy, some dogs have morning sickness. Scientists see this as evidence that the mother is minimizing her fetuses' exposure to toxins. Hormonal changes also lead to bitches developing food aversions during pregnancy. Avoid unnecessary drugs and herbs during pregnancy, because they may be harmful to the fetuses.

First Food of Life

A pup grows phenomenally during the first months of life. It can increase from less than 1 lb (450 g) at birth to 50 lb (22 kg) by its first birthday. Large breeds can reach double

that size in the same time. High levels of nutrients are needed to support this 50-fold increase in body mass. A bitch's milk is ideal for these growth demands. It has twice the nutritional value of cows' or goats' milk. Unfortunately, our intervention in dog breeding has led to increased litter size or decreased "mother size" in some breeds. Some mothers cannot produce enough milk for their pups without putting themselves in danger of suffering from a sudden calcium deficiency. When a mother cannot provide enough milk for her pups, supplement her milk with canine-milk replacer. The following home formula is fine in emergency situations:

The Working Dog

Working dogs that herd, guard, or search need 1.5 to 2.5 times more food energy than pet dogs. In the most extreme circumstances of winter sled-dog races, a sled dog may need 10,000 calories per day. Unlike humans, dogs need increased fat rather than carbohydrate in their diet for the stamina of hard work. Feed a high-fat, digestible, energy-dense diet in two or more portions daily. Provide a meal about one hour before working and feed the largest meal after hard work.

Canine Milk Supplement

- 1 can condensed milk
- An equal quantity of water (1 can)
- 2 tbs live yogurt
- 2 tbs mayonnaise
- 2 tsp glucose powder
- 25 g gelatin granules

Bring the water to the boil and whisk in the gelatin granules. Remove from the heat and add the condensed milk, then the yogurt, mayonnaise, and glucose powder, whisking thoroughly. Allow to cool, then refrigerate. The mixture thickens in the fridge. Bring back to liquid consistency in the microwave or using a double boiler.

During growth, a puppy's diet should contain at least 22 percent protein and 5 percent fat on a dry-matter basis. Dry-matter means "water removed from food." Dry-matter comparisons of one diet and another are difficult, but are the only valid way for you to compare the nutrient values of different foods (*see pages 48-49*). "Dry" dog foods have up to 10 percent moisture while "wet," or canned, foods can contain more than 80 percent. Fresh meat has about the same amount of moisture as canned foods. Puppies need the same nutrients that adults do, but in different quantities.

MAINTAINING NOT GAINING

If puppies ingest too much energy-dense food they may be heading toward lifelong obesity. Too much energy-dense food early in life creates a larger number of fat cells in the adult. It is harder to reduce the number of fat cells than it is the size of fat cells. Avoid plumpness in puppies. It looks cute but it is not healthy in the long term.

On a dry-weight basis, feed your dog a diet containing around 18 percent protein and 5 percent fat. Many foods available for your dog, either commercially produced or home-prepared, contain more than enough nutrients and are very tasty. If these nutrient-rich diets are fed on demand, obesity is the natural outcome. It is your responsibility to control your dog's food consumption. By some estimates, about one third of all dogs are obese (*see pages 44-45*).

AGING, HEALTH, AND DIET

The effects of natural aging, or of one of the specific health problems to which older dogs are susceptible, may demand changes to an existing diet. Generally speaking, an older dog needs about 20 percent fewer calories than it required in its prime, but more daily vitamins and minerals. As dogs mature, some individuals gain weight. This often occurs because the energy we supply them, in the form of food, is not being used up through exercise. Sometimes this weight gain

will be caused by an underactive thyroid gland. If your elderly dog is gaining or losing weight, make sure it has a clean bill of health from your vet before adjusting its diet.

CHANGING NEEDS

Your dog's nutritional needs gradually change throughout its life. Switching from one source of nutrients to another should be carried out in an equally gradual way. Plan diet changes to occur over a five- to 10-day period. Sudden diet changes affect the living environment of microorganisms in your dog's intestines. This is why diarrhea can occur if you abruptly change from one food to another. Begin by adding a little of the new food to your dog's existing diet. Gradually increase the proportion of new food over the following days.

Like us, dogs, especially small ones, have their own preferences for odors, textures, and flavors, but finicky eaters are made, not born. From early in life, offer your dog a nutritious variety of food but do not let it dictate its diet. As time moves on, modify that diet according to your dog's unique demands. Weigh your dog routinely. Steady weight is one of the best signs of good health. Weight increases or losses mean that the natural balance has been upset. Something is likely to be wrong, and adjusting nutrition may be central to resolving the problem.

MILK DRINKING

Milk is the staple of life. Puppies produce special enzymes in their intestines to digest lactose, the sugar in milk, but by maturity these enzymes naturally diminish. This can lead to milk causing diarrhea in older dogs. If this is a problem, offer lactose-free milk, available from supermarkets.

HIGH ENERGY
You need to vary your dog's diet according to its energy demands and environment. During youth, dogs need energy to grow as well as to maintain themselves. Dogs that live in cold climates will need extra nutrients to fuel their energy needs.

NATURAL DEVELOPMENT

NATURAL TRAINING

NATURAL NUTRITION

NATURAL HEALTH CARE

HEALTH DISORDERS

ASSESSING BODY CONDITION

FOR MOST OF US, our dogs become so familiar that we take for granted that they are happy and healthy. Most dogs are content with this arrangement because life is easy and food, comfort, and security are always available. Two potential problems can occur when we treat our dogs this way. We forget that, given the chance, they eat in excess, and that they need exercise to burn up excess energy.

SUBTLE CHANGES

I admit it. My Golden Retrievers are slightly overweight. I didn't think they were. They enjoyed vigorous daily exercise. They only ate their own meals and were never given tidbits from the table. And they looked good. Athletic but warm and cuddly. I knew they were overweight when, one day, while they were exercising in the park, one of them tore a ligament behind her knee. This was personally embarrassing because I warn clients with fat pooches of this potential medical consequence of their dog being overweight. If a dog carries more weight than it should, it runs the risk of rupturing a cruciate ligament when it is between seven and 10 years of age. My dog's optimum weight is 66 lb (30 kg). When she tore her ligament she weighed 73 lb (33 kg). Even 10 percent above the optimum can be harmful.

OVERWEIGHT DOGS

Obesity is overwhelmingly the most common nutritional problem in dogs. Puppies under one year of age are sometimes encouraged to

BREED DIFFERENCES

Body condition is strongly influenced by genetic factors. So too is obesity. In the United States, American Cocker Spaniels, Basset Hounds, Beagles, Cairn Terriers, Cavalier King Charles Spaniels, Dachshunds, Labrador Retrievers, Norwegian Elkhounds, Rough Collies, and Shetland Sheepdogs, are most prone to obesity. If you have one of these breeds, you will need to be extra-vigilant about the amount you feed your dog.

become overweight simply because roly-poly puppies look cute. Obesity is increasingly a problem because we don't exercise our dogs enough. It is also a "new" problem because we often feed our dogs food that is too rich in energy. In the last decade, pet food manufacturers have been extraordinarily successful in creating nutrient-rich, highly palatable energy foods for dogs. Some of these commercial diets are wholesome, but when fed freely provide far more energy than is necessary for a pet dog's lifestyle. Energy-dense, high-quality, commercial dog foods reduce the amount of waste that a dog passes. For urban dog owners, this means less clearing up, which is an attractive bonus. But in order to maintain our dogs at their optimum weight we must be extra careful not to feed too much of these tasty foods.

UNDERWEIGHT DOGS

During or after illness, after pregnancy, or when working, dogs have increased energy demands. By assessing your dog's body condition you can determine whether it needs more energy-dense food. Fat is twice as energy-dense as protein. Feed as you would a pregnant or lactating bitch, increasing trace elements as well (see pages 48-49).

An important cause of loss of body condition during illness is often dehydration. This may occur even when a dog continues drinking its normal amount of fluid. Water absorbs water-soluble vitamins and is absorbed by fiber to add beneficial bulk to your dog's diet. Always provide fresh, easily accessible water. A well-hydrated dog has taut skin. If you gently pinch the skin on its neck it snaps back into its normal position. If the skin remains "tented," retracting more slowly than normal, your dog is dehydrated.

THE IMPORTANCE OF EXERCISE

A modern urban lifestyle is not what dogs were made for; they tend to find it dull and unstimulating. The most exciting event is feeding time. Deep down, many dog owners suspect their dogs are unsatisfied. We know we are often not providing our dogs with the type of physical exercise they really want. Regardless of breed, virtually any young dog has boundless energy and will enjoy running and leaping around for hours on end.

We know this, and we feel a little guilty because we are too busy to let them do what nature prepared them for. So what do we do instead? We give them snacks. Put a little extra food in the bowl. Share a donut or a sandwich. Insidiously, without you noticing at first, your dog's body shape starts to change. The hourglass figure disappears as the belly line becomes more horizontal. From above, the hips and shoulders widen.

If your dog is fat, get to the root of the problem. Play with it more. Make life more stimulating, physically and mentally. Dogs were bred to be most efficient and most healthy at their optimum weight. Extra weight puts extra strain on a dog's joints as well as its heart and lungs. Obesity may also increase risks during anesthesia and surgery.

ADJUSTING YOUR DOG'S DIET

Use the illustrations (*see right*) to assess your dog's body condition. If your dog appears to be emaciated or thin, see your veterinarian. Cared-for dogs are rarely underweight due to diet alone. There will often be a medical explanation. If your dog is overweight or obese, the reason is likely to lie with you. Carefully examine its diet to determine where you have gone wrong. When changing your dog's diet, it is important that you do it gradually. A too-rapid shift can lead to bowel problems or, more frequently, to your dog becoming confused and unsettled because you have altered its routine.

Once you have assessed your dog's body condition and know what has caused its weight gain or loss, you are in a position to determine what to do about it. This involves an understanding of the different sources of calories, protein, fat, and carbohydrate, and how to balance the energy in calories that these sources supply with the energy demands of your dog 's life (*see pages 46-47*).

ASSESSING YOUR DOG

Use this chart to assess your dog's body condition. Compare top and side views with the pictures below. If your dog is at either extreme, consult your vet for advice on the cause and treament of its condition.

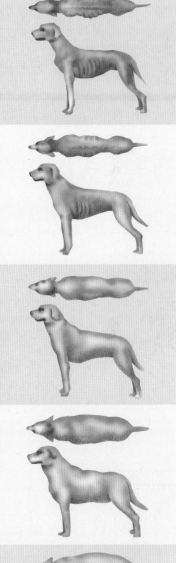

BODY CONDITIONS	BODY SHAPES
EMACIATED • Ribs showing, no fat cover • Severe abdominal tuck • Bones at base of tail raised with no tissue between skin and bone • No palpable abdominal fat	
THIN • Ribs easily felt with minimal fat cover • Waist obvious behind ribs • Bones at base of tail raised, and covered in minimal fat • Minimal abdominal fat	
IDEAL • Slight fat cover on ribs • Waist can be seen behind ribs • Bones at base of tail smooth, covered in thin layer of fat • Minimal abdominal fat	
OVERWEIGHT • Ribs not easily felt, with moderate fat cover • Waist hardly discernable • Bones at base of tail felt under moderate layer of fat • Moderate abdominal fat	
OBESE • Ribs not felt due to thick fat cover • No waist, abdomen distended • Bones at base of tail difficult to feel through fat • Extensive abdominal fat	

NATURAL DEVELOPMENT

NATURAL TRAINING

NATURAL NUTRITION

NATURAL HEALTH CARE

HEALTH DISORDERS

WHERE ENERGY COMES FROM

HUNGER IS A DOG'S NATURAL STATE, hunger for energy in the form of food. Energy comes from the protein, fat, and carbohydrate eaten by your dog. Protein, transported via the blood, helps tissues grow or repair. Fat is essential for healthy cells and an efficient immune system. Carbohydrates are converted to sugar and provide instant energy. The energy provided by food is calculated in kilocalories (kcals).

CHECKLIST
- Do not feed dogs only cat food. It contains more protein than a dog needs.
- Avoid raw meat. It may contain parasites or be contaminated by bacteria.
- A dog is able to survive on a vegetarian diet if it is carefully balanced.
- Increase dietary fat if your dog needs extra energy.

ENERGY NEEDS
Dogs need good quality protein to grow and maintain and repair body tissues. Proteins are complex molecules made up of a variety of amino acids. Dogs, like us, can acquire all the amino acids they need from vegetable-derived protein. The dog can live on a vegetarian diet, although from the perspective of evolution this is not natural, because a dog's gastrointestinal system works most efficiently with meat. Vegetable protein is less efficient than animal protein for providing dogs with the essential amino acids that are needed for body maintenance.

Fat provides energy and palatability in a dog's diet. Recent nutrition studies show that the type and amount of fat your dog eats affects not only its weight but also the efficiency of its immune system (see pages 50-51). In the table below is a list of animal-derived foods. All of these foods are good sources of energy for dogs, but equal quantities do not translate into equal kilocalories. If you want to change from one

PROTEIN AND FAT SOURCES OF ENERGY
Meat from different sources varies in the amount of energy that comes from its muscle or fat. This table gives the energy content of different meats, and how much of that energy comes from protein or fat. For most dogs, fat is an excellent energy source.

FOOD SOURCES (100 g/3.5 oz)	ENERGY (kcals)	PROTEIN (g)	FAT (g)	CARBO-HYDRATE (g)
Chicken meat	121	20.5	4.3	0
Chicken meat with skin	230	17.6	17.7	0
Duck meat	122	19.7	5	0
Duck meat with skin	430	11.3	42.7	0
Lean beef	123	20	4.6	0
Lamb	162	21	9	0
Pork	147	20.7	7	0
Turkey without skin	107	22	2.2	0
Venison	198	35	6.4	0
Rabbit	124	22	4	0
Tripe	6	9.4	2.5	0
Cod	76	17.4	0.7	0
Herring	234	17	18.5	0
Egg	47	12.5	11	Trace
Cottage cheese	98	14	4	2.4
Low fat plain yogurt	56	5	0.8	7.5

source of protein to another, use this table to compare the number of kcals provided by similar quantities of different foods.

Carbohydrates are not an important natural energy source for dogs, but there is some evidence that they are a good source of energy during pregnancy and lactation. Starch is the most common source of carbohydrate. Cooked starch is easily digested. The table below shows that 100 g of different starch foods produce different amounts of energy.

THE IMPORTANCE OF FIBER
Fiber is a natural part of a dog's diet when it eats the fur or viscera contents of other mammals. It stimulates saliva and gastric-juice production. Soluble fiber slows down digestion and absorption of food in the small intestine, while insoluble fiber stimulates "intestinal hurry." Fiber may be beneficial for preventing and treating constipation, sugar diabetes, obesity, inflammatory bowel disease, and excess fat in the bloodstream. Fermentable fiber creates substances in the intestines that may inhibit harmful bacteria.

Beet pulp, chicory, rice bran, and bran breakfast cereals are common sources of fermentable and non-fermentable fiber. Psyllium is an excellent source of soluble fiber.

ENERGY SOURCES
The intestinal contents of prey are a source of fiber and carbohydrate, both valuable for efficient digestion, but this type of "natural" eating is often impractical for household pets. You can improve upon nature's sources of energy.

DANGEROUS FOODS
Never feed your dog a meat-only diet. It might seem natural to you, but plain meat lacks balance in its calcium-phosphorus ratio. This type of diet leads to serious bone disorders and can eventually cause heart failure. Even from the most hygienic sources, assume that raw meat, eggs, or dairy products may be contaminated with Salmonella bacteria. All animal-derived sources of energy should be cooked before feeding them to your dog.

CARBOHYDRATE SOURCES OF ENERGY
Use this chart if changing your dog's source of carbohydrate. Note that different amounts of carbohydrate provide the same amount of energy. For example you need to feed your dog far more cooked potato to equal the energy provided by 100 g of cooked rice.

FOOD SOURCES (100 g/3.5 oz)	ENERGY (kcals)	PROTEIN (g)	FAT (g)	CARBO-HYDRATE (g)
White rice (uncooked)	383	7.3	3.6	86
Brown rice (uncooked)	357	6.7	2.8	81.3
Potato (boiled)	75	1.5	0.3	17.8
Yam (boiled)	133	1.7	0.3	33
White bread	235	8.4	1.9	49
Brown bread	218	8.5	2	44
Egg noodles (uncooked)	391	12	8.2	72

ESSENTIAL WATER
Of course, water is the essence of life. It is the largest component of most of the cells of the dog's body. Water absorbs water-soluble vitamins and is absorbed by fiber to add beneficial bulk to your dog's diet. Always provide fresh, clean, and easily accessible water.

NATURAL DEVELOPMENT

NATURAL TRAINING

NATURAL NUTRITION

NATURAL HEALTH CARE

HEALTH DISORDERS

ADJUSTING ENERGY INTAKE

MODERATE OVER-NOURISHMENT is common in dogs. After all, the species evolved to eat competitively with the rest of the pack. Today, we feed our dogs large amounts of extremely palatable food and often we fail to exercise them sufficiently. It is up to us, not our dogs, to ensure that the amount of energy that a dog consumes is virtually equal to the amount it needs for its personal lifestyle.

CHECKLIST

- Determine your dog's basic energy needs.
- Increase energy consumption during pregnancy and lactation.
- Increase energy consumption during growth.
- To overcome obesity, don't just reduce energy consumption.
- Eliminate the social causes of obesity.
- Ensure that all diets contain correct amounts of micronutrients.

CALCULATING ENERGY

The energy requirements of dogs can range from as little as 200 kilocalories (kcals) per day for an inactive Chihuahua to more than 6,000 kcals a day for a lactating "giant" mother. See the box below for guidelines to energy requirements for different-sized dogs.

If you feed your dog fresh food, you can use the table on page 46 to calculate how many kcals you are providing it. Determining how many kcals there are in commercial dog food can be more difficult because very few manufacturers give this information on the label. As a guideline, a standard 14 oz (400 g) can of dog food contains up to 400 kcals. Nutritionists calculate energy on a dry-matter basis but, unfortunately, dog food labels do not give this information so it is difficult to compare the nutritional content of one dog food to another. To calculate the nutritional value of food, you first need to know its moisture content.

TACKLING CANINE OBESITY

Keep a record of exactly what your dog eats, including all the tidbits. This makes you more conscious of all the extras it receives. Feed low-fat, high-fiber foods. This will lower calories while maintaining bulk. Fiber or water added to food "dilutes" the calories in it. Feed and exercise with your dog frequently. This might accelerate its basic metabolic rate. Avoid crash diets: they upset your dog and only drive its metabolism to be more efficient and fat-storing in the future. You may need as much help sticking to a healthy dog's diet as your dog does. If you are being stared at with mournful brown eyes, discuss the problem with your veterinary staff. In these circumstances they make understanding counselors.

Then you work out dry-matter content with a calculator. Here is what you do. First, read the manufacturer's Guaranteed Analysis, which appears on the label of the pet food. It gives the moisture content, as well as protein, fat, and fiber levels in percentages.

A TYPICAL LABEL

- Crude protein ....7.5 %
- Crude fat ....5 %
- Fiber ....0.2 %
- Moisture ....80 %

AVERAGE ENERGY REQUIREMENTS FOR DIFFERENT BODY WEIGHTS

These are guideline kilocalorie requirements for mature dogs with different lifestyles. An inactive lifestyle is one where a dog goes for short walks on a leash, while an active lifestyle would describe a dog that has at least an hour a day running off its leash. Note that dogs in cool climates need slightly increased kcal intake to keep warm.

ADULT WEIGHT	4–11 LB (2–5 KG)	13–22 LB (6–10 KG)	24–44 LB (11–20 KG)	46–66 LB (21–30 KG)	68–88 LB (31–40 KG)	90–110 LB (41–50 KG)
Inactive life style	185–370	420–620	665–1,040	1,080–1,410	1,445–1,750	1,780–2,070
Active life style	210–420	480–705	775–1,180	1,225–1,600	1,640–1,990	2,025–2,350
Working	295–590	675–990	1,065–1,665	1,725–2,255	2,310–2,800	2,850–3,310
Senior	150–300	345–505	545–850	885–1,155	1,180–1,430	1,460–1,690
Pregnant female	220–440	505–740	800–1,250	1,295–1,690	1,735–2,100	2,140–2,480

ENERGY REQUIREMENTS DURING LACTATION

During lactation a mother's energy needs soar. A bitch's milk contains about 40 percent more energy than cow's milk. To produce it requires a considerable increase in energy consumption. Even after her pups reduce their milk consumption, her energy demands remain 50 percent above what is required to maintain her normal weight.

ADULT WEIGHT	4–11 LB (2–5 KG)	13–22 LB (6–10 KG)	24–44 LB (11–20 KG)	46–66 LB (21–30 KG)	68–88 LB (31–40 KG)	90–110 LB (41–50 KG)
Lactation weeks 1–2	370–735	845–1,235	1,330–2,080	2,160–2,820	2,890–3,500	3,565–4,135
Lactation weeks 3–4	555–1,105	1,255–1,855	1,995–3,120	3,235–4,230	4,335–5,250	5,345–6,205
Lactation weeks 5–6	370–735	845–1,235	1,330–2,080	2,160–2,820	2,890–3,500	3,565–4,135

The dry-matter content is what remains when moisture is removed. In this example, if the food is 80 percent moisture, it must be 20 percent dry matter. Next comes more advanced but still simple arithmetic. Calculate the dry-matter nutrient content for protein, fat, and fiber using this formula.

FORMULA TO CALCULATE NUTRITION IN COMMERCIAL FOODS

• Dry-matter nutrient content =

$$\frac{\text{The label's nutrient percentage x 100}}{\text{Dry-matter content percentage}}$$

Therefore:

• Crude protein = $\frac{7.5 \times 100}{20}$ .... = 37.5 %

• Crude fat = $\frac{5 \times 100}{20}$ .... = 25 %

• Crude fiber = $\frac{0.2 \times 100}{20}$ .... = 1 %

By doing these calculations you can compare commercial dog foods with one another. This is important when you are switching from one source of nutrients to another in order to adjust your dog's energy intake.

CHANGING NEEDS

Almost everywhere in the world where dogs are fed by us, obesity is a problem. Neutering, living life on a leash, and access to tasty food are all implicated. The health of an overweight dog is at risk. Use the table on page 48 to assess your dog's correct food intake and adjust it accordingly. If your dog is underweight you should consult your vet, who will try to find out the reason.

MOTHERS AND PUPS

Energy requirements remain stable during the first five weeks of pregnancy, then increase by 10 percent per week in the last four weeks. By the end of pregnancy the requirement is 50 percent above maintenance. See the table above for energy needs during lactation.

From birth until a puppy reaches half its adult size, it needs about twice the amount of energy needed for body maintenance and during the remainder of its growth it needs 50 percent more energy. For simplicity, assume that dogs up to 12 kg finish growing by six months. Those up to 20 kg finish by nine months, and those up to 45 kg at a year. Check the calories needed for its grown weight in the table on page 48, then increase this by 100 percent for the first half of a puppy's growing period, then by 50 percent until it is mature. At this point, its energy needs drop to normal for the first time.

GERIATRIC DIETS

Older dogs have varying needs. Most will thrive on their adult maintenance diet supplemented with vitamins and minerals. Overweight elderlies should be gradually slimmed, while underweight seniors or those recovering from illness will benefit from an increase in energy food.

LOSING WEIGHT
Most dogs today have no gainful employment. If there is nothing else to occupy them, many dogs work on getting fat. For these individuals, eating becomes the most interesting aspect of life. Slimming diets alone do not correct the problem. Increase your dog's mental and physical exercise, and improve your relationship, with games and training.

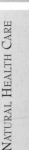

THE IMPORTANCE OF MICRONUTRIENTS

FOOD NEEDS CONVERSION. Cascades of chemical reactions in the dog's body turn protein, fat, and carbohydrate, the "macronutrients," into the essentials of life. These reactions rely upon vitamins and minerals, the "micronutrients." Nutritional synergy is only as efficient as the weakest link in the chain. Extra micronutrients are useful when a dog is stressed through illness, medication, or advancing years.

THE ROLE OF VITAMINS

Vitamins are nutrients that are needed as catalysts for the dog's metabolism. For convenience they are divided into fat-soluble and water-soluble groups. The fat-soluble vitamins enter the body with dietary fat and are stored in the liver. If too much is stored, a dog may become toxic and ill.

FAT-SOLUBLE VITAMINS

Vitamins that are fat-soluble include vitamins A, D, E, and K. Vitamin A serves many roles including maintaining healthy eyesight. Dogs can make it from substances called carotenoids, which are found in plant cells, but they get most of their natural vitamin A from eating the livers of other animals. Fish oils, milk, and egg yolk are good sources of vitamin A. Some Cocker Spaniels have a problem making enough vitamin A, leading to oily skin conditions. Dogs can synthesize vitamin D in their skin. Deficiency, causing rickets, is now rare.

VARY THE DIET
Dogs do not always choose to eat what is nutritionally best. For example, an all-meat diet has a poor calcium-phosphorus ratio that leads to pain, skeletal deformities, and then heart failure. Don't let your dog dictate what it eats.

Excess vitamin D is regrettably common, and leads to calcium deposits in soft tissue and skeleton deformities. Vitamin E, with the mineral selenium, acts as an antioxidant (*see box, page 51*), neutralizing free radicals that can damage cell membranes. Vitamin E acts as an anti-inflammatory for some dogs with skin disorders, and may be of benefit for vascular, heart, or neurological conditions. Stressed and hard-working dogs have a higher requirement for vitamin E.

Vitamin K is needed for blood coagulation. Some vitamin K is manufactured by bacteria in the dog's intestines. Dogs on prolonged antibiotic therapy may need a vitamin K supplementation. Deficiencies rarely occur.

WATER-SOLUBLE VITAMINS

There is little risk of overdosing with the water-soluble vitamins. If food is deficient in vitamin B complex, yeast-based tablets are a safe supplement. Some Giant Schnauzers suffer from a condition that interferes with vitamin B12 absorption. They need their B12 given by injection. Many of the B vitamins are synthesized by bacteria in the dog's intestines. Because antibiotics interfere with the bacteria that manufacture these vitamins, your dog might benefit from yeast tablets if it has been prescribed antibiotics.

Folic acid plays a vital role in the synthesis of prostaglandins, chemicals with many roles in the body including protection of the stomach lining. A deficiency can lead to increased levels of the amino acid homocysteine.

While we cannot manufacture our own vitamin C, dogs can. The dog's liver makes ascorbic acid from glucose, and it is likely that dogs have the capacity to increase vitamin C production when under the stress of illness. We (and guinea pigs) are unusual in the animal world in that we don't have the ability to manufacture our own vitamin C. We have to consume it in our food. Take care if giving a vitamin C supplement to your dog. When given in excess, vitamin C is excreted in the urine as a substance called oxalate. This can form into bladder stones.

MINERALS

Like vitamins, minerals play vital roles at the cellular level. Calcium and phosphorus are necessary for growth and maintenance of the skeleton and for cell-membrane and neuro-muscular function. Meat-only diets (low in calcium) lead to over-stimulation of the parathyroid gland and eventual swollen, painful joints. Lactation can result in low blood calcium leading to eclampsia, while diets high in calcium during pregnancy may increase the risk of eclampsia during lactation. Excess dietary calcium may induce zinc deficiency if fed over a prolonged period.

Selenium is an essential part of the enzyme systems that maintain healthy body tissue. It may also play a role in the immune system, and help neutralize carcinogens.

Copper is stored in the liver and, with iron, is associated with the transport of oxygen around the body in red blood cells. Some breeds of dogs, such as the Dobermann and Cocker Spaniel, may have an inherited copper-storage disease, leading to copper poisoning.

Zinc is vital for healthy skin, for an efficient immune system, and for competent taste buds. Zinc deficiency in the diet is sometimes called "generic dry dog food disease" because of the low zinc levels in poorly formulated dry dog food. Some Alaskan Malamutes and Siberian Huskies have an inherited zinc metabolism disorder where zinc absorption is poor.

BALANCED NUTRIENTS

Take great care when supplementing your dog's diet with added vitamins and minerals. High levels of some nutrients reduce the absorption of others. It is potentially dangerous to give large amounts of any single mineral. When a high dose of a single nutrient is needed, use a broad-spectrum vitamin and mineral supplement formulated especially for dogs. This helps to maintain a proper balance by raising the nutritional levels of other nutrients as well.

Iodine is necessary for efficient thyroid gland functioning. Although "hypothyroidism," an underactivity of the thyroid gland, is probably the most common hormonal imbalance that dogs suffer from, it is rarely associated with a deficiency of iodine in the diet.

ESSENTIAL FATTY ACIDS

Important discoveries have been made in the last decade that explain the vital role of essential fatty acids (EFAs) in controlling allergy, arthritis, inflammation, heart disease, auto-immune disease, kidney and nervous system function, dermatitis, and even cancer. Most of the EFAs known as omega 6 are associated with cell inflammation, and they may also suppress the immune system. Another group, called omega 3, are associated with reduced cellular inflammation. Omega-3 EFAs do not suppress the immune system. In both people and dogs, dietary omega-3 fatty acids enhance the efficiency of the immune system. Dogs need a good supply of animal or vegetable-derived linoleic acid, which is an omega-6 EFA, for body growth, wound healing, and liver function. Dogs can convert linoleic acid to another omega 6 called arachidonic acid, which is necessary for blood clotting, coat condition, and efficient reproduction. Feeding diets that are rich in omega-3 fatty acids results in changes in the composition of cell walls. As a consequence, the cell is less at risk of becoming inflamed.

"When given in excess, vitamin C is excreted in the urine as a substance called oxalate. This can form into bladder stones."

BALANCED NUTRIENTS

When supplementing your dog's diet with vitamins and minerals, note that high levels of some nutrients reduce the absorption of others. When a high dose of a single nutrient is needed, use a broad-spectrum supplement. This maintains a proper balance by raising the nutritional levels of other nutrients as well.

ANTIOXIDANTS

An antioxidant is a substance (such as vitamins C and E) that destroys free radicals. Free radicals are atoms in the body that destroy cell membranes. Dogs have their own natural free-radical scavenging systems. Consuming extra antioxidants may boost these natural systems.

IRON SOURCE
Iron is essential for red blood cell production. If you feed your dog fresh food, make sure you include green, leafy vegetables such as spinach.

NATURAL DEVELOPMENT

NATURAL TRAINING

NATURAL NUTRITION

NATURAL HEALTH CARE

HEALTH DISORDERS

PREPARING HOME RECIPES

WHOLESOMENESS IS THE MOST important ingredient in a home-made diet. Use high-quality, fresh ingredients. Prepare your dog's food daily and serve at room, not refrigerator, temperature. Increase or decrease the energy and micronutrient levels of the food according to seasonal changes and your dog's health. Treats should not provide more than 10 percent of the energy in your dog's diet.

RAW OR COOKED?

Puppies fed raw meat have slightly better growth rates than puppies fed cooked meat. This is not surprising considering that their digestion evolved to cope with raw rather than cooked meals, but there are disadvantages to uncooked meat. Because of modern abattoir methods we simply have to assume that raw meat, even though it is "fit for human consumption" may be contaminated with harmful Salmonella bacteria. Consuming these bacteria may or may not cause illness in your dog, but it may become a carrier of bacteria harmful to us. Uncooked freshwater fish can carry a tapeworm (*Diphyllobothrium latum*). Raw meat can carry parasites dangerous for dogs and ultimately dangerous for us. Dogs like raw meat, but there is little else to recommend feeding it to your dog.

GOOD INGREDIENTS

When selecting what to feed your dog, always use ingredients fit for human consumption. Meat alone is not a balanced food unless fed in whole carcass form including the skeleton and viscera. Plain muscle-meat and fish are rich sources of protein and fat but low in calcium, vitamin A, and vitamin D. Choose your meat source according to how saturated you want the fat to be. Beef is the most saturated, then, in decreasing order, lamb, pork, poultry, and fish. Remember, like us (but unlike cats), dogs can obtain their essential fatty acids from vegetable sources.

Below is a recipe for a typical adult dog. Because of its universal availability I have chosen chicken as a good source of protein.

A STANDARD HOME-MADE DIET

- Chicken ....2 oz
- Liver ....1 oz
- Uncooked rice ....¾ cup
- Sterilized bone meal ....1 tbs
- Iodized salt.................................pinch
- Sunflower or corn oil ....⅛ tsp

Cook the rice, bone meal, salt, and corn oil in twice the volume of water. Simmer for 20 minutes. Add the chicken and liver, simmering for another 10 minutes. Allow to cool before giving the meal to your dog. This recipe produces about 800 kcal of energy, enough to feed an active 22 lb (10 kg) dog for a day. Energy is in the form of 17 percent protein, 31 percent fat, and 53 percent carbohydrate on a dry-weight basis.

For weight control, you can replace the medium-fat chicken with either very lean poultry or flaky white fish such as coley or cod. Reduce the vegetable oil by half. For extra fiber, add ⅔ cup (40 g) of wheat bran to this recipe and increase the water for cooking by 50 percent. If you are feeding cereal grains for added fiber, remember that these are poorly digested by dogs. Cook a cup of grain in 2.5 cups of water for 75 minutes over low heat. If you see any grain in your dog's stool, it hasn't been digested properly. To avoid this, try soaking the grain in water overnight, cooking it longer, using more water, or using flaked or cracked grain instead of whole grain.

DOG TREATS ARE NOURISHING
If you love your dog, it is likely that you love giving it treats. It is simply human nature. There's nothing wrong with treats unless you give them in excess. Never let treats make up more than 10 percent of the energy in your dog's diet and take account of those calories when preparing the rest of its daily food.

GIVING BONES

All dogs love bones. Gnawing on a bone exercises the jaw muscles, massages the gums, and cleans the teeth. Unfortunately, bones can also cause serious internal problems and fracture teeth. Probably every vet in practice has, at one time or another, had to operate on a dog seriously ill because of eating bones. If you plan to feed bones, introduce them to your pup as early as possible. Offer only very hard bones and don't permit your dog to become possessive over them.

FOODS TO AVOID

Tofu can be difficult for dogs to digest and causes them to produce loose, pasty stools. Tofu may also increase mucus congestion in dogs' lungs. Avoid tofu in deep-chested dogs such as Irish Setters and Great Danes. Tofu and other bean products may increase a tendency toward life-threatening bloat (*see pages 134–135*). Adult dogs usually like milk but they do not actually need it and lack an enzyme necessary to digest it. If cows' milk causes diarrhea in your dog, give it lactose-free milk, available for lactose-sensitive children, from supermarkets.

GOOD SUPPLEMENTS

Supplements are usually unnecessary if a diet is well balanced, but when one is needed, a meal can be prepared from liver, bone meal, iodized salt, and fish oil that will contain all the micronutrients a dog needs. If feeding individual supplements, do not exceed the following amounts. Brewer's yeast is an excellent source of B-group vitamins and minerals: feed 1 tsp (5 g) daily per 22 lb (10 kg) body weight. Vitamin E in the form of "d-alpha tocopherol" is given at 50 IU (International Units) per 22 lb (10 kg) daily. Kelp (*Fucus vesiculosis*) is rich in minerals, especially iodine, which stimulates the thyroid gland: give no more than ½ tsp (2.5 g) daily. Cod-liver oil and halibut-liver oil contain the antioxidants vitamin E and beta carotene. Feed no more than 100 mg per 11 lb (5 kg) daily.

HOW TO FEED

Hunger is the natural state of dogs, unless they learn how to manipulate their owners. There are seldom problems feeding large-breed individuals. Through natural selection they are voracious eaters. Small dogs are another matter. Breeds such as Yorkshire Terriers and Chihuahuas can become picky eaters. Your dog is probably manipulating you when it pretends it would rather starve than eat the nutritious, palatable diet you offer.

Whether you use a ceramic, stainless steel, or plastic bowl, make sure it does not slip on the floor. If your dog has long facial hair or droopy ears, use a suitably sized bowl that prevents food getting on your dog. Wash your dog's food and water bowls daily but avoid bleaches or detergents with citrus or pine smells. They are likely to repel rather than attract your dog to its next meal.

A VEGETARIAN DIET?

The dog's digestive system is that of a food-gorging carnivore. It has a large holding-tank stomach and a relatively short intestinal tract. The natural diet for dogs is animal tissue, but when this is not available dogs convert vegetable fat and protein for their body needs. Dogs can survive on a vegetarian diet, but if you plan to feed your dog in this way for ethical reasons, think seriously before transferring your own beliefs onto the life-style of another species that depends upon you for its care, well-being, and quality of life.

ALGAE-BASED SUPPLEMENTS

Algae are plants without roots, stems, or leaves. Like other plants, algae contain vitamins, minerals, and trace elements such as iron, zinc, and iodine. Some blue-green algae are toxic, causing gastro-intestinal upset. Commercial algae-based supplements do no harm, but are no better than other nutrient sources.

GOOD MANNERS
Always feed your dog from its own food bowl, never directly from your table or elsewhere on the floor. Eating solely from its bowl conditions your dog to expect food only at food times and only from one source. You and your dog may be eating the same meal but your dog will not beg for yours.

NATURAL DEVELOPMENT

NATURAL TRAINING

NATURAL NUTRITION

NATURAL HEALTH CARE

HEALTH DISORDERS

COMMERCIALLY PRODUCED FOOD

DEVELOPING AN UNDERSTANDING of the dog's nutritional needs, and meeting them with home-cooked foods daily, are impossible ideals for many dog owners. Much as they would like to, they simply do not have the time. Some commercial pet food companies understand this dilemma and use the healthiest products, safest manufacturing processes and, most important, carry out extensive feeding trials.

CHECKLIST

- With the aid of a calculator, work out the nutrient content of dog foods on a dry-matter basis (*see pages 48-49*).

- Only use products tested by extensive feeding trials.

- Contact the manufacturer to get ingredient information that is not on the label.

- It is best to buy products from manufacturers with long-term research programs.

- Pay attention to your dog's opinion about any food.

WHAT IS IN DOG FOOD?

Reputable pet food manufacturers only use surplus nutrients from the human food chain in their products. Less reputable manufacturers may use products that have been deemed unfit for human consumption. At the premium end of the commercial dog food market, manufacturers compete with human-food producers for ingredients.

Whether canned or dry, dog food recipes will follow either variable or fixed formulas. Fixed formulas remain constant and they form the premium end of the market. Manufacturers make no substitutions. A variable formula product is not necessarily inferior as long as the variety of ingredients remains of high quality and nutritional value. What is in dog food is listed on the label. Unfortunately, this often needs to be interpreted by the manufacturer.

HOW TO INTERPRET A LABEL

Labels give information on:
Typical or Guaranteed Analysis This should list the minimum amount of protein and fat, and the maximum amount of fiber and moisture. It says little about the quality of a product.
Ingredients This gives you more information on quality but usually fails to be specific. Constituents are given in descending order of weight. Meat means muscle. Meat by-products or derivatives means viscera, bone, and marrow, natural components of a dog's diet. Meat meal means dry products rendered from animal tissues.
Feeding Guidelines These recommendations are only suggestions. Your dog may need more or less than what is recommended.

"LOW CALORIE" AND "LITE"

Manufacturers seldom state the calorie content of their dog food, even when it is promoted as "low calorie" or "litesavory In EU countries it is not actually permitted to state the energy content on the majority of dog foods! As a rule of thumb, assume that a "lite" food has about 15 to 25 percent fewer calories than the average from that manufacturer. If a label gives only "minimum" information and you want to know the "maximum" level for fat or other ingredients, contact the producer. If a label does not state the metabolizable energy per kilogram of product, manufacturers should provide you with this information.

Nutritional Adequacy Statement Look for the phrase "animal feeding tests" on North American manufactured foods. If the label says "formulated to meet the nutritional profiles..." this means that the manufacturer is relying upon laboratory analysis, not feeding trials, to determine the food's nutritional content.

SELECTING A COMMERCIAL FOOD

Most of the world's commercial dog foods are manufactured either in Europe or North America or to standards that have been set on those continents. European food labels state what preservatives have been added, although they are not required to state what preservatives are present in "preprocessed" ingredients. All European dog foods include a "best before" date that usually corresponds to the shelf life of the fat-soluble vitamins in the product.

In the United States, dog foods and their labels conform to regulations prepared by the Association of American Feed Control Officials (AAFCO). In Canada, a voluntary certification scheme is monitored by the Canadian Veterinary Medical Association. Manufacturers who comply with the official standards provide more information on their food labels about ingredients and they must substantiate any claims they make.

POTENTIAL PROBLEMS

Knowledge never stands still. It was not until 1980 that it was discovered that cheap, dry commercial diets were often deficient in zinc. Inadequate knowledge about canine nutrition is a potential problem with some commercial dog foods. It is possible for nutrients to be lost during food preparation. Manufacturing mistakes sometimes happen. Formula errors can and occasionally do occur. And there are unknown factors that can arise, too. For example, an allergic dog may respond to a fresh lamb and rice diet, but its allergies may return on a premium, commercially made lamb and rice diet. However, the greatest potential problem with commercially produced dog food will be spoilage in the package.

SHELF LIFE

Heat, humidity, light, even oxygen can spoil dog food. Of all the nutrients your dog eats, fat spoils fastest. Heat sterilization and vacuum sealing prevent spoilage of canned food but dry dog food needs preservatives. Antioxidants are excellent preservatives. Vitamin E (tocopherols) and vitamin C (ascorbic acid) are usually called "natural" although they are sometimes synthesized. Truly synthetic antioxidants such as BHA, BHT, and ethoxyquin are also used. BHA and BHT in excess may be associated with liver and kidney problems.

The United States Food and Drug Administration has recommended a maximum of 75 parts per million (ppm) of ethoxyquin in dog food, rather than the permitted 150 ppm, after tests showed that 170 ppm caused increased liver pigment levels in lactating bitches.

Natural antioxidants do not last as long as synthetic ones. To avoid feeding your dog potentially rancid food, buy commercial foods from retailers with a high inventory turnover. Whenever possible, try to use dry food products within six months of their manufacture date. Store your dog's dry food in a sealed container in a cool, dry location.

FEEDING TRIALS

Laboratory analysis is not sufficient to reveal unexpected problems with any commercial diet. Only feed your dog commercial food that has undergone extensive feeding trials. It is in the interest of reputable manufacturers that they discover potential problems before you do.

NATURAL DOG FOODS

Some pet food manufacturers use the word "natural" on their processed dog foods. Of course, a dog's true "natural" diet is fresh, warm rabbit or squirrel. Manufacturers of "natural" dog foods include natural rather than man-made antioxidants in their dry foods. In the United States, the world's largest source of dog food, the Food and Drug Administration has no official definition of what "natural" or "preservative free" means, although guidelines will be developed.

DANGEROUS ADDITIVES

Benzoic acid and benzoates, used as preservatives in food for human consumption, are banned from pet food because dogs cannot detoxify these substances. Propylene glycol was permitted in semi-moist foods, but is now banned because of its effect on red blood-cell survival.

TYPES OF FOOD

CANNED FOOD

Canned food is palatable to most dogs but gives little exercise to teeth and gums. It is best for dogs to chew and crunch food. Wet food is prone to contamination if not eaten immediately.

DRY FOOD

These foods are cooked under pressure, then dried. Fat is applied to the surface of the particles for palatability. Nutrients can be lost after a package is opened, so buy it in small packs and use immediately.

NATURAL HEALTH CARE

Over millions of years the dog evolved natural ways to maintain its health. When conditions permit, organs, cells, even molecules repair themselves. We should harness these evolutionary defenses, not depress them, when providing health care. Throughout our own history we developed numerous ways of caring for ourselves, involving touch or movement, medication, and techniques for influencing our mind and emotions. Some of these methods may be beneficial for dogs, too. The objective of any form of therapy is to enhance natural defenses and promote repair. Use a therapy to treat a dog only if it meets these objectives.

Exercise is vital for a dog's mental and physical health.

THE ORIGINS OF GOOD HEALTH

DURING EVERY SECOND of every day of your dog's life its body is defending and repairing itself. Organs, cells, and molecules are capable of self-diagnosis. In the best of circumstances your dog's body recognizes damage and then proceeds to remove, repair, or replace the damage. This is the basis of good health. Only when your dog's natural defenses fail does illness ensue.

NATURAL HEALING

My role as a veterinarian is not to heal animals. Dogs are outstandingly efficient at healing themselves. A vet's job is to create the circumstances in which an animal's body repairs itself. This is done by recommending a good diet, by prescribing medicines to help the body overcome attack or organ failure, by surgical interventions such as setting a broken bone, and, most complex of all, by creating a social, or even emotional, environment that promotes natural healing.

Obvious healing occurs at the visible level. Let us say a dog suffers a skin puncture in a fight with another dog. Over the next two weeks the skin naturally repairs itself. You can watch and marvel as the damage disappears. All of us are familiar with the

"Your responsibility in caring for your dog, and mine as its veterinarian, is to ensure the best circumstances for maintaining good health."

inflammation that occurs around a puncture, the formation of a scab, and the growth of new skin under the scab to fill the defect. The real repair, however is less visible.

GUARDIANS OF GOOD HEALTH

At all times, white blood cells circulate in the bloodstream, waiting for accidents to happen. When an injury occurs, such as the skin puncture wound, the "infantry" arrive. Cells called neutrophils, the body's most populous white blood cells, converge at the spot where the defensive line of the skin has been breached. They kill germs that have got

through. This creates debris, but almost immediately other white blood cells, called macrophages, quite literally "big eaters," arrive, engulf, and digest the debris. Pus consists of white cells that have "committed suicide" defending the body. At the same time, new cell formation begins at the margin of the wound. These new cells grow across the wound, under the protection of the carapace-like blood clot that has formed. New blood vessels sprout from the closest intact vessels and grow with the new cells.

HARMONIOUS ACTIVITY

All of these activities are controlled by recently discovered chemical regulators called cytokines, proteins so small and so scarce they are almost impossible to detect. Some cytokines stimulate cell growth, while others inhibit it. There is a natural, well-regulated balance between these opposing cytokines. If you consider that the entire lining of your dog's digestive system is virtually renewed several times each week, that gives you an idea of how coordinated these activities are. This natural balance of cytokine activity is influenced by hormones and by the nervous system, by the "state of mind." One state of mind encourages a homeostatic balance of cytokine activity. Another state of mind results in cytokine disharmony. This is how "stress" affects good health.

CELLULAR GOOD HEALTH

The wall of a cell is, like a dog's skin, its first and most important line of defence. It is not a permanent structure, but a membrane made up of proteins embedded in a fatty substance. Recent research into omega-3 (anti-inflammatory) and omega-6 (pro-inflammatory) fatty acids has shown how a dog's diet influences the levels of these fatty acids in cell membranes. Cells with more omega-3 fatty acids in their walls are less likely to become inflamed than those with a preponderance of omega-6 fatty acids. Cell walls are covered with special receptor sites that are designed to recognize and bind certain nutrients, hormones, and other substances to the cell. To ensure that the receptor sites are always kept in pristine condition, bits of the cell wall with their receptor sites are continually withdrawn into the cell where they are examined, repaired if necessary, and then returned to the cell's surface. Inside the cells, scavengers called lysosomes recognize and eliminate defective sections of the cell wall. This is natural healing at the cellular level.

MOLECULAR GOOD HEALTH

Dogs have trillions of cells in their bodies and millions are replaced every single day. Cells make new cells by passing on their genetic information, their DNA, from one generation to the next. Technically, DNA also transcribes information into another related molecule called RNA that can travel out of a cell nucleus. RNA translates the information it acquired from DNA and directs cells to manufacture specific proteins that determine the form and function of all aspects of life. These processes of replication, transcription, and translation of information are the most basic processes of life and are profoundly "homeostatic."

THE ROLE OF ENZYMES

Overseeing DNA activity is a group of proteins called enzymes. Enzymes cut up DNA molecules, dissect out bits, add other bits, and put it all back together with amazing precision and speed. But lots can go wrong. A DNA molecule might be injured by radiation, or ultraviolet light, or any of hundreds of chemicals to which the body can be exposed. When this happens, it makes a mistake when it copies itself. The new cell is "wrong." If it is not detected, it multiplies "wrong" and could become a cancer. But molecular troops are waiting for mistakes to happen. When DNA copying goes wrong, special enzymes snip out the damaged bit of DNA, fill the gap with a correct version, then paste the whole system back together.

Molecular mistakes occur daily and each one is a potential cancer. Virtually all are caught in time. This is natural good health at the molecular level. Your dog's body evolved to heal itself. Your responsibility in caring for your dog, and mine as its vet, is to ensure the best circumstances for the maintenance of good health, but also to work with natural defenses when help is needed to overcome adversity.

WOUND REPAIR

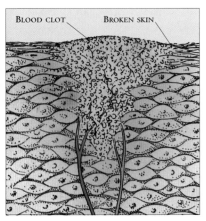

THE SKIN
When skin damage occurs, defensive white blood cells converge at the site of injury. Some kill germs that have invaded the injury, others digest debris.

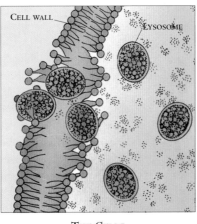

THE CELLS
The wall of each cell protects the interior. Inside each cell, scavengers called lysosomes monitor the health of the cell wall, eliminating defective sections.

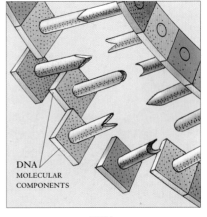

DNA
DNA copying is carried out in each cell's nucleus. When it goes wrong, special enzymes snip out the damage and fill the gap with the correct version.

NATURAL DEVELOPMENT

NATURAL TRAINING

NATURAL NUTRITION

NATURAL HEALTH CARE

HEALTH DISORDERS

WORKING WITH NATURAL DEFENSES

MODERN VETERINARY MEDICINE has saved millions of dogs that otherwise would have died from infection or injury. We tend to credit modern treatments for this success, but this is only partly true. Modern medicine removes obstacles but does not in itself repair. Healing comes from within the dog and depends upon an efficient immune system and an uncompromised capacity for self-repair.

ADVANCES IN MODERN MEDICINE

In this century, spectacular advances in drug therapy have created a vast armory of weapons we can use to treat diseases. These treatments have their downside. Drug therapy has misled us into thinking in a simple "cause and effect" way. If vomiting occurs, give an anti-emetic. If a dog coughs, give an anti-tussive. If histamine is released in an allergic reaction, give an antihistamine. If a painful inflammation occurs, give an anti-inflammatory. Treating the clinical signs of disease is simple, but when we do so, we may be suppressing the dog's natural defenses. We forget that these defenses evolved to fight injury and infection.

THE CAUSE AND EFFECT OF ILLNESS

Some of the most common problems vets are asked to treat are vomiting, diarrhea, coughing, and limping. These are not diseases but your dog's natural defenses

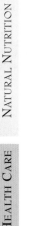

DIMINISHED DEFENSES
Many breeds were developed from a small genetic base. Selective breeding has created inherited predispositions to illness. This Bernese Mountain Dog has poorer natural defenses against cancer, heart problems, and joint diseases than do many other breeds of dog.

reacting when confronted with something that upsets its equilibrium. Dogs vomit readily because they are natural scavengers. Vomiting is the most efficient way to rid the stomach of something potentially harmful should it travel further through the gastro-intestinal system. Diarrhea serves the same purpose. Toxins in the intestines are removed as quickly as possible. Intestinal irritants may be covered in mucus when expelled, a sign that the large intestine is reacting defensively.

Coughing actively expels from the air passages any material that has accumulated as part of the body's natural reaction to infection. Coughing may also occur when a dog's heart is not functioning well and fluid accumulates in the lungs. Limping is a natural way to rest an injured limb. Bearing weight on the other legs gives the injured leg a chance to heal. A common mistake we all make is to suppress these natural defenses rather than work with them to fight the threat to equilibrium.

TREATING THE WHOLE DOG

A permanent struggle exists between your dog's natural defenses and elements that, if left unchecked, could overcome them. Cancer cells multiply if natural defenses don't recognize their presence. Germs enter the body and cause disease if defenses don't detect and destroy them. When we think about how to work with a dog's defenses, regardless of the type of threat to a dog's health, we need to answer a few questions:

1. Is the medical condition genetic or inherited?
Cures are not possible when conditions are genetic. Our best way to enhance natural defences is to avoid selective breeding that leads to known inherited illnesses. If a dog carries the genetic potential for an inherited disease, it will not necessarily develop that condition — environmental factors play a role. We can help the dog avoid the circumstances that allow the genetic potential for a problem to develop, although we seldom know exactly what those circumstances are.

2. Have design changes increased susceptibility?
The risk of suffering from some medical problems increases when we deviate away from natural dog design. For example, dogs with long backs and short legs tend to be susceptible to slipped discs. We can enhance the natural defenses of these individuals with careful exercise and by supplying nutrients to maintain healthy spinal columns.

3. Does the dog's environment cause the problem?
The dog's ancestor, the wolf, only meets unrelated wolves on occasions of territory disputes and the risk of transmission of disease is therefore low. This risk increases when unrelated dogs congregate, as when they are kenneled together. This is why the most common form of upper respiratory tract infection is called "kennel cough," We can enhance defences by vaccinating against transmissible diseases (*see pages 120-121*).

4. How is the problem manifested?
Using pneumonia as an example, difficulty in breathing is a manifestation of the harm caused to lung tissue by an infectious virus, parasites, bacteria, or fungus.

5. What part of the condition is the dog's defense?
Using the above example, coughing is the dog's natural defense to help expel mucus and debris, by-products of the dog's defensive systems, from its air passages. Rather than suppressing a cough, we should work with it.

6. What are the dog's natural defenses?
A dog might develop a fever and lose its appetite when it has an infection. These are natural defenses, reducing the germ's ability to multiply. We should not eliminate these defenses but rather work with them.

7. How does the illness outflank the dog's defenses?
Diseases constantly evolve to cope with the threats directed at them. For example, bacteria breed to develop resistance to antibiotics. We need to be aware of the tactics of the enemy when planning to assist a dog's natural defenses.

ENVIRONMENTAL THREATS
The dog evolved to live in small groups. Protection against the common diseases within a group was inherited. Mixing dogs from different environments brings different diseases together. Some dogs do not have natural protection and epidemics occur.

HELPING SELF-REPAIR
In this age of drug therapy we tend to think that drugs alone are responsible for recoveries from illness. When an abscess is treated with antibiotics and the abscess disappears, we credit the antibiotic therapy with the recovery. Antibiotics are powerfully important drugs but they only ever reduce the number of bacteria. Antibiotics give the immune system time to prepare its counterattack, to deploy natural killer cells, macrophages, and other components of the natural defense system. The real source of the cure is the immune system, aided and abetted by antibiotics.

HEALING FROM WITHIN
Drug therapies do not cure. They facilitate repair. Treatments originate outside the body but healing comes from within. Before the development of modern technologies, medicine relied upon the drugs in plants and the power of the mind to overcome disease. The fact that emotion is able to modify the behavior of your body cells, and modify the efficiency of your immune system, is accepted in human medicine. This raises the question of whether complementary forms of veterinary medicine can also enhance your dog's defenses.

CHECKLIST
Selective breeding can have the effect of reducing natural defenses. This leads to hereditary health problems such as:

- Cancer in Bernese Mountain Dogs, Boxers, Flat-coated Retrievers, and St. Bernards.

- Heart conditions in Cavalier King Charles Spaniels, Newfoundlands, Dobermanns, and Irish Wolfhounds.

- Joint problems in Rottweilers, Labradors, German Shepherds, Golden Retrievers, and Yorkshire Terriers.

WHAT IS COMPLEMENTARY MEDICINE?

CONVENTIONAL MEDICINE treats the body as an exquisitely evolved piece of machinery, while complementary medicine approaches health from a more spiritual viewpoint. The objectives of both forms of medicine are the same: to return the body to a state of balance. Implementing the spiritual aspects of complementary medicine, however, is more problematic when applied to dogs than to humans.

WHY SO LITTLE RESEARCH?

Double-blind studies in which neither the vet nor the dog owner (nor, of course, the dog) know what is being used therapeutically, are difficult to set up for many forms of complementary medicine. Also, until recently, there has been little impetus for research from within the fields of complementary or conventional veterinary medicine.

DEFINING MEDICINE

How you define what medicine is or does influences your attitude to different forms of diagnosis and treatment. A dictionary might define medicine as the science of diagnosing and treating disease or damage to the body or mind. Carvel Tiekert, executive director of the American Holistic Veterinary Medical Association defines medicine as "anything that works." To clarify what I am writing about, here are the definitions I use.

Conventional veterinary medicine, also called orthodox, scientific, modern, or Western medicine, uses scientific principles and techniques to diagnose and treat illness. It is the form of care that is most readily available to dog owners in the West.

DIFFERENT SYMBOLS, COMMON MEANING
Equilibrium is the aim of all forms of medicine. The Western emblem of medicine, the intertwined snakes of the caduceus (left), *and the Chinese symbol of yin and yang* (above, centre), *both represent opposites held in harmonious balance.*

Complementary, alternative, or integrative veterinary medicine covers a wide variety of systems of diagnosis and treatment that are separate from conventional veterinary medicine. Treatments are less interventionist than conventional treatments, and often have a spiritual component. Most complementary treatments are fully compatible with those of conventional medicine.

Traditional forms of veterinary medicine use historic methods that may pre-date the scientific era for the diagnosis and treatment of illness. Traditional veterinary medicine includes Far Eastern forms such as Chinese and Japanese, Indian (Ayurvedic), European folk medicine, and indigenous forms of medicine that are still practiced in Africa, the Americas, and elsewhere. In poor regions of the world, traditional veterinary medicine still remains the most common form of care for agricultural animals. It is a major branch of complementary veterinary medicine.

HOLISTIC VETERINARY MEDICINE

Holistic medicine (the word is derived from the Greek *holos* meaning "whole") recognizes the interplay of mind, body, and spirit and considers that the whole is greater than the sum of its parts. There is a common belief that holistic medicine is the preserve of the complementary therapies, but in fact it is rapidly being integrated into conventional veterinary medicine. Practicing vets know that nutrition, environment, and social relationships can affect health.

While conventional veterinarians talk of "homeostatic balance," vets who practice complementary therapies are interested in "harmony." Conventional vets want to know and understand, right down to the molecular level, what happens when things go wrong in the body, and the homeostatic balance is upset. Complementary vets, and people who choose complementary therapies for themselves or for their dogs, feel uneasy with this approach because simply breaking down disease into its biochemical components denies the influence of the soul.

To describe medicine in this mechanical way is to deny the spirituality of life, the essence of many complementary forms of medicine.

The European medical philosophy that evolved into modern medicine has its origins in the 17th-century tension between the Church and the emerging notion of factual science. The philosopher René Descartes accommodated factual science and religious belief by creating the mind-body philosophy that still influences Western medicine today. Care of the mind, in the form of the soul, was given to the Church, while care of the body was given to medical science. Under this division, medicine evolved to regard illness as a mechanical breakdown of body parts. Spirituality – the mind and the soul – played no role, as these aspects of life and personality previously did, and still do in traditional forms of medicine.

Descartes believed that only humans had souls; animals are automata, functioning by instinct, incapable of experiencing pleasure or pain. His philosophy survives today in the minds of many Western-trained vets. When I carried out a survey of British vets' attitude to pet death, one out of four practicing small-animal vets answered that dogs are not sentient beings – they are unaware of their own feelings and emotions. When the same survey was applied to veterinarians in Japan, not one of them believed that to be true.

SYMPTOMS AND SIGNS

With words we describe how we feel. I might say I have a headache, or cannot sleep, or feel depressed. These are my symptoms, my subjective feelings. My doctor might then take my pulse or look at the color of my tongue. My heart rate or pallidness are my clinical signs. Like pediatricians, it is not possible for vets to ask their patients about their symptoms. If I see a dog with its head low, squinting in bright light, I might guess that it has a headache, but it is only a guess. Dogs cannot tell us about their symptoms. Vets rely completely on clinical signs when making diagnoses.

WHAT ABOUT THE EVIDENCE?

There is a proverb, sometimes attributed to the Chinese, at other times to the Jewish Talmud, that says, "To be uncertain is to be uncomfortable, to be certain is ridiculous." In veterinary medicine, the clinician's state is one of uncomfortableness. Whenever I make a diagnosis, I have to be a little uncertain.

In the early 1990s, a fresh concept, called evidence-based medicine, was developed at McMaster University's Medical School in Canada. The concept suggests that doctors (or vets) have to accept uncertainty. It explains that for many medical questions good research findings will never be available. In these circumstances, we need to rely upon our own, an expert's, or collective experience for the evidence that a treatment is useful.

CONSTANT REASSESSMENT

The McMaster clinicians say that doctors and vets need to constantly assess what they are doing and the outcomes of their actions. Let me give you an example: Cystitis or bladder inflammation causes a dog to urinate more frequently. If I give antibiotics, the frequency of urinating diminishes. Logically, I assume that the antibiotic killed the bacteria causing the medical condition. But it is now known that a bacterial cause for cystitis is, in fact, rare. Yet dogs improve on antibiotics.

The answer may be that the antibiotic happens to do something else that, by sheer good fortune, is beneficial. Some antibiotics can reduce spasm in the urinary tract and provide relief from discomfort. Evidence-based medicine says we should evaluate not only what we know, but what we do not know. If treating a dog for cystitis with a herbal remedy results in the dog straining less, evidence-based medicine says use it, rather than wait for the explanation.

Throughout history, people who have practiced medicine have used treatments long before understanding them. A considerable problem with our dogs, however, is to know which of the complementary therapies we should use and in what circumstances.

SPECIFIC OR HOLISTIC?
Conventional veterinary medicine often aims to restore equilibrium or balance by targeting specific problems with specific drugs. Complementary therapies also aim to restore balance, or harmony, but often use combinations of substances as found in whole herbs.

NATURAL DEVELOPMENT

NATURAL TRAINING

NATURAL NUTRITION

NATURAL HEALTH CARE

HEALTH DISORDERS

COMPLEMENTARY THERAPIES

A VARIETY OF THERAPIES are available to preserve good canine health or to treat illness when it occurs. Rather than separate conventional from complementary therapies, for any therapy you consider, ask instead, "Is it safe?" and "Does it work?" Pet-owner demand for complementary therapies is increasing. Use these therapies to complement the best that conventional medicine has to offer.

CHECKLIST

- Complementary therapies often work on the assumption that disease is a result of the interaction between the dog and its environment.

- Complementary therapies are particularly useful for chronic conditions.

- Just because a therapy is "natural" does not mean it is safe. Some herbs are toxic to dogs.

- If your dog is ill or in pain, always consult your vet before embarking on any form of home treatment.

THE RISE IN POPULARITY

The success of conventional veterinary medicine may be partly responsible for the rising popularity of complementary therapies. When I began practicing veterinary medicine almost 30 years ago, I saw about three dogs each week with clinical distemper. Most died from the disease. Today, because the majority of dogs are vaccinated against distemper, cases are rare. Because the disease no longer appears to be a threat, some people turn to nosodes – homeopathic remedies – for protection and, because their dogs do not develop distemper, feel that the nosode offers protection (*see pages 92–93*).

ONE OR THE OTHER?

In 1942, one of the most articulate fathers of modern medicine, Sir William Osler, wrote, "The philosophies of one age become the absurdities of the next and the foolishness of yesterday has become the wisdom of tomorrow." Do not be dogmatic about what is best for your dog. Conventional medicine can be mechanical and dispassionate, but it saves lives. It has been inherently suspicious of complementary therapies but is beginning to adopt Osler's open mind. In 1996, the American Veterinary Medical Association reclassified acupuncture as a conventional rather than a complementary therapy.

RELYING ON FAITH

While most of us are reluctant to allow any conventional therapy to be used on ourselves or our dogs until the procedure or drug has been subjected to vigorous studies, many of us will happily take complementary therapies on trust. We are attracted to the idea that swallowing something natural, or undergoing

COMMON CAUSES FOR A VISIT TO THE VET

When veterinarians at the University of Minnesota surveyed American veterinary clinics they learned that dogs are taken to vets mostly for minor reasons. Here are the most common reasons for dogs of different ages being taken to the vet.

0–7 YEARS OLD		7–10 YEARS OLD		OVER 10 YEARS OLD	
No medical problems	32%	No medical problems	15%	Mouth problems	14%
Mouth problems	6%	Mouth problems	14%	No medical problem	7%
Ear disease	6%	Ear disease	6%	Age-related eye changes	3%
Skin problems	4%	Skin problems	3%	Arthritis	3%
Lameness	1%	Tumor	2%	Tumor	3%
Worms	1%	Fatty lump (lipoma)	2%	Ear problems	3%
Eye inflammation	1%	Eye inflammation	1%	Heart murmour	2%
Fleas	1%	Arthritis	1%	Fatty lump (lipoma)	2%
Skin Lacerations	1%	Anal sac blockage	1%	Cataracts	2%
Anal sac blockage	1%	Lameness	1%	Skin problems	1%

form of medical therapy that is thousands of years old, will enhance good health. We know the downside of conventional medicine: the drug reactions; dogs treated as cases, not individuals; and the aggressive desire to prolong life's length without consideration of life's quality. We question the objectives of conventional medicine, but equally we should question the basis of complementary therapies. Blind faith in any therapy is not in your dog's interest. Ask questions. How long will it take to see results? If there appears to be no improvement, at what point do you accept that the therapy may not be working?

CONVENTIONAL MEDICINE

Most conventional vets treat all medical problems in the same "fire-brigade" way: there is a fire burning, so douse it. This is by far the best way to treat some but not all conditions. Conventional veterinary medicine should always be your treatment of choice in the following circumstances:

- To manage physical injury and trauma
- To treat medical and surgical emergencies
- To treat acute bacterial and fungal infections and parasitic infestations
- To immunize and prevent infectious disease
- To diagnose and correct hormonal upsets.

Conventional medicine is not as good for curing a variety of chronic conditions. These are the areas where, increasingly, dog owners turn to complementary therapies for help:

- Chronic pain or degenerative disease
- Viral diseases and chronic infections
- Chronic allergic disorders
- Heart disease, debility, and fatigue
- Behavioral and psychosomatic disorders
- Cancer.

Owners of dogs with any of these problems are often willing to try to tackle the root of the problem by, for example, altering their dog's lifestyle. They want therapies that do not harm other parts of their dog's well-being.

MIXING OLD AND NEW
Conventional medicine is not always successful at treating chronic conditions such as allergy. Complementary therapies based upon traditional herbal treatments are useful. For example, oatmeal-based shampoos have become integrated into conventional veterinary therapy for allergic itch.

COMPLEMENTARY THERAPIES

When someone asks me about treating their dog with a complementary therapy, it tells me that the owner has a specific philosophy of life and wants to apply it to his or her dog. It also tells me the owner is prepared for a long treatment and does not expect an instant cure.

Complementary therapies can be divided into three categories; touch and movement (physical), medicinal, and mind and emotion. Touch and movement therapies are only beneficial with those dogs that actively enjoy physical attention from their owners. When animals are manipulated against their will, the stress inhibits their natural killer cells from performing their defensive functions.

If you plan to use any medicinal therapies, remember that a dog's physiology is different to ours. A herb that is safe for us may be toxic to dogs. Whenever possible, use supplements or nutrients in appropriate quantities for dogs. These can be quite different from the quantities that are beneficial for us.

Mind and emotion therapies depend upon an ability to think in the abstract. The mind-body relationship is increasingly understood by conventional medicine, but what is good for our inner needs does not necessarily apply to dogs. Never force a dog to undergo any type of mind-body therapy it does not enjoy.

WHERE TO GO

Dogs have different nutritional, medical, and emotional needs to our own. The best way you can help your dog is to seek advice from a qualified vet who understands the different needs of pets. He or she will refer you to a vet who specializes in the appropriate complementary therapy.

THE MIND-BODY RELATIONSHIP

NATURAL DEVELOPMENT

NATURAL TRAINING

NATURAL NUTRITION

NATURAL HEALTH CARE

HEALTH DISORDERS

IN HUMAN MEDICINE the relationship between health and personality, long recognized in Eastern medical systems, is now broadly accepted by conventional medicine. Confident, positive personalities cope better with poor health than introverted, negative personalities. Although it is more difficult to study this phenomenon in dogs than people, there is no reason why it should not apply to them too.

CONVENTIONAL PROBLEMS

It is true that until recently, conventional veterinary medicine used to be primarily interested in physical cause and effect. There was little interest in the influence of personality on behavior, health, or illness simply did not exist. This is changing. There is a converging interest in the role that stress and personality play in a dog's health.

MIND AND BODY MEDICINE

The interrelationship between mind and body has been accepted for centuries in traditional forms of medicine throughout the world. In traditional Chinese medicine, the life force, *qi*, directs and coordinates the flows of energy and is central to a dog's health, personality, and individuality. Practitioners of traditional Indian medicine believe that three *doshas* "vital energies" – *vata*, *pitta*, and *kapha* – not only govern health but also shape the personality.

In modern veterinary medicine, the branch called psychoneuroimmunology (PNI) studies the interrelations between an animal's mind ("psycho"), its nervous and hormonal systems ("neuro"), and its immune system ("immuno"). PNI investigates 24-hour circadian rhythms, biofeedback, and neuroendocrines and cytokines (proteins that stimulate or inhibit cell activity).

The differences in the explanations of traditional medicine and modern Western medicine may seem overwhelming. *Qi* and *doshas* are mysterious, even spiritual, while

PNI is dry, arcane, and pedantic, but both Eastern and Western medical systems make a connection between the mind and body.

In all forms of traditional medicine, the way you think and feel is believed to have a direct effect on how your body responds to illness. In conventional medicine, it is known that the number of circulating natural killer cells, vital for good health, is affected by emotion. When university students are under the stress of exams, the fighting power of the killer cells in their immune system is known to drop. Emotions have a direct effect on the immune system.

THE PLACEBO RESPONSE

In sociable species such as humans and dogs the mind-body relationship can be affected in many ways. One of the most intriguing ways is through the placebo response.

In human medicine, surgically tying an artery in the chest in individuals with angina eliminated pain for many of them. But so too did just surgically opening and closing the skin without tying the artery! Ultrasound was found to reduce wisdom-tooth pain, but so did the ultrasound machine when it was set to produce no ultrasound. Dr. Harold Koenig from Duke University in North Carolina discovered that churchgoers have better functioning immune systems than non churchgoers.

These are placebo responses: benefits that arise for non-physical or non-material reasons. Whether you believe in God, in complementary therapies, or in orthodox Western medicine, belief itself appears to plays a role in your body's natural defenses. All of us, regardless of our individual personality, can benefit from the placebo response. There is a common denominator, however, which is expectation. A doctor's or a veterinarian's expectation is infectious. If your doctor is convinced that a treatment will work, and convinces you, the treatment has a better chance of working. The question is whether dogs can experience expectation, the basis of the placebo response.

SWEET PLACEBO

When mice were given, with saccharin, a drug by mouth to suppress their immune system, their defensive capacity faltered. Later, just giving saccharin without the drug caused immune failure. Animals are capable of experiencing a placebo response.

LIKE OWNER LIKE DOG?

Studies of dog owners in the United States and Britain show that your personality can have a direct effect on your dog's behavior. Among Cocker Spaniel owners, tense, shy and anxious people are more likely to have aggressive dogs. What this interesting study showed was the possible relationship between how you treat your dog and its attitude towards life. I'm sure that most people who work with dogs understand that an owner's personality affects a dog's behavior. Whether your relationship with your dog can affect its state of mind and its health simply isn't known. I see no reason why it should not.

PLACEBO RESPONSE IN ANIMALS

Expectation is a conditioned response. Pavlov conditioned his dogs to salivate at the sound of a bell. They learned to expect a food treat in conjunction with the ringing sound.

Even physiological body processes can be changed through learned conditioning. Over 20 years ago, studies of mice showed that when they were given insulin, which lowered their blood sugar, they produced more sugar. Later, salt water injections instead of insulin injections also stimulated them to produce more sugar. The salt water was a placebo that provoked a physiological response. The mice had been "conditioned" to experience a surge in blood sugar, even though salt water would not cause this effect.

YOUR VALUE AS A PLACEBO

People with a natural desire to please their doctor are likely to enjoy a placebo effect, while hostility decreases the placebo response. Does this mean that Labradors and German Shepherds, breeds that want to please their masters, are more likely to benefit from a placebo than, say, the Chow Chow, a more independent, even hostile, breed?

It seems to me that the placebo effect occurs when someone is conditioned to it. If this is the case, then it certainly applies to dogs because conditioning is the basis of our relationship with them. A study by Professor Brenda Bonnett in Ontario showed that 40 percent of dogs suffering from joint pain improved, according to their vet's assessment, when they were given nothing more than capsules of rice flour. I think it is likely that many of these dogs genuinely did improve in mobility. There are two dimensions to pain, unpleasantness and intensity. The placebo response does not affect intensity but does affect low-level unpleasantness. In Professor Bonnett's study, I think that just by paying more attention to them, the owners conditioned their dogs to feel less low-level unpleasantness. A dog's natural defense against pain was heightened because of its relationship with its owners

YOUR DOG'S IMMUNE SYSTEM

In Britain, where for decades the common cold was studied, only 20 percent of the volunteers exposed to the cold virus became infected. Of these, 25 percent developed symptoms. Your likelihood of developing infection depends in part on your personality. How optimistic you are, and even whether you are extroverted or introverted, affects how well your immune system works.

Similarly, a group of dogs can be exposed to kennel cough but not all the dogs will develop the disease. This is because the efficiency of a dog's immune system plays a vital role in whether a dog picks up an infection. Our dogs' personalities and states of health are interrelated, just as ours are.

LOOK ALIKE
Selective breeding has created breeds that share both looks and personality profiles but within each breed there are often profound personality differences between dogs.

ASSESSING YOUR DOG'S PERSONALITY

DIFFERENT EMOTIONAL STATES affect how well a dog copes with illness. Your dog's unique personality is an important factor to consider before embarking upon any form of conventional or complementary therapy. Assessing your dog's personality helps you decide which therapies may be beneficial and which should be avoided unless there are no suitable and effective alternatives.

CHECKLIST

- A dog's personality is partly inherited and partly formed by its environment.
- For thousands of years dogs were bred for personality and function rather than looks.
- Differences in personality exist between breeds and between the sexes, as well as between individuals.
- Selective breeding can enhance or diminish a dog's ability to defend its good health.

THERAPY AND PERSONALITY

In his book, *How the Mind Works*, Professor Steven Pinker explains how evolutionary pressures shaped not just how an animal's body functions but also how it thinks. He explains how emotions are part of the interlocking systems that evolved to help individuals survive. This suggests that your dog's personality has an integral role in its health, one that it is vital to take into account when your dog is not well.

Many traditional therapies will consider the personality type or constitution before deciding on the treatment. Personalities are described by statement, rather than critique, as "strong" or "weak." Types of herbs, or even the amount of pressure applied during manipulations, are altered according to an individual's personality. For instance, in Ayurvedic therapies, dogs are divided into three personality groups: *kapha* dogs are well-muscled,

strong, stable, patient, and possessive; *pitta* dogs are evenly proportioned, confident, and aggressively competitive; and *vata* dogs are lithe, lanky, quick, and creative but energy-wasting. More generally, dogs are described as having "excess" or "deficient" personalities. An "excess" dog is assertive, hard-muscled, confident, with a strong voice, and demands attention. A "deficient" dog is shy, timid, introverted, will bark rarely, and suffers poor digestion and frequent illness. If overweight, the dog will have pudgy fat and weak muscles. If thin, it tends to have a slight bone structure and small muscles.

CHOOSING A THERAPY

Assessing your dog's personality enables you to judge the suitability of certain therapies. Many of the physical therapies, such as chiropractic, osteopathy, and hydrotherapy will require the dog to be comfortable when it is handled by strangers. Some dogs might snap at a practitioner when they are being manipulated, while other dogs will be tense and terrified. If your dog is likely to react in either way to a physical therapy there is no point continuing. The fear your dog feels will cause its stress levels to rise and its immune system will be compromised.

Most dogs will accept medicinal therapies but it may take some time before you know if the treatment is effective. Like mind and emotion therapies, some medicinal therapies may involve the placebo response (*see pages 66–67*). If your dog is very responsive to you, and you believe that a therapy will work, your dog may respond to your belief, and to the treatment.

EXCESS OR DEFICIENT?
In Ayurvedic medicine, the strong personality of an "excess" dog such as this Rhodesian Ridgeback (far left) is believed to make it less prone to illness than an introverted "deficient" dog, such as this Cocker Spaniel (left).

QUESTIONNAIRE

The questionnaire below is designed to help you assess the personality of your dog. Does your dog greet your guests, or does it disappear until visitors have left your home? Is your dog always asking to play, or is it content to snooze in its bed for hours on end? The questionnaire also addresses your dog's general health in order to assess the efficacy of its immune system.

Different factors are presented in the column on the left, while on the right you will find lists of related statements. Consider your dog and score each statement accordingly, using the scoring system given in the box on the right. When you have finished, add up the scores and check the total in the box at bottom right. Your dog's result will indicate how it is likely to respond to complementary therapies.

SCORE

Almost always	5
Usually	4
Sometimes	3
Rarely	2
Almost never	1

FACTOR	ASSESSMENT
SOCIABLE WITH PEOPLE Many therapies involve active participation by people. Therapies such as acupuncture and massage should be used only on dogs that have high scores on sociability with people.	*My dog:* • Likes to be with its human family • Greets strangers with a wagging tail • Enjoys being petted • Joins with children in play
ACTIVE Just as our own physical fitness is an important factor in overcoming ill health, active dogs are best equipped to maintain good health, and to recover quickly from injury or illness.	*My dog:* • Enjoys physical activity • Plays games with its human family • Gets active daily exercise off the leash • Demands attention
RISK-TAKER A risk-taking dog increases its risk of physical injury, but risk-taking individuals' curiosity and enthusiasm may help them to recover most efficiently from states of poor health.	*My dog:* • Willingly investigates new surroundings • Approaches other animals without fear • Is relaxed when visiting the vet • Is not frightened by new experiences
GOOD HEALTH General good health is the best sign that a dog's immune system functions efficiently. A high score here means that your dog's defenses have generally been working well.	*My dog:* • Is generally physically well • Recovers quickly from minor illnesses • Does not complain about minor injuries • Is not very sensitive to pain
TRAINABILITY The placebo response is a potent component of all forms of medicine. Dogs with high scores in trainability may respond best to mind-emotion therapies, or others where placebo is important.	*My dog:* • Enjoys learning new commands • Is relaxed during training • Retains its training • Is fully house trained
SOCIABLE WITH OTHER DOGS Sociability with other dogs indicates a positive attitude, which is crucial for any therapy. Because of the dog's pack-animal heritage, enjoying the presence of other dogs can be a spur to recovery.	*My dog:* • Enjoys the company of other family dogs • Encourages play with unfamiliar dogs • Shows no aggression to unfamiliar dogs • Is not submissive to unfamiliar dogs

TOTAL SCORE

24–55 Your dog is reserved and wary of strangers. It is unlikely to accept many conventional or complementary therapies.

56–89 Taking into account where your dog scored highly, you can selectively use some complementary therapies.

90–120 Your dog has a confident and outgoing nature. It will accept many forms of complementary therapy.

NATURAL DEVELOPMENT

NATURAL TRAINING

NATURAL NUTRITION

NATURAL HEALTH CARE

HEALTH DISORDERS

TOUCH AND MOVEMENT THERAPIES

TOUCH IS A DOG'S MOST PRIMITIVE SENSE. A newborn will first finds its mother through touch, maintaining contact with her and the rest of the litter for warmth and security. Harry Harlow's cruel experiments with monkeys at the University of Wisconsin in the 1950s showed how vital touch is to good health. Using a glass partition, Harlow separated newborn monkeys from their mothers at birth. The baby monkeys were well nourished but had no physical contact with their mothers or any other animals. When they matured, they developed physical, behavioral, and medical problems.

Throughout a dog's life, touch retains its ability to reward. Mothers lick their young and both are physically and psychologically rewarded by their actions. In adulthood, dogs continue to touch each other through licking or simply lying in close physical contact. Our intervention in their lives potentiates the value of touch. When your own dog is petted by you or someone else known to it, its blood pressure drops, its heart rate slows, its skin temperature lowers, and its state of arousal diminishes. These physiological changes are good for its health. Most of us intuitively understand that touch is beneficial because we are ourselves rewarded when we touch our dogs.

HYDROTHERAPY
Most dogs love the water and it is beneficial for healthy dogs to wade and swim. Dogs that are recovering from bone and joint injuries may be referred to specialized hydrotherapy pools.

ACUPUNCTURE
Used for a wide variety of problems, acupuncture stimulates the brain's endorphins, bringing natural pain relief.

In the 1970s, Dr. Aaron Katcher, a psychiatrist at the University of Pennsylvania, observed that pet owners experience a drop in blood pressure when they stroke their own dogs. Dr. Constance Perin at the Massachusetts Institute of Technology postulated that touching and petting our dogs is subconsciously reminiscent of our own infancy, giving us the same physiological rewards that we experienced when we were in physical contact with our mothers.

Touch and movement therapies are especially appealing to dog owners who have turned to complementary therapies as a refuge from the unwanted side effects and technological obsessions of conventional veterinary medicine. Acupuncture and acupressure are the most widely available of all the touch therapies, while veterinary chiropractic is more widespread than osteopathy. Hydrotherapy is used for a range of conditions in parts of Japan and is available as a physiotherapy in Britain and the rest of Europe, North America, Australia, and wherever a swimming pool is available. The simplest and most common touch therapy is massage, and this can be carried out at home. Massage is perhaps the most effective of all contact treatments.

TTOUCH THERAPY
TTouch was developed by Linda Tellington-Jones, initially as a training method. The gentle, rhythmic stroking relaxes and focuses the animal.

NATURAL DEVELOPMENT

NATURAL TRAINING

NATURAL NUTRITION

NATURAL HEALTH CARE

HEALTH DISORDERS

ACUPUNCTURE

THE TRADITIONAL CHINESE Medicine (TCM) concept of *yin* and *yang* describes the principle of the opposite aspects of life. The basis of good health is the appropriate balance of *yin* and *yang* as they interact in the body. An imbalance results in illness. Acupuncture, the insertion of fine needles at specific points in the body, was developed in the East out of this philosophy.

QUESTIONS TO ASK

- Will my dog resent treatment?
- How long does a session last?
- How do I know if my dog is improving?
- How many sessions will be needed?
- Will there be after-effects?
- What will it cost?

HISTORY

Veterinary acupuncture is probably as old as acupuncture itself. In India, a treatise on the use of acupuncture on elephants, thought to be 3,000 years old, was found in Sri Lanka in 1979. In China, a rock carving that is over 2,000 years old depicts soldiers performing acupuncture with swords on their horses. Outside China, modern interest in veterinary acupuncture developed during the 1970s, and the International Veterinary Acupuncture Society (IVAS) was formed in 1975. This organization provides extensive courses for veterinarians, and a vet who has completed IVAS training has a good understanding of the theory and practice of acupuncture.

HOW IT WORKS

There are two radically different theories, Chinese and Western, about how acupuncture works. In Traditional Chinese Medicine acupuncture is one element in a range of recognized therapies that also include herbs, acupressure, exercise, and diet. Fundamental to the philosophy of TCM is the concept of a vital force called *qi*, an invisible "life energy" that flows along meridians, or channels, through the body. *Qi* is maintained by *yin* and *yang*, opposite but complementary forces whose perfect balance keeps the body in harmony. Along the meridians are points where *qi* is concentrated. Humans have 670 acupoints. In dogs there are 112 traditional acupoints. Inserting a fine needle at any of these points stimulates or suppresses the flow of energy. The role of the traditional acupuncturist is to determine the imbalance of *qi* and to use appropriate acupuncture points to stimulate or suppress it.

In Western veterinary acupuncture, vets may find the philosophy of TCM appealing, but they will also use the scientific means at their disposal to make a diagnosis: a physical

TREATING AN INJURED FORELEG

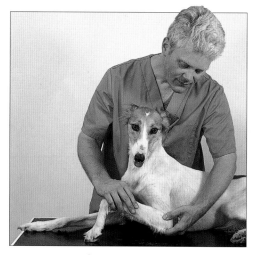

1 The practitioner first examines the patient, and a full history of the current problem, plus details of previous illnesses and injuries, is taken from the pet owner. The dog is examined for signs of pain or discomfort, or imbalance in any part of its body.

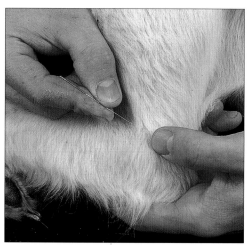

2 On the basis of the examination and history, the minimal number of points possible is selected for the treatment. This can also be based on experience, intuition, and especially in the case of nervous dogs, their tolerance to being handled and restricted.

WHERE IT IS AVAILABLE

Acupuncture for dogs is a medical procedure and can only be performed by a qualified veterinary acupuncturist. Do not have the procedure carried out by someone who performs acupuncture solely on people. Your vet should be able to recommend a colleague who carries out this procedure. If not, write to the International Veterinary Acupuncture Society for veterinary acupuncturists in your locality. Do not use acupuncture as an alternative to drugs or surgery for the treatment of severe or acute pain, and do not take a dog in pain on long car trips for acupuncture therapy. The journeys might increase your dog's discomfort.

examination, laboratory tests, x-rays, and other modern techniques such as ultrasound. Once the diagnosis is made, acupuncture is performed at selected points used for treating the disease or pathological condition. The typically Western approach is to insert the needles in the region where the animal feels chronic pain rather than in classic acupoints elsewhere on its body.

WHAT IS IT USED FOR?

Acupuncture is used most frequently for problems such as arthritis, back pain, tendon injuries, and physical problems of the nervous system. Although most commonly used as a non-chemical method for reducing pain, some veterinary acupuncturists use this method to promote healing of damaged tissue.

VETERINARY OPINION

Painkilling drugs work by mimicking the brain's pain-killing chemicals, the endorphins. Acupuncture stimulates the release of the brain's endorphins, bringing natural pain relief. It is now considered an integral part of conventional veterinary medicine.

As a rule, quiet dogs accept the insertion of needles surprisingly well. Some become relaxed and tranquil, and may even sleep while the needles remain in place. Sensitive breeds such as Cavalier King Charles Spaniels and Chihuahuas are more likely to become agitated, while dominant dogs may resent treatment. Do not use acupuncture on a dog that resents or is upset by the procedure. You will cause more harm than good.

NEEDLES
The thin, flexible acupuncture needles used on dogs range in length from 0.5–1.5 in (1–4 cm).

HOW OFTEN?
Therapy usually begins with weekly sessions for the first month, extending to less frequent intervals when continuing therapy is beneficial. If no improvement is seen after three sessions, it is unlikely that any further acupuncture will be beneficial.

4 After the treatment the needles are removed. Some dogs need time to "wake up" and a gentle massage helps to complete their treatment. Most dogs finish each treatment in a relaxed state and usually happily accept their next treatment. The vet may show the pet owner acupressure points (*see page 74*) on the dog's body to which they can apply pressure in between acupuncture sessions. This may help to maintain the benefits of the treatment.

3 Needles are placed at various depths according to location and size of patient. The patient is left as quiet as possible during the treatment, which may last up to half an hour. Most pets relax deeply, some even sleeping soundly during the session.

NATURAL DEVELOPMENT

NATURAL TRAINING

NATURAL NUTRITION

NATURAL HEALTH CARE

HEALTH DISORDERS

ACUPRESSURE

ACUPRESSURE IS BELIEVED to predate its sister therapy, acupuncture (*see page 72*), but is less well known in the West. It works on the same principle, that *qi*, "life energy," flows along meridians around the body. Pressure is applied with the fingers to points on the meridians. It is perhaps more suitable for dogs than acupuncture, and has the advantage that, with training, dog owners can apply it at home.

CHECKLIST

- Done incorrectly, a manipulation can increase pain and worsen a condition. Ask your practitioner to show you how to apply finger pressure.

- Do not use a manipulation therapy to control overt pain.

- Control your dog's discomfort with effective painkilling medications.

- Never proceed with any type of manipulation therapy that your dog resents.

HISTORY

Many Chinese doctors practice acupressure, and it is a popular form of self-help, but it is infrequently used in veterinary medicine. Historically, several styles of acupressure developed, the most common of which is *tuina*, which involves finger pressure but also rubbing, kneading, and rolling. The Japanese form of acupressure, *anma*, developed into what is now called shiatsu (*see page 75*).

HOW IT WORKS

Your dog's muscles are rather like slings, ropes, and pulleys that move various parts of its body. Muscles lie in layers that run in certain directions. You can liken them to the pile of a carpet that, if rubbed one way, becomes smooth, and if rubbed the opposite way, becomes rough. Acupressure, using straight fingers, presses muscles in the "right" direction. Touch begins on the acupoints in natural "valleys" in the musculature, using

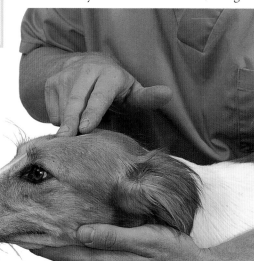

PRESSURE APPLIED
Acupressure is easily performed at home and is an excellent way for owners to become involved in and continue their dog's treatment.

the middle finger and and forefinger, or the thumb and forefinger. Pressure intensifies until the dog's muscles start to resist. At this point the pressure is relieved slightly, and then held on the point for five seconds.

Other variations of the sister therapies, acupuncture and acupressure, are used on people but are rarely applied to dogs. Moxibustion is as old as acupressure. The herb mugwort, *Artemisia vulgaris*, called moxa in Chinese, is dried, cured, and mortar-ground. Applied as a cone-shaped plug to the top of an inserted needle, the moxa is set alight, heating the needle and causing local skin inflammation.

A modern variation of this heat therapy is electro-acupuncture. Electrodes are attached to inserted needles and a low-voltage electric current passes into the dog's body. Laser light is also sometimes used as an alternative to the physical insertion of needles or to finger pressure (*see page 83*). Laser equipment is expensive and its usefulness depends upon a dog remaining still long enough for the laser to be positioned and used. Laser therapy is used more on horses than on other animals. No conclusive evidence has been published showing the benefits of these therapies.

VETERINARY OPINION

Acupressure is sometimes used on dogs that resent the insertion of acupuncture needles. Acupuncture points do not need to be stimulated by needles alone and the use of light finger pressure on the points can be a relaxing and effective treatment. Vets apply acupressure to relax a dog before it undergoes acupuncture. No evidence has been published that proves acupressure does anything more than relieve pain by relaxing muscles.

WHERE IT IS AVAILABLE

Veterinary acupuncturists sometimes use acupressure as part of their therapy. They will often show dog owners how to apply finger-tip or even finger-nail pressure to acupoints. This is believed to maintain the value of therapy between veterinary visits.

Shiatsu

SHIATSU, A FORM OF finger-pressure therapy, has its basis in Traditional Chinese Medicine and follows the same philosophical principles of "life energy" and meridians as acupuncture and acupressure. Therapists use fingers and thumbs, applying pressure at key points to stimulate muscle relaxation and blood circulation. Shiatsu is mainly practiced on dogs in Japan, Australia, and the United States.

LISTEN TO YOUR DOG

Let your dog tell you whether or not to continue with acupressure or shiatsu. Manipulation can be comforting to some dogs and aggravating to others. Always reward relaxed behavior with kind words and, whenever possible, a food snack.

HISTORY

Shiatsu, Japanese for "finger pressure," has its origins in Traditional Chinese Medicine, which was introduced into Japan 1,500 years ago. Early in the 20th century in Japan, a massage practitioner named Tamai Tempaku, combined the millenia-old practice of acupressure with a modern understanding of medical anatomy and physiology, creating shiatsu. Shiatsu has been successful in Japan and is now widespread there. It has become a popular therapy in Australia, and on the west coast of North America, but is less commonly practiced in Europe.

HOW IT WORKS

There is a considerable gulf between the theory and practicality of shiatsu for dogs. Some Japanese practitioners consider that it works in just the same way as acupuncture does, by stimulating the "life force," *ki*, (*ki* in Japanese, *qi* in Chinese) along the meridians. Australian and other Western practitioners, on the other hand, tend to use physiological terms to describe the effect of their therapy, claiming that shiatsu massage enhances the body's self-healing capabilities by aiding relaxation and regulating the components of the circulation system.

Shiatsu massage covers the whole body. The practitioner stretches and massages the dog's trunk, limbs, and head. Manipulation begins gently but becomes firmer if the dog allows. The end of a session, which usually lasts 20 minutes, is followed by a rest period to allow the dog to absorb the benefits of treatment. Needless to say, the dog decides whether or not to accept shiatsu.

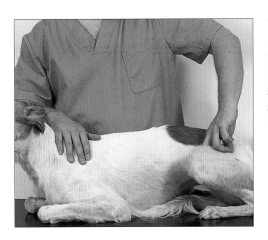

TAKING THE PULSE
Shiatsu practitioners use modern medical techniques such as monitoring the pulse, both to diagnose a problem and to assess the effects of therapy.

VETERINARY OPINION

Shiatsu is believed to release muscle tension, promote deep relaxation, and aid healing by improving circulation. There have been no published studies of its value. It is not well known in Europe, but practitioners in Australia claim that it is superior to acupressure because it is based upon modern knowledge of canine anatomy. Practitioners ask the owner about the dog's medical history, its diet, and personality, and watch the dog's movement as it walks around, before taking its pulse and beginning the shiatsu massage.

WHERE IT IS AVAILABLE

Shiatsu is available from therapists with a knowledge of canine health, anatomy, and behavior. There are forms of shiatsu, for example, *Do-in* finger pressure, that rely upon self-assessment by the patient of a condition such as indigestion or headache. Because it is difficult to diagnose these states in dogs accurately, such forms of shiatsu are hard to apply in veterinary care.

TRIGGER POINT THERAPY

ALTHOUGH MUSCLE ACCOUNTS for 40 percent or more of your dog's weight, muscle problems receive scant attention in conventional veterinary textbooks. Muscle is subject to daily wear and tear but veterinarians usually concentrate on the body's superstructure – the bones, joints, and ligaments – when treating pain. Trigger point (TP) therapy is a physical treatment of the sites of muscle pain.

TERRIER SENSITIVITY

Some breeds of terrier, Scotties in particular, suffer from jaw pain while they are pups and are unable to eat without the assistance of pain-killing drugs. This condition is called cranio-mandibular osteo-arthropathy. A similar condition in people is considered to be a TP condition and is treated with TP therapy.

HISTORY

Trigger point therapy comes from China and is now beginning to be accepted in Western conventional medical teaching. Until recent decades, if physicians found no laboratory or radiological evidence for the source of a patient's muscle or "myofascial" pain, they considered it to be in the person's mind, rather than the muscles. The discovery that pain is often felt, not at the site of injury but at a different or "referred" site, lead to TP therapy being re-evaluated.

While classic acupuncture points are always at specific sites, TPs are not. However, over 70 percent of common TP points are near classic acupuncture points. It seems possible that the Chinese physicians who determined the acupuncture points for pain also encountered and included a number of the common "myofascial" TP locations. If this is so, acupressure often works because it affects TPs.

HOW IT WORKS

Scientific research suggests that trigger points in muscles are sites of increased metabolism and nerve sensitivity, but of reduced blood circulation. Left untreated, the muscle cells become damaged and a source of chronic pain. Muscle consists of two types of fibers called "slow" and "fast." Throbbing pain comes from "fast" fibers. TP pressure will stimulate these fibers, add to the pain for an instant, and then relieve it.

A dog naturally shifts its weight to avoid using a painful limb. It may also tense its muscles as a way of trying to cope with joint discomfort. Either way, it overuses certain muscles, which then develop painful trigger points. If a dog permits, firm finger pressure is applied on the TP point.

The response to local therapy is usually immediate for tenderness that has started only recently. Chronic pain, which has been felt for a long time, takes longer to control. Hot packs are sometimes applied to the muscle for a few minutes after therapy, which helps to reduce muscle soreness and enhance circulation. Relief is more likely to be long-lasting when all the treated muscles are used in their full range after a therapy session.

VETERINARY OPINION

Working at Murdoch University's veterinary school in Perth, Australia, Dr. Liz Frank uses TP therapy on dogs, to relieve discomfort associated with pathological damage and for pain relief in young dogs that have exercised too vigorously. TP therapy is used when a taut, and probably tender, band can be felt in a specific muscle. Dr. Luc Janssens in Belgium concentrates his treatments on seven specific trigger points and describes them as feeling "like marbles in mud."

WHERE IT IS AVAILABLE

Although muscle injury is a significant cause of pain, it tends to be neglected and TP therapy currently has limited availability. Experienced therapists work in Australia, Belgium, and the United States.

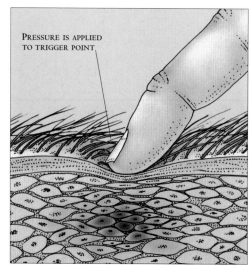

PRESSURE IS APPLIED TO TRIGGER POINT

POINT OF PAIN

Trigger points are found in the neck, shoulders, and hips. Pain is not always felt at a trigger point, but projected to a "referred" site. TP pain is a deep ache in people. The pain heightens when finger pressure is applied, before being relieved.

TTOUCH THERAPY

TTOUCH IS A TERM used to describe a gentle physical therapy for animals developed by Linda Tellington-Jones. It evolved from the light movements of the Feldenkrais method, which helps people become more aware of their bodies. Random, circular, finger touches are used over a dog's body to relax and prepare it for training. It is particular advocated for calming frightened dogs.

TTOUCH TECHNIQUES

To make learning easy, TTouch uses animal names to describe different methods. For example, Raccoon TTouch is quick, gentle, and light while Bear TTouch is deep and slow. The basic circular touch used most often on dogs is called Clouded Leopard, signifying softness with strength.

HISTORY

In 1972 the Israeli engineer and writer Moshe Feldenkrais published a book called *Awareness through Movement*, in which he promoted his concept that the brain learns to direct the body to move in certain ways, and that these ways are not necessarily the best ones. Linda Tellington-Jones, a Canadian horse-trainer, successfully adapted the Feldenkrais Method to horse training. In 1978, she created the TTEAM, meaning Tellington-Jones Equine Awareness Method. When her training techniques were later applied to cats, dogs, and other animals, the words behind the acronym were changed to Tellington-Jones Every Animal Method. In 1984, she introduced TTouch, a method of gentle, rhythmic stroking that relaxes and focuses animals by stimulating the nervous system.

HOW IT WORKS

TTouch therapy manipulates only the skin, not deeper tissues. With relaxed fingers the dog's skin is gently and slowly pushed around in a small, tight circle, beginning at the six o'clock position and completing a circle and a quarter, finishing at eight o'clock. These circling actions are done in connected lines over the dog's body. Pressure is adjusted for different dogs and different parts of the body, depending upon what is comfortable and non-threatening to the dog.

VETERINARY OPINION

While there is no formal evidence that TTouch has therapeutic value, trainers who use it say that animals become relaxed and more focused on their training sessions.

Zoos in San Diego in the United States, and in Zurich, Switzerland, include Tellington-Jones methods in their programs for wild animals. Dogs that enjoy contact and petting from their owners are likely to find this form of touch therapy relaxing. Frightened or nervous dogs that need to be handled may be calmed with TTouch because the movements that are used tend to be slow, repetitive, and non-threatening.

WHERE IT IS AVAILABLE

TTouch practitioners are widely available in Canada and the United States, and they can also be found in the UK. However, a professional therapist is not always needed for this treatment. TTouch is not difficult to learn. The gentle strokes and manipulations can be applied by dog owners to their own pets or by veterinary nurses to hospitalized individuals. Books and videos are available that explain the techniques.

GENTLE MOVEMENT
Here Linda Tellington-Jones gently rubs the inside of a dog's lips and makes tiny circles on the gums. This aims to cure dogs that are anxious or aggressive.

CHIROPRACTIC

CHIROPRACTIC HAD DUBIOUS beginnings but has matured into an effective form of physical therapy that may have applications for dogs. It considers the backbone or spinal column as the defender of the spinal cord and structural focus of the body. When the spine and other parts of the skeletal system function smoothly, the entire system of bones, joints, and muscles works in harmony.

DANIEL PALMER
Canadian-born Daniel Palmer (1845–1913) founded the Palmer School of Chiropractic in Iowa in 1898. He was jailed in 1906 for practicing medicine without a license, but his son, B.J., continued his work.

DO-IT-YOURSELF?

Trained veterinary chiropractors and osteopaths know and understand canine anatomy. They know where muscles are attached to bones and where nerves, ligaments and tendons are located. Never attempt to use thrusting or rapid manipulations on your dog. A careless manipulation can cause pain. In some circumstances it can paralyze.

HISTORY

Chiropractic was developed in Canada in 1895 by Daniel Palmer and perpetuated by his son, B.J. Palmer. Early chiropractors invented a curious terminology and theory of action for their work that led to it being condemned, in the 1960s, as an "unscientific cult." Condemnation forced chiropractors to carry out properly controlled studies on their clients. The results, worldwide, were so encouraging that chiropractic manipulation is today accepted as a safe technique for alleviating conditions such as lower-back pain. In the 1950s, John McTimoney, a British chiropractor, developed a gentle form of manipulation and applied it to animals. His is the most popular form of veterinary chiropractic in Britain.

HOW IT WORKS

Modern chiropractors examine the spinal column and pelvis and also look at other relevant joints for misalignments or muscle spasm. Using hands only, the problem areas are treated with palpation and manipulation.

Aftercare usually involves rest or very limited exercise for several days. Depending upon the injury, one or more treatments may be needed, with half-yearly or yearly re-examinations.

VETERINARY OPINION

In 1996, the American Veterinary Medical Association reported, "Sufficient clinical and anecdotal evidence exists to indicate that veterinary chiropractic can be beneficial." Chiropractic can be used for canine athletes. Greyhounds racing on tight tracks tend to put abnormal strain on their spinal columns. Agility dogs encountering obstacles on tight courses may also suffer from spinal-column tension. Individual dogs, especially if they are overweight, or short-legged and long-backed, may also benefit from chiropractic manipulation, and it can be therapeutic for dogs during the recovery stage after road traffic accidents and other physical mishaps.

WHERE IT IS AVAILABLE

Few veterinarians are trained in chiropractic manipulation. The American Veterinary Chiropractic Association holds courses both for veterinarians and chiropractors in the United States and Canada. The McTimoney Chiropractic Association trains and certifies animal chiropractors in Britain. McTimoney practitioners only work on animals that have been referred to them by a qualified vet.

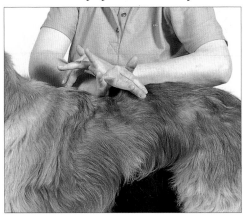

SPINAL ADJUSTMENT
Chiropractors work along the spine from the atlas to the lumbar region. They palpate each area and make adjustments where they find bones and joints are out of alignment.

OSTEOPATHY

OSTEOPATHY AND CHIROPRACTIC are the most widely practiced forms of human complementary medicine in the West. Studies show that manipulations based upon a firm understanding of anatomy are effective for limiting human back pain. Joint pain, including spinal column discomfort, is common in dogs. Veterinary medicine has been slow to accept manipulation as a valid form of pain control.

HISTORY

Osteopathy, like chiropractic, evolved out of bone setting. While chiropractic initially concentrated wholly on the spinal column, osteopathy used touch and manipulation to treat all parts of the muscular-skeletal system. This therapy was developed by Dr. Andrew Taylor Still. He was an Army doctor in the American Civil War who later in life, in 1892, founded the American School of Osteopathy. A British School of Osteopathy was founded in 1917. Osteopaths have not been as organized as chiropractors in their approach towards treating dogs and other animals. In Britain, some osteopaths are members of the recently formed Association of Chartered Physiotherapists in Animal Therapy (ACPAT). Individuals belonging to this group will only take animal referrals from practicing veterinarians.

HOW IT WORKS

Osteopaths are interested in why there is a fault in the muscular-skeletal system as well as how to overcome or cope with it. The techniques that they use are manual, and are sometimes similar to those of chiropractors to improve the mobility of muscles and joints. But while chiropractic concentrates mainly on the manipulation of misaligned joints, osteopathy places more emphasis on soft-tissue treatment. The aim of this treatment is to bring back mobility by making the muscles relax. Equine osteopaths occasionally use ropes as well as their hands to manipulate joints, but practitioners manipulating dogs use methods similar to those used on people.

VETERINARY OPINION

Virtually no research has been carried out on the value of osteopathy for dogs, but anecdotal evidence from veterinarians who refer individuals such as Dachshunds with back pain to osteopaths say they are pleased with the results. Osteopathic procedures may be helpful in the recovery phase after trauma from road traffic accidents, especially injuries involving fractures. Like people, dogs can suffer from degenerative joint diseases and osteopathic treatment for these conditions can be very helpful. The natural role of osteopathy in conventional veterinary medicine has not yet been seriously examined.

WHERE IT IS AVAILABLE

Now established alongside conventional medicine in the United States, and practiced in Europe and Australasia, osteopathy is widely available for us but still limited in availability for dogs. Your vet may refer you to a chiropractor or an osteopath, depending upon which is available.

PRECAUTIONS

Never force a dog to undergo any kind of physical manipulation. If it does not enjoy the experience you will do more harm than good. Beware of making your dog feel uncomfortable in order that it can experience the value of a manipulation. For example, a long walk or car journey to the "physio" may make your dog's condition worse. If rest is important to recovery, this takes precedent over any manipulation. Manipulations are appropriate after the rest stage of recovery.

SUPPORT SYSTEM
Practitioners emphasize the importance of the musculo-skeletal system in well-being. If bones and joints are correctly aligned, the body is free of stress.

THERAPEUTIC MASSAGE

MASSAGE DOES MORE THAN exercise and strengthen your dog's muscles. It stimulates blood and lymph circulation, disperses pain, and helps restore mobility and flexibility. Massage is especially beneficial for athletic dogs and has subtle values over and above the obvious physical ones. Massaging your dog helps to build trust and makes you aware of subtle changes in your dog's physical condition.

HISTORY

Massage may be the oldest and most natural form of medical care. It is an important element of all forms of medicine, including Traditional Chinese, Ayurvedic, Persian, Arab, Greek, and ancient Roman. In modern Western medicine, the concept of massage was restored to favor by the Swedish gymnast Per Henrik Ling at the end of the 19th century. His Swedish massage methods then became the basis for physiotherapy.

Therapeutic massage is used more frequently on canine athletes than on typical housedogs because their form and lifestyle predisposes them to greater need. Massage oils are not used on dogs.

HOW IT WORKS

Touch is perceived through the skin, the dog's largest sensory organ. Gentle massage triggers the release of cytokines, chemicals that exist in such small quantities that they were not known to exist until 20 years ago. These chemicals affect the dog's hormonal system, bringing down the levels of stress hormones that weaken the immune system.

Massage also stimulates blood circulation, which increases the amount of oxygen that reaches tissue and flushes out toxins and waste. Massage probably induces cells at the site being massaged to release cytokines. The cytokines then instruct the brain to release pain-killing endorphins.

Different forms of massage can be used, depending on a dog's need. "Effleurage" is the most common, which is stroking in one direction. It is used at the beginning of a therapeutic session and serves to calm the dog. "Petrissage" involves specific skin and muscle tissues being stretched, rolled, gently pinched, kneaded, even ever-so-slightly wrung. Hand movements may be circular or back and forth. Percussive forms of therapeutic massage

TOUCH HEALING

Almost every society in the world has a tradition of healing by "laying on of hands." Most touch healers are ordinary people who say they discover accidentally that they have special gifts which work not only on humans but on other animals too.

MASSAGING A DOG

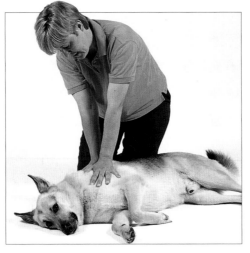

1 The first stage of massage is effleurage, which entails stroking the dog gently in one direction. Slow stroking aids relaxation, while fast stroking will stimulate the dog. Steadily slow the pace until your dog is completely relaxed.

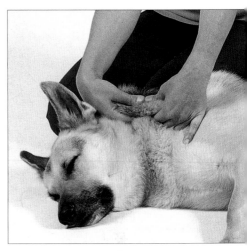

2 Once your dog is relaxed, move on to petrissage an aid to circulation. "Kneading" the dog involves applying circular pressure with the palm, all over its body. Follow this with "picking up" the soft tissues between the fingers and thumb and then releasing.

such as tapping may be used occasionally, but the more physically robust actions of clapping and hacking that are commonly used for people are only used for large, heavy dogs whose frames are not too delicate.

VETERINARY OPINION

Early and frequent touch leads to reduced glucocorticoid production later in life. Translated out of medical jargon, dogs that are frequently touched when they are young experience less stress when they are older. In theory, this means that dogs that are routinely massaged should have fewer immune system problems than other dogs.

Massage is therapeutic at a variety of different levels. On its own, it can reduce pain and discomfort, and increase blood circulation. On a secondary level, regularly massaging your dog helps you uncover early signs of problems such as muscle tenderness, swelling, or shrinkage. On a third level, if you massage your own dog, it strengthens the bond between you and your pet, and is actually good for you too, dropping your heart rate and lowering your blood pressure.

PRECAUTIONS
Never massage inflamed, infected, swollen, torn, or bruised areas. Similarly, never massage a dog with a fever, in clinical shock, or suffering from heatstroke. Do not massage near tumors, bone fractures, dislocations, or ligament tears. Never massage an injured neck or back. Unwittingly, you may make the condition far worse.

From the point of view of the veterinarian, dogs that accept regular massage will make better patients. They are easier to examine and treat because they are relaxed about being handled and manipulated.

WHERE IT IS AVAILABLE

Massage can be carried out at home if your dog is willing and in general good health. If your dog is recovering from an injury and needs remedial massage, it should only be administered by a registered therapist who is familiar with canine anatomy. Your vet should be able to refer you to someone in your area.

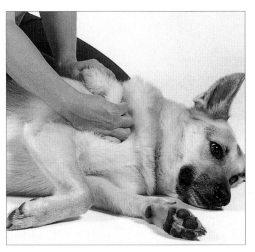

3 If your dog still appears happy with the massage, move onto "wringing," gently pushing and pulling the skin in both hands, followed by "rolling," the final stage of petrissage, where the skin is pushed away and then pulled toward you.

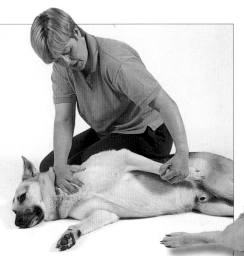

4 If your dog allows, you can gently stretch its limbs. The front and back legs are stretched forward then backward, each stretch being held for no more than six to 10 seconds. Stretching will wake up your dog, so finish with effleurage to relax it again.

HYDROTHERAPY

IN TRADITIONAL HYDROTHERAPY, water in all its forms, hot or cold, steam or ice, is used to revitalize and restore the body. Water is also an ideal medium for any physical therapy. Whirlpools and waterjets, when available, can be used to stimulate muscles and joints after physical injuries or surgery. Cold and heat in the form of ice packs or warm compresses are also used to treat local conditions.

HOW HOT?

Ensure that water is not too hot. A dog's coat retains and exaggerates the effect of overheated water. It is best to avoid hydrotherapy for dogs that dislike getting wet. Avoid any form of heat for dogs with high blood pressure.

HISTORY

Virtually all mammals enjoy the feeling of floating in water and will enter ponds, lakes, rivers, or the sea for the simple satisfaction of wading and swimming. Historically, warm water bathing has been used therapeutically throughout the world wherever there are natural hot springs. Hydrotherapy for dogs originated when vets in Japan arranged for dogs to be treated for a variety of medical conditions at hot spring spas in Hakone.

HOW IT WORKS

Water is an ideal vehicle for heat and cold. Cold water stimulates surface blood vessels to constrict, which inhibits blood flow and the cascade of chemical events that causes inflammation. External cold water redirects blood toward the internal organs, helping them to function more efficiently. Warm water dilates blood vessels, increasing blood flow to the skin and muscles and easing stiffness. Improved circulation brings more oxygen, nutrients, and elements of the immune system to the body's cells. It helps remove waste products. Increased blood flow to the skin also reduces blood pressure.

VETERINARY OPINION

Conventional veterinarians understand the value of buoyancy and water resistance for exercising injured dogs. Where hydrotherapy swimming pools are available, vets routinely refer dogs to hydrotherapists and consider the treatment to be an effective form of physiotherapy. Japanese vets appreciate the value of natural sulfur springs for treating dogs with certain skin conditions such as oily seborrhoea. Where hydrotherapy facilities for dogs exist they are frequently used.

WHERE IT IS AVAILABLE

Your vet may advise you of a designated pool in your area if your dog needs hydrotherapy. Otherwise, swimming in a lake or the sea will be beneficial for any dog that enjoys it.

NATURAL SWIMMERS
Dogs that have degenerative joint problems or are recovering from injuries are often helped by hydrotherapy. At specialized pools, dogs wear buoyancy jackets so that they can swim gently, avoiding any further strain on the injured limb.

OTHER PHYSICAL THERAPIES

A PHYSICAL THERAPIST thinks of an injury as a process, rather than an event. The process often begins acutely and continues for a variable length of time. The therapist modifies his or her treatment during the course of the process, rather than maintaining a standardized therapy throughout. A variety of new technologies are used as complementary forms of physical therapy for dogs.

PRECAUTIONS
All of these physical therapies have limitations and carry the potential for doing harm. Increasing tissue temperature is supposed to increase the pain threshold, but, in excess, these therapies destroy tissue. Do not apply them to your dog yourself.

HISTORY
In 1973, in his book *Horse Injuries*, Charles Strong first advocated the use of electrical stimulation to treat pain in animals. Since then, other physical therapies, including laser, electrical stimulation, magnetic therapy, and therapeutic ultrasound have been advocated as therapies for dogs. The American Veterinary Medical Association now includes these technologies, as well as hydrotherapy, stretching, and massage in its definition of physical therapies.

HOW THEY WORK
A wide variety of technical appliances are available to veterinarians but all have the same purpose — to relieve pain. Therapeutic lasers first appeared on the market about 30 years ago. In human medicine, since 1990, over 2,500 articles have been published on the use of low-level laser therapy (LLLT). LLLT is the internationally accepted term for lasers that do not burn. These devices do not raise cell temperature but are thought to cause chemical reactions within cells. They are more frequently used in horses than dogs.

Various high- and low-voltage electrical stimulators are marketed for pain relief. The most popular are low-voltage transcutaneous, electrical nerve-stimulator units or TENS units. These provide sensory stimulation in much the same way that electro-acupuncture does (*see page 74*).

Small ultrasound units make use of ultra-high-frequency sound waves to "heat" tissue such as ligaments, tendons, or scar tissue. The intensity of ultrasound varies according to what the practitioner wants to achieve.

Lower intensities are used to reduce pain, to relieve spasms, and to disperse excessive inflammation. Higher intensities are used to heat tissues before stretching and massage. Ultrasound is usually applied through a gel, to damaged tissue.

VETERINARY OPINION
Laser light is capable of penetrating tissue but there is some doubt as to whether LLLT radiation has the capacity to penetrate to a sufficient depth to be therapeutic. Electrical stimulation does appear to stimulate blood flow. It has been reported to increase the contractile force of muscle fibers, improving muscle strength after injury.

While advocates say that LLLT reduces pain, clinical trials have not substantiated this suggestion. TENS units are perhaps more frequently used than other physical therapies and they may well stimulate a dog's endorphins much as electro-acupuncture does. A report published in 1995 found that ultrasound reduced the development of excess fibrous tissue in dogs with femur fractures. However, in clinical trials sham ultrasound (the machine is on but no ultrasound is being emitted) has been as therapeutic as therapeutic ultrasound.

WHERE THEY ARE AVAILABLE
If you are interested in these therapies for use in controlling your dog's pain, find a vet who is experienced with the equipment used in the therapy in question. If experience is not available, use another therapy that is known to be effective and does not carry the potential risks of these treatments.

CHECKLIST
- Lack of exercise causes muscles to shrink and joints to tighten.
- Physical therapies are useful methods of manipulating muscles and reversing atrophy.
- Pain is serving a useful purpose. It conditions a dog to rest the injured part of its body.
- Excess pain may be controlled by various forms of physical therapy.

NATURAL DEVELOPMENT

NATURAL TRAINING

NATURAL NUTRITION

NATURAL HEALTH CARE

HEALTH DISORDERS

Natural Development

Natural Training

Natural Nutrition

Natural Health Care

Health Disorders

Medicinal Therapies

THE BASIS OF GOOD HEALTH is well-balanced body biochemistry. Illness is associated with abnormal body chemistry. In many circumstances, these abnormalities are corrected by providing the body with specific substances. Throughout history, people have used a great variety of natural products as medicinal therapies; Western culture takes this tradition in a scientific direction, purifying specific substances. The objective of all forms of medicine, complementary and traditional, is to return the body to a state of equilibrium. However, there are philosophical differences in how this is best achieved.

Western medicine investigates how the body works, down to its most elemental level. Scientists want to know what is happening, not just to organs or cells, but to molecules. They feel that if they understand how balance is upset at the most basic level of life, they can formulate specific therapies at that level.

GIVING MEDICINE
Medicines have been given to dogs for as long as dogs have lived with us. Herbs were and still are used as purgatives, emetics, and fever reducers, and to return the dog's body to a state of harmony.

A NATURAL SALT LICK
Owners believe their dogs lick them as a sign of affection, but they are actually attracted to our salty sweat and are using us as mobile salt licks.

Complementary veterinarians say this is fine as long as the diagnosis is correct, but the very nature of illness means that diagnostics remains "educated guesswork." They argue that more general manipulative, herbal, or mind therapies are safer and more realistic than target-specific therapies.

Herbal medicine evolved wherever people lived. Today, over 75 percent of the world's population still rely upon herbal medicines for basic body care. Dogs, too, learn that eating certain plants is beneficial. Where I live, dogs are particularly attracted to a weed called pig thistle and selectively eat it, perhaps for its therapeutic value. The pharmaceutical basis of Western medicine evolved from herbal traditions. A report published in 1975 by the American National Academy of Sciences suggests that Chinese herbal medicine has a 50 percent "success" rate, higher than any other type of indigenous herbal medicine that has been studied. For example, Amerindian medicine has a 25 percent success rate. Regardless of what type of medicinal therapy you plan to use on your dog, remember, what works for us may be unsuitable for dogs. Always take advice from therapists who are experienced in using that medicine for dogs.

NATURE'S MEDICINE
Evolution taught dogs that eating certain vegetation can be beneficial. Some dogs eat grass to induce vomiting when unwell, in order to rid the stomach of potential toxins.

NUTRITIONAL THERAPIES

NUTRITIONAL THERAPIES ARE the basis of natural dog care but can be difficult to implement because so much still needs to be learned about the dietary management of good health. Nutritional therapies are beneficial not only when there are nutritional deficiencies but also when food itself is the cause of a problem. Eating disorders, on the other hand, are human, not canine problems.

HISTORY

The concept of nutritional therapy evolved out of naturopathy, which is the science of treating disease and promoting good health through nourishing, non-allergenic foods, clean water, fresh air, and an uncontaminated environment, achieving equilibrium and good health in the body's internal environment. The basic concept of naturopathy has been adopted by conventional veterinary medicine and is the basis of preventative medicine today. Nutritional therapies concentrate on overcoming health problems through fasting and clinical nutrition.

HOW THEY WORK

Not eating, a central component of "nature cures," appears to be an excellent strategy that all animals developed over the centuries

MEGAVITAMIN THERAPY

Pioneered by the Nobel prize-winning scientist Linus Pauling, megavitamin or orthomolecular therapy involves giving large doses of vitamins as a medication rather than as nutritional therapy. In his book *Vitamin C and the Common Cold*, Pauling argued that large doses of the antioxidant vitamin C mopped up free-radical molecules that cause cellular damage. While we obtain our vitamin C only from what we eat, dogs manufacture their own. A megadose may do no harm, but it may upset the balance of acid and alkali in a dog's body.

to help overcome illness. When challenged by infection, cytokines in a dog's brain turn off the brain's hunger center. Consequent fasting benefits the ill dog in two ways. By not eating, bacteria that invaded the body are starved of the minerals they need. More important, a fasting dog will not use up precious energy looking for food. The dog rests, reduces heat loss, and fights infection.

Controlled fasting is beneficial for most mammals. Mice that are fasted for two days before an infection are more likely to survive the infection than mice that are not fasted.

FOOD SENSITIVE
Itchiness and diarrhea are common manifestations of food sensitivity. A diet that is good for most dogs but induces sensitivity in one individual simply reveals that dog's underlying nutrient sensitivity.

DIET-INDUCED PROBLEMS

A dog's diet may be the actual cause of a medical or behavioral problem. A diet may be deficient in macro- or micronutrients. It may be toxic to a dog, contaminated with hazardous materials, contain antinutrients, or be imbalanced. Diet-induced problems can be caused when we, or manufacturers of dog food, formulate diets incorrectly. Processing problems and post-processing mistakes also lead to diet-induced problems, usually deficiencies. Diet-induced problems are uncommon, a consequence of the dog's superb nutritional adaptability and the quality of most food we feed dogs today.

NUTRIENT SENSITIVITIES

Each dog is a unique individual with its own idiosyncratic responses to the foods it eats. Some individuals tolerate almost any foods, while other dogs develop a variety of food intolerances. Nutrient-sensitive diseases occur, not when there is a defect in the diet, but rather when there is a defect in the dog.

Nutrient-sensitive diseases include food allergies, heart, liver, and kidney diseases, and some forms of urinary tract disease. Food sensitivities occur more often in some breeds, such as the Shetland Sheepdog and the Golden Retriever, than others. Regardless of breed, the likelihood of a dog developing a food sensitivity increases with age.

Treating a nutrient-sensitivity condition can be risky because any diet change is usually a permanent one. Without careful planning, a nutrient-sensitivity problem can be turned into a nutrient-deficiency condition.

FEEDING-RELATED DISORDERS

Overfeeding is the most common feeding-related disorder in dogs. A feeding-related problem is a responsibility of the owner, rather than of the dog. And, frustratingly, the only treatment for this nutritional problem is to educate the owner, a far more difficult task than changing a dog's diet. Feeding-related problems include obesity, growth disorders, and reproductive failure.

VETERINARY OPINION

Historically, veterinarians have understood the link between nutrition and health, but it is only in the last 20 years that nutritional therapy has become a component of clinical veterinary care. Food grown in poor soil may lack nutrients, crops sprayed with pesticides may contain toxic chemicals, or meat that has been passed as unfit for human consumption can end up in dog food. Poor food may alter the balance of bacteria in the gut, which is thought to be a cause of the increased incidence of allergic conditions in dogs.

WHAT DIETS ARE AVAILABLE?

In reaction to information concerning the way livestock are treated, the drugs they are given to promote their growth, and the risks of disease meat poses to us, increasing numbers of people are giving up meat and eating vegetarian diets. A vegetarian diet is safe for dogs, also, but by no means natural.

Some dog owners feel that raw food diets are most natural. This is true, although dogs have difficulty digesting raw vegetables and grains. Raw meat contains nutrients that are unaltered by cooking but may also contain harmful bacteria such as Salmonella.

Beginning in the 1980s, and accelerating rapidly in the 1990s, pet food manufacturers produced a range of therapeutic diets for dogs. Responding to a more refined demand, dog food manufacturers use ingredients from the "human food" chain in their dog foods, and avoid synthetic preservatives and colorants. The best of the therapeutic diets utilize the nutritionist's knowledge of practices such as modifying gut flora to secure health benefits. Some dog food manufacturers have responded to owner concerns about nutrition faster than human convenience-food makers.

Regardless of what nutritional therapy your dog needs, any strict diet fed over a long period may lead to malnutrition. Always talk to your vet and obtain a canine nutritionist's advice before embarking on any form of nutritional therapy for your dog, especially if it is growing, pregnant, or elderly.

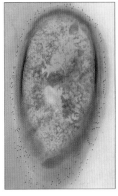

BENEFICIAL BACTERIA
Certain types of bacteria in the intestines, such as Lactobacillus brevis *(above), aid digestion, and some of them enhance the immune system. An incorrect diet alters intestinal bacteria and reduces natural defences.*

CHECKLIST

- Use nutritional therapy to support the immune system.

- Never force a dog to eat when it doesn't want to.

- Always get a veterinarian's advice before changing a dog's diet.

Understand what you are feeding your dog. Differentiate between:

- Diet-induced problems caused by the diet itself.

- Particular nutrient sensitivities that are personal to an individual dog.

- Feeding-related disorders that are caused by how we feed dogs.

NATURAL DEVELOPMENT

NATURAL TRAINING

NATURAL NUTRITION

NATURAL HEALTH CARE

HEALTH DISORDERS

HERBALISM

WHILE HERBS ARE A MAJOR SOURCE of pharmaceuticals, herbal remedies differ from conventional drugs in using parts of the whole plant rather than isolating single active ingredients. In traditional forms of herbalism, the choice of herbs depends upon the dog's personality as well as its medical condition. In modern herbalism, there is greater emphasis on the chemical constituents of the herb itself.

DANGERS IN NATURE

All medicines, whether they are natural herbs or synthesized by pharmaceutical companies, are potentially toxic in excess. The difference between therapeutic and dangerous doses for dogs can be minimal. Herbal does not mean safe. Use all medications for dogs with care and caution.

HISTORY

From the very earliest stages of evolution, animals learned that eating certain types of vegetation made them feel better. Dogs will eat grass in order to induce vomiting and remove any toxic food they have eaten.

Classical herbalism developed in all early human cultures but was best recorded in the ancient Hindu texts, the *Vedas*, starting about 4,500 years ago. Ayurveda, the traditional holistic healing system of the Indian subcontinent, shares herbs with Traditional Chinese Medicine (TCM), where legend tells how animals guided humans to discover the medicinal values of plants. Herbalism also flourished in Europe and was augmented by Persian and Islamic physicians.

When Europeans arrived in the Americas, Africa, and Australasia, their herbal armories were expanded by herbs used by native peoples. The first flu epidemics in the new American colonies were often treated with

sage (*Salvia officinalis*) and boneset (*Eupatorium perfoliatum*). Even today, in most parts of the world, herbs remains a vital ingredient of traditional medicine both for people and for the animals in their care.

HOW THEY WORK

In traditional forms of medicine, herbal treatments are tailored to an individual's personality. Ayurvedic medicine stipulates the need for balance between the "energies" within and without the body. Ayurveda's five great elements – ether, air, fire, water, and earth – are contained in three *doshas*, or energies, that every person, animal, food, and environment is made up of in varying degrees. Because each animal is a unique composite of *doshas*, its illness is treated with herbal prescriptions not only according to the disease, but also according to its combination of *doshas*, its age, and even the time of day.

Herbalism in Traditional Chinese Medicine follows similar patterns. Illness is regarded as a "pattern of disharmony." There are herbs for sweating, vomiting, draining downward, warming, clearing, reducing, harmonizing, and that have a tonic effect, and these are used according to the blend of *yin* and *yang* both of the patient and of the herbs, in order to restore harmony. For example, ginseng is believed to act as a tonic to the *yang* tendencies of the body, which are male and assertive. Herbal treatments are tailored to the individual animal.

SYMBOLISM IN MEDICATION

Like conventional drugs, the dispensing of herbs is imbued with symbolism, much of which is understated but nevertheless understood both by the herbalist and the dog owner. A herb can be:

- A sign of the herbalist's power to heal
- A symbol of the mystical power of the herbalist
- A sign that the dog is "really ill"
- A fulfillment of the contract between you, as the owner of the dog, and the herbalist

HERBALISM AND FOODS

Traditional associations with herbs influenced regional cuisine. Indian cookery reflects Ayurvedic alchemy. The water-generating nature of coriander is used to balance the heating qualities of chilis, while cardamom reduces the mucus-forming qualities of other foods.

CHILIS

CARDAMOM　　CORIANDER

- A sign that you can control the dog's health

- An indication of the herbalist's understanding and concern

- A way in which the herbalist can communicate with you

- A way of satisfying your goal to use traditional medicine such as herbs

- A source of satisfaction for the herbalist

There is far more to the dispensing of a herb or a drug than just the substance itself.

VETERINARY OPINION

Modern herbalism, under its scientific name of phytotherapy, is the basis of conventional drug therapy. While many modern drugs have been isolated from herbal extracts, for example, aspirin from willow-tree bark, modern herbalists contend that therapeutic herbal plants are complex mixtures of chemicals, all of which contribute to the beneficial effects of their use. Herbalists argue that chemicals that have been isolated and refined from herbs are much more likely to be toxic than their botanical sources; these isolated chemicals produce effects that have a rapid onset and a greater intensity, which can lead to unwanted side effects.

Conventional veterinarians understand and accept the medicinal values of herbal therapies but find it difficult to accept the ancient concepts that underlie traditional herbalism. They find the herbalist's emphasis on promoting balance and harmony in the body through preventative health care, diet, and lifestyle compatible with modern trends in conventional veterinary medicine.

However, dogs' sensitivities to herbal substances are likely to be quite different to our own. Because toxic doses for dogs have not been calculated for most herbs, vets are concerned about possible side effects of certain remedies.

In many parts of the world, traditional herbalism remains the treatment of choice for livestock animals, although this form of traditionalism has been abandoned for pet animals, which are now generally treated with modern pharmaceutical therapies. When I had the opportunity to visit East Java recently, veterinarians there told me that with the advent of Western veterinary medicine, centuries of trial-and-error understanding of the value of local herbs for treating animals would probably die out within one generation.

WHERE THEY ARE AVAILABLE

Herbs are available worldwide and often are promoted for benefits that have never been evaluated or proven. In most countries, there is little control over how herbs are sold. In Germany, however, the German Federal Health Authority's Commission E publishes information on the composition, use, interaction with other drugs, side effects, and dosages of marketed herbs. This allows herbs to be marketed as "over-the-counter" drugs in Germany, and enables doctors and veterinarians to use common sense and to prescribe what they feel is best for their patient. In Germany, 50 percent of the total sales of herbal products are prescribed by doctors, and more St. John's wort (*Hypericum perforatum*) is purchased as an anti-depressant than the widely promoted drug Prozac. Where such information is not available, be cautious when considering herbal treatments for your dog. Few have been evaluated. Some are dangerous, even life-threatening.

STILL ACTIVE?
Herbs have a short shelf life. Use products labeled with a harvest or expiration date. The label should explain the parts of the herb used and list any other ingredients, such as fillers or containers.

CHECKLIST

- Herbal therapies provide chemical building blocks for body cells.

- They interfere with dangerous microorganisms.

- They maintain effective defenses.

- As knowledge increases, herbal therapies evolve.

- Herbalism evolved into modern pharmaceuticals.

- The nutrient side of herbalism is evolving into "nutraceuticals."

- Proven therapies are the best kind, irrespective of whether they are old ones or new.

WILLOW LEAVES

WHOLE HERBS
Many herbalists use whole herbs, for instance, the bark of the willow tree (right). Others feel that toxins in herbs decrease the activity of the desired ingredients and prefer to use synthesized ingredients. Willow bark is a source of salicin, from which aspirin is derived.

WILLOW BARK

ASPIRIN

HERBAL THERAPIES

HERBAL THERAPIES ARE OFTEN used to correct body functions and are given in short courses. Some dogs are not disposed to eat fresh or dried herbs, so herbal tablets tend to be used. Herbs may be good as skin treatments for people but can be dangerous for dogs, as they may lick them off and poison themselves. Put an Elizabethan collar on your dog if applying any medication to its skin.

HAWTHORN

PEPPERMINT
LEAF

MOTHERWORT
HERB

CHECKLIST
- Be extremely cautious with herbs.
- Apply to your dog's coat only herbs known to be safe if ingested.
- Dogs do not have good natural systems to detoxify a range of natural substances.

HERBAL PREPARATIONS

The medicinal parts of plants can be prepared in a variety of ways. Infused oils, ointments, and creams are made for topical use (applied to the surface of the body).

Decoctions, tinctures, and infusions are more appropriate than topical preparations for dogs because they are made from herbs that are known to be safe if taken internally. Decoctions are prepared by boiling in water the tough parts of plants such as bark, roots, and berries. The liquid is strained and consumed either hot or cold. Tinctures are made by soaking a herb in alcohol and water, usually for a few weeks, and then straining it. Tinctures are usually stored in dark bottles and can be kept for up to two years. Infusions are made like tea, from the leaves and flowers of the herb.

THE USES OF HERBS

In order to survive, plants produce chemicals for their own protection. Some of these chemicals are beneficial for other forms of life, including dogs. For example, garlic, the world's most popular herb, contains at least 200 different compounds, many of which are said to be useful for dogs. Garlic lowers blood pressure, accelerates the breakdown of waste matter from cells, and may even act as a mild flea repellent. Ginkgo (*Ginkgo biloba*) leaves contain substances called flavonoids that are said to be effective at scavenging free radicals. Siberian ginseng (*Eleutherococcus senticosus*) may help regulate blood sugar and affect the adrenal glands. *Ashwaghanda* (*Withania somnifera*), popular in Ayurvedic herbalism, is reported to increase hemoglobin and red blood cell counts, countering anemia.

HERBAL HOME-CARE KIT

Some herbal remedies are especially effective for minor accidents and illnesses. These herbs have been used with safety on dogs and constitute a basic home-care kit.

They can be found at most pharmacies and herbal shops. Only use herbs recognized as safe for dogs, preferably those specially prepared for veterinary use.

COMFREY
Comfrey (Symphytum) is soothing and healing. Used to help heal wounds, burns, bruises, and strains.

LAVENDER
Lavender (Lavandula) is claimed to be antiseptic and calming. Used on the site of insect bites and for burns.

POT MARIGOLD
Pot Marigold (Calendula) is used to soothe inflamed skin. Infusions are given for digestive disorders.

GARLIC
Garlic (Allium sativum) is given for mild infections, upper respiratory conditions, and digestive disorders.

ECHINACEA
Echinacea (Echinacea purpurea) may act as an antibiotic and stimulate the immune system.

BARBERRY
BARK

HORSETAIL
HERB

CINNAMON
BARK

Oil of cedar (*Cedrus*) is reported to have antibacterial, antifungal, and acaridical (mite-killing) properties. Seed oil extracted from neem (*Azadirachta indica*) is antibacterial and, according to published reports, inhibits ringworm. Scientific studies suggest that aloe vera has anti-inflammatory, analgesic, and anti-microbial effects, while studies in horses suggest it stimulates the immune system.

Cancer treatments have been developed from herbal products. For example, the Madagascar periwinkle (*Catharanthus roseus*) contains vincristine, which shrinks certain types of cancers. When it was available only as a plant extract it was very expensive, but laboratory synthesis of vincristine has reduced the cost, and made it available for controlling white blood-cell cancers in dogs.

PREPARING AN HERBAL INFUSION

For immediate soothing and antiseptic use for wounds or skin infections, or for the relief of mild gastroenteric problems, an infusion of peppermint leaf or Roman chamomile flower can be made at home:

- Heat a clean (well washed and rinsed) cup with boiling water.
- Pour away the water and add I tsp of dried or 2 tsp of fresh herb to the heated cup.
- Fill to three-quarters level with boiling water.
- Cover and leave to steep for 10 minutes.
- Remove the cover, pouring condensation inside the cover back into the cup.
- Strain and use or store covered in a cool place.

COMMON HERBAL THERAPIES

If not used correctly, herbal substances can be just as dangerous as wrongly prescribed modern drugs. Do not make your own diagnoses or use any of these herbs without professional guidance.

CONDITIONS	HERBAL THERAPIES
CANCER *(prevention)*	• Lemon balm *Melissa officinalis* • Mistletoe leaf *Viscum album* • Barberry bark *Berberis vulgaris* • Roman chamomile flower *Chamaemelum nobile* • Comfrey leaf *Symphytum officinale* • Echinacea root *Echinacea purpurea* • Fenugreek seed *Trigonella foenum-graecum*
ITCHY SKIN	• German chamomile flower *Chamomilla recutita* • Burdock root *Arctium lappa* • Curled dock root *Rumex crispus* • Licorice root *Glycyrrhiza glabra* • Southernwood *Artemisia abrotanum*
SKIN ABRASIONS	• Turmeric root *Curcuma longa* • Yarrow *Achillea millefolium* • Peppermint *Mentha x piperita* • Comfrey leaf *Symphytum officinale*
COLITIS	• Marsh mallow root *Althaea officinalis* • Nutmeg seed *Myristica fragrans* • Turmeric root *Curcuma longa*
HEART DISEASE	• Hawthorn *Crataegus laevigata* • Motherwort *Leonurus cardiaca* • Dandelion leaf *Taraxacum officinale*
URINARY TRACT DISORDERS	• Stone root *Collinsonia canadensis* • Field horsetail *Equisetum arvense* • Quack grass *Elymus repens* • Bearberry leaf *Arctostaphylos uva-ursi* • Juniper berry *Juniperus communis* • Marsh mallow root *Althaea officinalis*
KIDNEY IMPAIRMENT	• Cinnamon bark *Cinnamomum zeylanicum* • Rehmannia root *Rehmannia glutinosa* • Comfrey leaf *Symphytum officinale* • Celery seed *Apium graveolens*

WARNING

Be wary of imported Chinese herbs. The desired herb may be contaminated with other herbs that are potentially toxic to dogs. Only use herbs from reliable, established suppliers who carry out batch assessments for consistency and quality control.

HOMEOPATHY

HOMEOPATHY IS ENJOYING A REVIVAL in both North America and Europe. The American Veterinary Medical Association says: "Clinical and anecdotal evidence exists to indicate that veterinary homeopathy may be beneficial." About 60 percent of the 2,500 homeopathic remedies come from plants. Current understanding of biology cannot explain scientifically how homeopathy works.

WARNING

Don't prepare your own homeopathic medicines. Some are deadly if not prepared properly. Don't experiment. Only use products recommended by an experienced homeopath, produced in safe conditions. The greater the dilution, the safer the solution.

HISTORY

The idea that "like cures like" is found in many forms of traditional medicine and was revived in the late 18th century by the German doctor Samuel Hahnemann. Critical of the invasive treatments, such as leeches and violent purges, used by his contemporaries, he developed "homeopathy," from the Greek *homoios* (same) and *pathos* (suffering). Homeopathic treatment of animals was later introduced by Baron von Boenninghausen in the early 19th century.

HOW IT WORKS

The body is in a constant state of self-repair, with all organs and cells constantly renewing themselves. Homeopaths believe that a "vital force" regulates the body, and maintains health. Clinical signs of disease

DO NOSODES PROTECT?

Some owners choose not to use biological vaccines to protect their pets from serious infectious diseases such as distemper, parvovirus, and rabies and rely upon homeopathic nosodes to render protection. At a recent meeting of the American Holistic Veterinary Medical Association, Dr. Susan Wynn gave the results of a study in which dogs were given nosodes to protect them against canine parvovirus. When exposed to parvovirus, all the dogs developed this serious disease. Homeopathic nosodes do not stimulate a dog's immune system to form protective antibodies.

are seen as indications that the body is fighting illness or injury. The homeopath determines how the body is trying to defend itself, before prescribing, according to the principle of "like cures like," a remedy that stimulates self-healing rather than suppresses the signs of disease. The result may be that symptoms work their way along the body from head to tail; or they move from inside to outside the body; or they move from the more important organs to the least important. Historically, "like cures like" has been called the "law of similars." This was and remains

POTENTIZATION

Hahnemann believed that the more a substance was diluted, the more potent it became. Remedies are made from plant, animal, and mineral extracts. The extract is

chopped or ground and then soaked in a mix of 90 percent alcohol and 10 percent distilled water. This mixture is shaken from time to time to dissolve the material.

1 Once the mixture has stood for two to four weeks, the mixture has become infused. It is strained into a dark glass bottle, and becomes known as the "mother tincture."

2 One drop of the tincture is then diluted in 99 drops of alcohol, then shaken rapidly – a process called succussion. Dilution and succussion are repeated.

3 After dilution and succussion have resulted in the required potency, a few drops are added to a jar of lactose tablets, which absorb the potentized remedy.

the central principle of homeopathy. The remedies consist of substances that, if taken undiluted by a healthy person, would cause symptoms similar to those of the disease being treated. For example, poison ivy, *Rhus toxicodendron*, naturally causes local skin irritation, so diluted *Rhus tox* is used to treat a skin irritation, caused, for example, by flea bites. All substances used in homeopathic remedies are diluted many times.

When used preventatively, homeopathic remedies are called nosodes. Nosodes are available to prevent infectious diseases such as respiratory infection and viral enteritis (*see box, left*). Diluting doses repeatedly limits possible harmful side effects and is believed to increase the potency of the solution. This is called the "law of potentization."

MODERN EXPLANATIONS

Chaos theory, which proposes that minute changes lead to huge differences, has been used to explain how homeopathy works. So too has resonance theory, which says that all matter consists of and radiates energy. Some homeopaths believe that water, the substance in which homeopathic medicines are made, is capable of storing energy. Others argue that diluting and shaking homeopathic remedies creates an electromagnetic state, and magnetite, an electromagnetic substance found in dogs' and other mammals' brains, is hypersensitive to the resulting mixture.

VETERINARY OPINION

An extensive review, published in the *British Medical Journal* in 1991, analyzed 107 controlled studies involving homeopathic medicines. It concluded that, although the studies were not well designed, 81 showed homeopathic medicines to be effective, 24 showed they were ineffective, and two were inconclusive. In 1994, a double-blind study published in the medical journal *The Lancet* reported that homeopathy was more useful than a placebo in treating hay fever. No high-caliber studies of homeopathic medicines have been carried out on dogs.

The number of veterinarians who include homeopathic remedies such as *Arnica 6c*, *Aconite 6c*, and *Hypericum 6c* in their medical arsenals is increasing in Europe, North America, and Australasia. Although they find it difficult to accept homeopathic theories, many vets are willing to accept evidence from owners that homeopathic remedies work. Most vets feel that, because homeopathic treatments are administered in such minute amounts, they can do no harm and will not upset any therapies directed at returning the body to homeostatic levels, for example, through intravenous fluid therapy. They do not consider remedies to be therapeutic.

WHERE IT IS AVAILABLE

Most homeopathic remedies are available in liquid and in pill form. Liquids are easy to administer to dogs using a pipette at the corner of the mouth, and pills are also easy although, unlike conventional medicines, they are not meant to be swallowed but rather to be dissolved in the mouth. My nurses give *Arnica 6c* to all surgical cases while animals are anaesthetized, placing the tiny pills under the tongue. Unfortunately, a dog's mouth becomes dry during anaesthesia, and the pills can take time to dissolve.

SAMUEL HAHNEMANN
In a lecture delivered in the early 1800s to the Leipzig Economic Society, Samuel Hahnemann, the founder of homeopathy, referred to the similarity of his methods as applied to animals and humans. Homeopathic treatment of animals was formally begun around this time by Baron von Boenninghausen.

HOMEOPATHIC HOMECARE KIT

Because homeopathic remedies are so diluted, there is little possibility of them causing side effects. These homeopathic remedies can be kept at home to form a basic home-remedy kit.

CONDITIONS	HOMEOPATHIC THERAPIES
Panic attacks and emotional stress	*Aconite 6c*
Flea bites and wasp stings	*Apis 6c*
Bruises and swelling	*Arnica 6c*
Flatulence and digestive disorders	*Carbo Veg 6c*
Skin grazes and superficial wounds	*Hypercium 6c*

BIOCHEMIC TISSUE SALTS

BIOCHEMIC TISSUE SALTS, sometimes called Schüssler salts, are homeopathic remedies prepared from mineral rather than animal or vegetable sources. While they are prepared in the same way as homeopathic remedies, rather than using them according to the homeopathic philosophy of "like curing like," biochemic tissue salts are given to correct perceived mineral deficiencies.

HOW THEY WORK

Therapists believe that an imbalance or lack of specific salts causes a range of medical conditions from emotional upsets to allergies. They believe that a small "homeopathic" dose, where the minerals are diluted so that they are no longer measurable, is easily absorbed by the body, restores balances, and helps the body to heal itself.

WARNING

Biochemic tissue salts are often made up as lactose-based tablets. If your dog has loose stools when it drinks milk, it may be "lactose-intolerant," sensitive to the natural sugar, lactose, in milk. In these circumstances do not give lactose-based tissue-salt tablets.

HISTORY

The concept of using tissue salts to correct the body's mineral imbalances was developed in the 1870s by a German homeopathic physician, Dr Wilhelm Schüssler, who also created the terms "biochemics" and "tissue salts." He named 12 essential salts, and described the medical conditions that his remedies should be used to treat, either singly or in combination. Biochemic tissue salts were incorporated into the existing range of organically-derived homeopathic remedies.

VETERINARY OPINION

Conventional medical research has shown that mineral salts are vital for good health, and conventional vets routinely measure mineral levels in the blood, especially those of sodium and potassium, to monitor a variety of illnesses. However, they feel there is no evidence that biochemic remedies, if diluted to homeopathic levels, will have any effect. Homeopathic vets will often prescribe biochemic tissue salts, along with nutritional advice, as treatment for minor illnesses.

BIOCHEMIC TISSUE SALTS

Tissue salts are used singly or in combination to treat conditions that a homeopathic vet feels are associated with specific mineral deficiencies. Tablets are given more frequently for new clinical signs and less frequently but for longer durations for chronic conditions.

CONDITION	NAME	SOURCE
Poor dental health	*Calc. fluor*	Calcium fluoride
Bone problems	*Calc. phos.*	Calcium phosphate
Catarrh	*Calc. sulph.*	Calcium sulfate
Early stage of inflammation	*Ferrum phos.*	Iron phosphate
Later stages of inflammation	*Kali mur.*	Potassium chloride
Emotional strains	*Kali phos.*	Potassium phosphate
Breathing problems	*Kali sulph.*	Potassium sulfate
Lower bowel conditions	*Mag. phos.*	Magnesium phosphate
Mouth problems	*Nat. mur.*	Sodium chloride
Upper bowel conditions	*Nat. phos.*	Sodium phosphate
Allergies	*Nat. sulph.*	Sodium sulfate
Neurological disorders	*Silica*	Silica dioxide

BACH FLOWER REMEDIES

FLOWER ESSENCES ARE prepared from petals, leaves, and stalks of plants and are used to treat canine emotional states, thought by the developers to be the main cause of disease states. Although similar to homeopathics in that they are physically dilute, flower essences are closer in form to herbal decoctions in that they are produced in relatively concentrated 1:10 or 1:100 dilutions.

ARE FLOWERS CALMING?

The relationship between emotion and disease is studied in psychoneuroimmunology (PNI). Some vets believe that Rescue Remedy reduces panic in some dogs. Others assume that giving a remedy causes the PNI effect: dog owners become less tense, which has a positive effect on their pets.

HISTORY

In the 1930s, an English bacteriologist and homeopath, Edward Bach, concluded that harmful emotions lead to physical disease. "Treat the mood of the patient," said Dr. Bach, "and the disease will disappear." Believing that essences from flowers could affect an individual's state of mind, Dr. Bach developed the first range of flower essences. He identified appropriate non-toxic flowers by cupping his hands over blooms of many varieties and intuitively divining which had healing properties. In 1936, Bach Flower Remedies were commercially marketed in Britain, fulfilling Bach's belief that patients should heal themselves. In the 1970s, a range of Californian Flower Remedies were marketed in the United States, and a decade later Australian Bush Flower Remedies were successfully launched in Australia.

HOW THEY WORK

Dr. Bach developed 38 flower essences, each of which is meant to deal with a specific emotional state or behavioral problem. For shock, panic, and hysteria he produced a multiple flower essence called Rescue Remedy, overwhelmingly the most popular flower essence given to dogs. Remedies are prepared by infusing flower heads and other flower parts in spring water for three hours in direct sunlight. The solution is preserved in brandy and sold in 10 and 20 ml phials.

VETERINARY OPINION

Clinical trials of Bach Flower Remedies began at the University of California's veterinary school in the early 1990s but the results were so discouraging that the project was dropped. No other clinical trials have been carried out. When Flower Remedies are analyzed, only spring water and alcohol are detected. Proponents attribute the beneficial effects of Flower Remedies to "molecular imprinting," one of the theories that is also applied to homeopathy.

WHERE THEY ARE AVAILABLE

Bach Flower Remedies are now available in health food shops and pharmacies around the world. Californian and Australian Bush flower remedies are primarily available in their countries of origin.

AWAY FROM LIGHT
Bach Flower Remedies come in airtight bottles made of dark glass with a pipette to measure the prescribed dose. They should be stored in a cool, dark place.

BACH FLOWER REMEDIES

It is easier to interpret your own emotional state than your dog's. A sudden change in your dog's behavior may have a physical cause. Consult your vet before prescribing any complementary therapy.

STATE OF MIND	FLOWER REMEDY
Shyness	Monkey flower
Apathy	Wild rose
Fear on behalf of the family	Chestnut
Lack of self confidence	Larch
Lack of concentration	Clematis
Melancholy	Mustard
Aloofness	Water violet
Excessive desire for companionship	Heather
Overprotectiveness	Chicory
Dominance	Vervain

MIND AND EMOTION THERAPIES

WHILE IT HAS BEEN KNOWN FOR DECADES that unnatural environments can create behavioral problems for dogs, it is only in the last decade that a relationship has been firmly established between the dog's mind and clinical diseases of the skin and the gastrointestinal and urinary systems. By gaining an understanding of how the mind and emotions affect disease, and by using therapies that can affect the dog's mind, it may be possible to treat some conditions without needing to resort to drugs.

The dog's emotions are really ancient mechanisms for marshaling the body's forces. Emotions, and the physiological changes that are associated with them, developed to cope with the vagaries of life, including threat. If a dog perceives a threat a cascade of chemical reactions is stimulated in its body, reactions that help it to cope with that threat. Even short-lived depression may be a natural and beneficial coping mechanism to deal with stress successfully. However, in the 1940s, Professor Hans Selye, of McGill University in Montreal, Canada, showed how long-term, chronic threat could cause heart problems, gastric disorders, and a breakdown of the immune system in animals. In experiments that would be considered ethically unacceptable today, Professor Selye demonstrated that if the stress response is activated for too long, the stress response itself overstretches the immune system, which in turn leads to the dog's health being compromised.

EXERCISE AND REST
Exercise is essential for a dog's mental and physical well-being. It also enhances sleep. Puppies build their muscles and bones during sleep, while an adult dog's body repairs and regenerates itself.

EARLY LEARNING IS VITAL
While your dog is still a pup, teach it to amuse itself in your absence. This reduces the likelihood of stress later in life when it is left alone for a period of time. When prevention has not been possible, attempt a mind therapy before resorting to drugs.

But stress is not necessarily a bad thing. Dogs thrive on positive, intermittent stress. Just think of the anticipation and excitement of a terrier or retriever that is waiting to chase a ball. The buzz of excitement, the stimulation of a challenge, these are good for dogs. A safe, boring life can be a chronic negative stress on some dogs. Dogs evolved to cope with intermittent stress, not chronic stress. People suffering chronic stress have a higher incidence of cancer, infectious disease, heart conditions, and strokes than people who are not chronically stressed. If we looked, we would probably find the same statistics for dogs. Chronic stress reduces natural resistance.

Relaxation techniques, controlled breathing, and sound sleep are known to be good for our health. Recently these therapies have been applied successfully to dogs. Biofeedback therapy is also used. Scent has a powerful effect on our emotions and has been used for thousands of years, but more applicable to dogs is the new study of the influence of pheromones, natural body odors, on the dog's mind. Other unusual therapies aimed at influencing the dog's mind are also used to enhance well-being in non-invasive ways.

THE IMPORTANCE OF PHEROMONES
Dogs and other animals are known to communicate by scenting each other's facial and anal glands. The glands secrete odor signals called pheromones, which transmit information such as identification.

NATURAL DEVELOPMENT

NATURAL TRAINING

NATURAL NUTRITION

NATURAL HEALTH CARE

HEALTH DISORDERS

NATURAL DEVELOPMENT

NATURAL TRAINING

NATURAL NUTRITION

NATURAL HEALTH CARE

HEALTH DISORDERS

RELAXATION THERAPY

THE ABILITY TO RELAX and the value of controlled breathing are considered important in human medicine. Breathing exercises can be taught that will lead to psychological and physical improvements for the individual. The same benefits apply to dogs but training methods are reversed. Dog owners reward their pets when they relax and breathe slower. Dogs learn to relax themselves to earn their rewards.

CHECKLIST

- Provide active daily exercise for your dog.

- Play games that require mental as well as physical coordination

- Practice relaxation techniques and always reward your dog for relaxed breathing and calm demeanor.

- Allow your dog to sleep without interrupting its dreams.

- Modify your dog's exercise according to its age and abilities.

- Provide mind games such as "find the ball" for elderly or convalescing dogs.

HISTORY

For thousands of years relaxation techniques have been an integral part of Eastern health systems, but it was not until the 1960s, when Dr. Herbert Benson of Harvard Medical School in Massachusetts began his research into the therapeutic effects of relaxation, that conventional medicine appreciated how it affects the body's physiology and reverses deleterious effects of stress. In the early 1990s, Professor Karen Overall, head of animal behavior at the University of

RELAXATION IS REWARDED

Natural relaxation is rewarded by kind words and physical contact from the owner. Stroking from its owner in turn enhances further relaxation by reducing the dog's state of arousal, including its blood pressure.

Pennsylvania's veterinary school, adapted relaxation techniques for dogs and showed that dogs respond better to training when they are relaxed. Relaxation therapy is now used in clinical situations to reduce stress for dogs with cardiovascular and other conditions.

HOW IT WORKS

When shallow, rapid breathing is excessive, too much carbon dioxide is removed from the blood. This leads to physiological and behavioral changes, including a lack of concentration. Dog owners are trained to reward their dogs for relaxing. They do so by watching their dog's ear position, eyes, and breathing rate. A dog is rewarded when the ears relax, the look to the eyes becomes less intense, and the breathing rate drops. Owners simply "condition" their dogs to realize that relaxation is rewarded.

Physiological responses to relaxation are substantial. Circulating levels of adrenalin, a stress hormone, drop, as does blood pressure and blood-sugar levels. As the dog's muscles relax, the lactic acid in them will diminish. Digestion improves, the immune system becomes more active, and alertness increases.

VETERINARY OPINION

Teaching dogs to relax in order to increase their alertness and enhance training has a marvelous logic. Because it is a new idea, most of the veterinary profession is unaware of its methods or value. However, there appears to be potential to incorporate this form of natural conditioning into conventional therapeutic regimes for a wide variety of medical problems.

WHERE IT IS AVAILABLE

Relaxation training is available primarily from the University of Pennsylvania's veterinary school, where it is used on dogs referred for behavioral conditions. Vets elsewhere instruct dog owners in relaxation therapy for dogs with physical problems such as heart disease or joint pain, or for those needing to relax while recovering from surgery.

EXERCISE AND REST

NOTHING IS MORE NATURAL for the well-being and good health of dogs than undisturbed rest and regular exercise. While most dogs get more than enough rest, many get less exercise than they should. This is one of the most unnatural aspects of dogs' lives today. Routine exercise is therapeutic for a dog's mind and its body. It enhances well-being and strengthens the immune system.

EXCESSIVE EXERCISE
Take care when increasing exercise in your dog's daily routine. Sudden exercise can be a burden on the heart, and overweight older dogs are susceptible to tearing ligaments behind their knees. Ask your vet to devise a nutrition and exercise plan suitable for your dog's age, weight, and state of health.

THE IMPORTANCE OF EXERCISE
The benefits of routine and appropriate exercise have been thoroughly researched and evidence in its favor is overwhelming. Exercise increases circulation, improves heart and lung function, strengthens muscles, keeps joints mobile, reduces the risk of diabetes, maintains natural weight, improves immune function, and encourages sound sleep.

All canine mental and physical activity depends upon the efficient availability of energy, which is derived from the food it eats and the oxygen it breathes. Compare the behavior of a well-exercised dog and an overweight, sedentary one. The differences are obvious. Sedentary dogs look, as well as act, less energetic than well-exercised canines.

WHAT HAPPENS DURING EXERCISE?
Routine exercise increases the body's ability to produce energy effectively and helps feed the brain with oxygen, maintaining mental alertness. Brain cells die if the brain does not receive sufficient amounts of oxygen and glucose. Some researchers believe that exercises requiring coordination and mental agility, such as hide-and-seek, generate more connections between brain cells. Exercise is nature's antidepressant. During exercise, body temperature rises and endorphins, the body's natural opiates, are released. Sustained exercise also burns the waste products that accumulates during stressful inactive periods.

THE IMPORTANCE OF SLEEP
Relaxed sleep is just as important as routine exercise. While eight hours a night is about right for most people, dogs need 12 hours of sleep each day. Sleep consists of Rapid Eye Movement (REM) sleep, when dreams occur, and Non-REM (NREM) or deep sleep. Deprived of either form of sleep a dog becomes confused and forgets its training.

WHAT HAPPENS DURING SLEEP?
During dreamless (NREM) sleep, your dog's body repairs and regenerates itself and the immune system strengthens and revitalizes. Puppies have more need of NREM sleep than adults because this is when they build their muscles and bones. With advancing years the need for NREM sleep diminishes.

During dream (REM) sleep a dog's eyes move behind the lids, its feet twitch, the whiskers on its face quiver, and sometimes it makes yelping sounds. About 20 percent of a dog's sleep is REM sleep. No one knows the exact purpose of sleep and dreams but both appear to be vital for dogs, and both activities should always be allowed to proceed without needless interruption.

NATURAL SLEEP
Sound sleep is therapeutic for dogs. Dogs dream during deep sleep, although why and what they dream remains a mystery. During light sleep, which consumes about 80 percent of sleep time, the dog's body repairs itself and the immune system is revitalized.

AROMA AND PHEROMONE THERAPY

THE INFLUENCE OF SCENT on a dog's behavior can be dramatic. One of the dog's close relatives, the Ethiopian wolf, coordinates heat (estrus) cycles in the pack through scent. The concept of influencing the dog's mind-body relationship by using natural scent messengers has gained popularity recently. By mimicking natural scents, aroma and pheromone therapy may modify behavior.

AROMATHERAPY AND ESSENTIAL OILS
Essential oils are extracted from the roots and flowers of plants. They can be heated, or diluted in steaming water, in order that they may be inhaled. If used for massage, they must first be diluted in a vegetable-based carrier oil.

TOXIC OILS

Some oils used for aromatherapy massage on people are potentially toxic to dogs if they are swallowed. Never use aromatherapy oils on a dog without advice from an expert on their potential toxicity. Never carry out a complementary procedure on a dog that increases its level of stress or agitation.

HISTORY

Herbal oils have been used for centuries in many cultures to treat illness and promote well-being, but it was not until 1910 that the French chemist Réné-Maurice Gattefossé coined the term "aromatherapy." Since that time, doctors in France have sometimes used essential oils (made up of fatty acids) to treat medical and behavioral conditions.

In the 1980s, Dr. Patrick Pageat, a French veterinarian who had studied pheromones in pigs, began to look at cats. He analyzed cat facial-gland secretions, finding 40 different components. Most of these consisted of simple fatty acids. After several years of trial-and-error investigations he found that one sub-group of fatty acids, when it was concentrated and applied where cats were spraying urine, inhibited that unwanted behavior. With the help of one of France's largest perfume manufacturers, he had this sub-group of fatty acids synthetically reproduced. This product has been marketed as a natural pheromone analogue that is used to dissuade cats from urine marking at home. Studies of canine pheromones are now being undertaken.

TRANSFERRING INFORMATION
In the animal world even a few molecules of scent, usually in the form of fatty acids, are capable of transmitting information from one member of a species to another. This is why dogs sniff each other intently when they meet.

HOW IT WORKS

Pheromones are the odor signals that animals use to communicate with each other. Dr. Pageat classifies natural dog pheromones into three groups. The first group contains pheromones found in urine. The second group consists of "alarm mark" pheromones that are found in anal-gland secretions. The third group are the identification pheromones found in facial and lip-gland secretions, the pheromones that dogs scent when they sniff each other's lips. Dr. Pageat speculates that, by spreading facial secretions in the environment, antagonism between dogs can be lessened.

VETERINARY OPINION

Scents released by oils act on the hypothalamus, the part of the brain that influences the hormone system. In theory, a scent might be able to affect mood or metabolism. Natural scents, such as pheromones, ought to be more effective than plant-derived scents for controlling a dog's mind. Studies of the use of pheromones to control unwanted behaviors such as urine-marking in cats are promising.

Aromatherapy is often requested by dog owners, but there are drawbacks to its use. Dilute oils can be massaged into a dog's armpit or inner thigh, but some dogs resent the odor and roll vigorously to cover it. Pheromone therapy, on the other hand, has been well received where it is available.

OTHER THERAPIES

A REMARKABLE ARRAY of mind-body therapies are used both to help people stay healthy and to enhance their body's response when they are unwell. Many of these therapies, for instance, color therapy, have no practical application for dogs. However, some complementary mind-body therapies, although impossible to study on creatures other than humans, may affect animals other than us.

WHERE'S THE EVIDENCE?

Many vets tend to view with suspicion information that does not fit existing theories, and demand higher levels of evidence to support new ideas. Remember that all through history we have found new treatments and used them before we have understood them. We do not know everything now.

MUSIC THERAPY

The eminent pediatrician Dr. T. Berry Brazelton has shown that music influences human babies even while still in the womb, while German studies conducted in the 1990s suggest that certain rhythms may reduce stress in people by lowering heart rate, blood pressure, and respiration.

Dr. Martin Seabrook at Nottingham University, England, carried out research that demonstrated that dairy cows produce more milk when they listen to gentle music such as Beethoven symphonies than when no music is played in the milking shed. The effect of music on canine health and behavior has not yet been studied.

LIGHT THERAPY

Natural light has been an important element of naturopathy (a therapy that emphasizes fresh air, sunlight, and exercise) for over a century, but it is only recently that medical science discovered how light plays a role in regulating the dog's biological clock. The dog's daily or "circadian" rhythms, which are influenced by light, control sleep, hormone production, and other functions. Yearly rhythms too, such as the seasonal shedding of hair or heat cycles, are influenced by increasing or decreasing daylight. Light therapy has not been studied in dogs.

MAGNETIC THERAPY

Some migrating birds successfully travel thousands of miles each year by following the position of the magnetic poles of the earth. Molecules of magnetite in the brain are thought to play a role in this "sixth

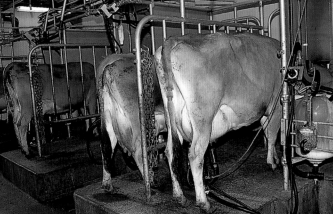

sense." Dogs also have magnetite in brain cells, but its function is unknown. Magnet therapy, utilizing electromagnetic fields, is used therapeutically in Europe, North America, and Australia to help heal bone fractures. Conventional veterinarians use magnetic resonance imaging (MRI) scans in diagnosis. They are safe and superior to x-rays, but more costly.

SPIRITUAL HEALING

Increased medical evidence shows that firm belief in your own religion, or in the powers of a spiritual healer, enhances your body's ability to defend itself. Faith healing is used on cats worldwide. Most reputable healers belong to national associations, for example, in the United Kingdom, healers follow a specific code of conduct, prepared by the Federation of Spiritual Healers, for the treatment of animals. How the positive value of spiritual belief affects animals in our care is unknown.

COWS RESPOND TO BEETHOVEN

If you ever hear the slow movement of Beethoven's Fifth Symphony as you enter a dairy farm milking shed, it means that the dairyman is familiar with studies indicating that cows release more milk when listening to soothing music.

NATURAL DEVELOPMENT

NATURAL TRAINING

NATURAL NUTRITION

NATURAL HEALTH CARE

HEALTH DISORDERS

THERAPEUTIC CARE

WHATEVER FORM OF THERAPY you choose for your dog, remember that the most important rule of care is "Do no harm." The key to recovery from illness is lack of stress, good nutrition, and responsive immune and repair systems. Do not inadvertently stress your dog by using a therapy that seems appropriate to you but distresses your dog. Do not be afraid of using successful conventional therapies.

CHECKLIST

- To reduce the risks of any form of therapy, either conventional or complementary, ask your vet these questions:

- What is the exact reason for using this therapy?

- How does the therapy work?

- Is the therapy absolutely necessary?

- What are the chances of success?

- Are there known potential side effects?

- Is there a choice of different therapies?

- What are the recognized alternative treatments?

CHANGES IN VETERINARY CARE

Many individuals can be exposed to an infection, yet only some will develop clinical signs of illness. If we take viral infections of the upper respiratory tract as an example, conventional veterinary medicine is excellent at diagnosing which infection a dog has, but it is not so good at explaining why a specific dog developed that specific disease in the first place. It is also not so good at creating an environment for recovery.

However, veterinary care is changing, and conventional and complementary forms of care are becoming integrated. The two approaches are no longer distinct and opposing philosophical entities.

ADVERSE DRUG REACTIONS

In the UK, the Suspected Adverse Reactions Surveillance Scheme recorded the following cases over the course of 1994.

DRUG	AMOUNT
External parasite control	41
Antibiotics and antifungals	40
Non-steroid anti-inflammatories	37
Live vaccines	36
Worming medicines	22
Hormones	10
Inactivated vaccines	8
Corticosteroid drugs	1
All other drugs	25

MARKET-DRIVEN CHANGES

Veterinarians are by nature conservative. This is logical, you could say, from an evolutionary viewpoint. If a vet has had success with a particular treatment, why venture into the unknown, especially the scientifically inexplicable unknown, and try another method of treatment? However, driven by public demand, conventional vets are now beginning to study complementary therapies in order to deal with stress-related and degenerative problems. These are increasingly common in dogs because dogs are now living longer, a result of good nourishment and effective vaccination against killer diseases such as distemper and canine parvovirus. Living into old age means they are more prone to degenerative disorders.

In my experience, most dog owners are intuitively sensible about what is best for their pets. They understand that dogs are not people and that different ethical precepts exist for deciding what should be done and how far you should go in treating a dog's medical condition. Compassionate dog owners innately understand that there are technological ways to prolong a dog's life, but also ask "What is best for my dog?"

CONVENTIONAL DRUGS

Owners often express concern about the incidence of adverse reactions to modern drugs. In many countries drug reactions are not centrally reported and compiled, but in the United Kingdom, the Suspected Adverse Reactions Surveillance Scheme recorded, in a typical year, that conventional drugs caused 220 suspected adverse reactions. The box (*see left*) gives the drug categories.

Outwardly, these are remarkably low figures considering that there are over six million dogs in the UK. However, the figures are misleading because they refer only to acute and severe adverse reactions. Drugs may be chronically harmful but there are no statistics compiled that collate potential long-term or chronic adverse reactions to conventional drug therapies.

NATURAL CARE ENHANCES RECOVERY
Provide warmth for your sick dog, let it rest where it chooses, even hand-feed it to ensure good nourishment. It will want to continue with this behavior once it is well, but with consistency on your part it will return to its former habits.

COMPLEMENTARY THERAPIES

A dog's needs are different to yours or mine, both physically and nutritionally. Ideally, only use someone recommended by your vet for any form of complementary therapy. Do not use a therapist that is only qualified to work with people. There are conventionally trained vets throughout the world who practise a variety of complementary therapies, often alongside conventional treatments. If you have problems locating one in your area, national and international associations for veterinary acupuncture, homeopathy, and holistic veterinary medicine may be tried.

The rise in popularity of complementary veterinary medicine is reflected in journals that are published and yearly academic meetings that are held. However, there are no statistics that exist for assessing acute or chronic adverse reactions to complementary therapies such as herbal medicines.

A HEALING ENVIRONMENT

When your dog is recuperating from illness or injury, create a supportive environment conducive to recovery. Your dog may seek out a special area where it feels comfortable. Ensure that this location is warm and draft-free. Provide soft bedding to prevent bed sores, and make sure water and food are within reach. Unless advised otherwise, chicken and rice is an ideal recovery diet. Do not expect your dog to play when it is ill, and do not allow children or fellow dogs to pester it. Do not scold your dog for soiling indoors.

NATURAL AGING

Age comes to all dogs. A 10-year-old dog is equivalent to a 60-year-old human, and from then on each dog year is equivalent to four human years. A 20-year-old dog is equivalent to a 100-year-old person. For them, like us, there is not a whole lot you can say about the advantages of aging. Personally, I like old dogs best, but from the dog's perspective age brings deteriorating eyesight, reduced strength and agility, harder hearing, joint pain, and more frequent medical problems and visits to the vet.

Anticipate the inevitable changes of aging by training your dog to respond to hand as well as word signals. Keep to daily routines as change is likely to confuse an old dog. Bathe and groom your dog more often, because its skin glands naturally produce less oil. Brush its teeth daily and provide more frequent toilet breaks. Watch the calories and arrange for a yearly "older dog" health checkup. Use effective therapies to reduce the discomforts of old age.

CARING FOR AN ILL DOG

You know how you feel when you are ill. Respect your dog's personal desire, whether it is to be left alone or to have your company. Dogs are not complainers. Always assume that a condition that is painful for us is painful for them too. A tucked-up belly, limping, difficulty standing or walking, all of these are frequently caused by pain. Take over natural cleaning responsibilities if your dog cannot groom itself normally when it is unwell. Make medicine-taking as pleasant as possible by hiding medicine in tasty food. When, inevitably, it comes about that a comfortable life is no longer possible, think first of your dog's quality of life. Death is an inevitability, but when your dog's life is irrevocably low, do not wait for a "natural" death. We have it in our power to make pet death a physically painless event. Most vets will do whatever they can to make the sad event as easy as possible for you, your family, and your dog.

HOSPITALIZING YOUR DOG

Hospitalizing your dog is unavoidable whenever intensive care is necessary — when help is needed emptying the bladder or bowels, when pain control is critical, or when diagnostics or therapeutics require constant monitoring. Otherwise, your dog will recuperate best in its own home. Keep hospitalization to a minimum.

GIVING MEDICINE
Minimize stress by making pill-taking a pleasure. Whenever possible, hide the pill in tasty food. Most dogs willingly consume a tidbit of bread, peanut butter, and a hidden pill. When using skin treatments, always reward your dog's compliant behavior.

HEALTH DISORDERS

There is a place for both conventional and complementary health care for your dog. Conventional medicine is at its best when acute conditions require treatment. Powerful drugs and modern surgical techniques are the methods of choice to treat acutely painful or life-threatening conditions. Complementary procedures can play a supporting role and may be useful for chronic or long-term disorders for which conventional veterinary care appears to have no remedy. When opting for any treatment, always consider the stress it places on your dog. What seems appropriate to you may not be right for your dog.

Dogs are stoical, but owners can often tell if something is wrong.

CONFRONTING HEALTH DISORDERS

THE MOST SUCCESSFUL WAY to combat a health disorder is to understand how it manages to overcome or bypass natural defenses. In veterinary medicine we often have to confront health problems without a clear understanding of who the enemy is, or even what its tactics are. This is where the diagnoses and treatments of conventional and complementary veterinary medicine differ.

CHECKLIST

Approach health problems in the following ways:

- As accurately as possible, define the problem.
- Minimize physical and psychological stress.
- Create an environment conducive to recovery.
- Integrate positive values of both conventional and complementary therapies.
- Locate complementary practitioners through holistic veterinarians.

DIFFERENT FORMS OF DIAGNOSIS

Veterinary care is like pediatrics. Your dog's well-being depends upon you noticing that something is wrong, and describing to your vet what you have seen, or felt, or smelled, or heard. For example, you might notice that your dog has difficulty climbing stairs. A conventional veterinarian looks for clinical signs. A raised temperature might mean infection. Unusual heart and lung sounds can mean cardiovascular disease. Resentment when its back or joints are manipulated can mean osteoarthritic injury and pain. Blood tests, x-rays, and ultrasound might be arranged. Your vet is looking for information that fits recognized patterns to allow him or her to name your dog's problem.

When a specific disease is identified, there may be a specific treatment. However, it can be difficult to identify some diseases. Your dog is certainly ill but the disease cannot be identified. When this happens it is called an "undifferentiated illness."

AN ALTERNATIVE APPROACH

For complementary vets, the presence of recognizable clinical signs is important but the absence of an accurate diagnosis is less of an obstacle to treatment. For each type of complementary therapy, undifferentiated illnesses — usually pain, lethargy, and various stress-related conditions — are given unique diagnostic labels, such as "weakened vital force," "excess *pitta,*" or "stuck liver *qi.*" Complementary vets have both general and specific therapies for these conditions, and the patient's personality, as well as its medical history, is a vital part of diagnosis.

THE RISKS OF TREATMENT

The first rule of medicine is as important today as it was when Hippocrates first formulated, it and it is worth mentioning again: *Primum non nocere* – First, do no harm. This must be the basis for all conventional and complementary therapies. Your dog's body wants to be healthy and to maintain homeostasis. The body's self-diagnosis, repair, and regeneration is the success story of evolution. Your dog has magnificent ways of repairing itself but you can help it to confront health disorders by reducing risk and augmenting its natural defenses. Prevention is better than cure. The best way to prevent disease is to reduce genetic and environmental risks (*see pages 108-109*).

CLINICAL SIGNS OF DISEASE

Do not treat your dog's clinical signs as the problem. Use them as a guide to the origin of the problem. Work with them rather than against them. A cough, for example, is a defense. It leads you to the throat, windpipe, lungs, and heart. In some circumstances, for example, foreign material in the air passages, suppressing a cough could be life-threatening. In others, such as congestive heart failure, the cough leads your vet to the true problem Again, suppressing the cough is not in your dog's interest. The cough naturally reduces when its heart condition is treated effectively.

"DO-IT-YOURSELF" IS DANGEROUS

Your dog's well-being depends entirely upon you. Complementary practitioners who are not qualified veterinarians are not trained to detect signs of disease in dogs. Seemingly minor conditions can become life-threatening problems if not treated properly. When seeking complementary treatments for your dog, use the services of a veterinarian trained in complementary therapies or an individual recommended by a qualified veterinarian. When seeking advice, always tell your vet what complementary treatments you have given to your dog.

MIND AND BODY INTEGRATION

Psychoneuroimmunology (PNI), one of the most exciting fields of medicine today, investigates the connection between the mind and body. Each white blood cell circulating in a dog's bloodstream has receptor sites on its surface for all the chemical messengers in its brain. Emotion, psychology, and behavior are all factors that should be considered and integrated into diagnosis and treatment. A medical problem may well be a physical condition but the root of the problem can be emotional or psychological.

USE SAFE TREATMENTS

Whenever possible, use the safest effective treatment. Some complementary therapies, such as homeopathy, are only minimally interventionist, as are some conventional veterinary therapies such as bed or cage rest. Other therapies are more "invasive." Conventional drugs have potential side effects. An antibiotic either destroys bacteria or prevents their further multiplication. Some dogs, when they swallow certain antibiotics, have a natural inclination to get rid of the "foreign" substance and vomit it back. This form of rejection applies to certain herbs too. We might find them natural but dogs don't. Do not define one form of medicine as safe and the other as dangerous. Assess the risks before deciding what is best for your dog.

TREAT CHRONIC CONDITIONS

Chronic problems are the backbone of complementary veterinary medicine. Long-lasting conditions of muscles, joints, the immune system, the gastrointestinal and urinary systems, and psychosomatic disorders are the fields where complementary therapies are most widely used. Other conditions, such as acute trauma, surgery, anaesthetics, severe infections, prosthetics, parasite control, dentistry, and vaccinations, and any illness that is intensely painful or life-threatening, is best treated with conventional methods.

MAINTAINING GOOD HEALTH

Confronting health disorders should not be done on a "fire brigade" basis. Prevention is the most important way to maintain health. Feed a diet that contains not only all the nutrients necessary for life but also the ingredients that are known to bolster your dog's natural defenses (*see pages 50-51*). Assess your dog's lifestyle and make sure that you are feeding the correct quantity and quality of food needed to maintain the dog's optimum weight and health (*see pages 48-49*).

There is no reason why the evidence that exercise is good for our health does not apply to dogs too. Provide your dog with the opportunity to exercise regularly every day, according to its wants and abilities. Routine mental and physical exercise nourish both the mind and body. When one is nourished, the other benefits.

MAINSTREAM ALTERNATIVE

Many dietary advances that are an integral part of conventional medicine today, such as the beneficial effects of fish oil on the immune system, of vegetable beta-carotenes in cardiovascular problems, and *Lactobacillus* bacteria to avoid antibiotic side effects, all have their origins in complementary therapies.

DEPENDING ON YOU
Your dog needs your help to overcome health disorders. Get advice from a vet you trust and only use therapies that are appropriate for your dog's condition.

NATURAL DEVELOPMENT

NATURAL TRAINING

NATURAL NUTRITION

NATURAL HEALTH CARE

HEALTH DISORDERS

THE CHANGING NATURE OF DISEASE

THE NATURE OF DISEASE is always changing. In my early years in clinical practice, before vaccines were widely available and when dogs wandered freely, infection and trauma were the most common veterinary problems. Vaccination and responsible pet ownership have changed the nature of disease. Today, genetic, metabolic, and geriatric disorders play dominant roles in veterinary care.

INEXPLICABLE

It is popular to try to explain that everything that occurs in the body is a result of evolutionary adaptation, and say that for everything there is a reason. Perhaps this is not so. The natural historian Stephen Jay Gould argues that sometimes aspects of life and evolution may be simply "accidental."

PARASITES AND MICROBES

Throughout the dog's evolutionary history, parasites and germs have adapted ways to overcome its natural defenses. Some adaptations are spectacularly effective. Rabies virus is a proficient and nasty example. After entering the dog's body, usually through a bite, the rabies virus confuses the dog's immune system by binding onto neurotransmitter chemicals in the nervous system and riding these chemicals, piggyback, from one cell to the next, until it reaches the brain. To get from the dog's brain into another animal, the virus does two things. It travels through nerves to the saliva glands, where it concentrates in multitudes. At the same time, it affects two specific parts of the dog's brain, the rage centre and the area responsible for the throat muscles, which become paralyzed. By residing in saliva, while making the dog aggressive and likely to bite and at the same

time paralyzing the ability to swallow, rabies virus efficiently enhances its likelihood of survival even though it may kill its "host" in the process. This is a formidable enemy. Only when Western medicine discovered how natural defenses try to cope with viruses by producing antibodies was the rabies virus controlled (*see pages 110-111*).

NEW GERM ADAPTATIONS

Biological vaccines changed the nature of viral diseases. Distemper was once the most common infectious cause of death in dogs. It killed one of my patients each week where I first practiced. Effective vaccination changed the nature of this disease but then, seemingly from nowhere, canine parvovirus swept through the world's dog population, killing thousands of puppies before vaccines for protection were developed.

While vaccines protect populations from dangerous viruses, antibiotics are used to kill bacteria and fungi, or prevent them from multiplying. Here we have created conditions ripe for mayhem. Antibiotics have rapidly accelerated bacterial evolution. Microbe evolution is now taking place at a faster pace than at any time in history. Germs are evolving faster than we can isolate and create new antibiotics to control "antibiotic-resistant" microbes. The nature of bacterial illness will continue to evolve, with the likelihood that bacteria resistant to all known antibiotics, a phenomenon that already exists with a human hospital strain of bacteria, will also occur with bacteria that affect dogs.

ENVIRONMENTAL PRESSURES

As we altered our own environment we altered the nature of canine diseases. The dog evolved to live outdoors, within a pack, getting nourished by eating other animals and vegetation. Dog diseases changed when we moved dogs away from their natural environment. Mixing dogs from different packs increased the risk of transmissible diseases. Cities increased the risk of road-traffic accidents. In some parts of some

DESIGN FLAWS
Through breeding selectively to satisfy our own ideas of beauty, we alter dogs' risk of disease. Because of its unnaturally flattened face, this Bulldog has a greater risk of heart disease, eye injuries, choking, and facial-skin infection than did its ancestors.

countries gunshot wounds are a common cause of traumatic injury. Simply living in our warm homes changed the nature of canine disease. In temperate zones, fleas are a more important cause of canine disease than they were previously, simply because they have found our homes ideal breeding grounds. Now there are more fleas.

GENETIC PRESSURES

In natural evolution genetic mutations are always occurring. Survival of the fittest means that beneficial genetic mutations are retained while deleterious ones die out. When we intervened in dog breeding we influenced genetic pressures. Unwittingly, kennel clubs, through beauty contests and breeding to written breed standards, accelerated evolutionary genetic changes in dogs in the same way that antibiotics accelerated evolutionary genetic changes in microbes. Many of our breeds today come from small genetic bases. Any genetic problem that existed in that small genetic base, for example, the West Highland White Terrier's genetic predisposition to skin allergy, is magnified through the breed population.

Other deleterious genetic changes in the nature of disease occurred because of the show success of an individual in a particular breed. Its unknown genetic medical defects were then spread to a larger-than-normal

NEW ENVIRONMENTS *Dogs evolved to live their whole lives outdoors. From an evolutionary viewpoint, they have had little time to adapt to indoor conditions. Dust and carpet mites abound in our warm homes and are increasingly responsible for allergic skin problems in dogs.*

population because of its popularity. We perpetuate problems, such as deafness in Dalmatians, because they are not thought to be critical to our requirements. Increasingly, genetics is at the root of many of the chronic conditions that I see each day in clinical practice.

THE NEW GERIATRICS

At one time, a dog's life expectancy was the same as the wolf's, typically about seven or eight years. Some individuals lived longer and the potential life expectancy was greater still, but the vagaries of life meant that few individuals lived longer than the average age.

Our care and attention to dogs changed that. Today many dogs reach their potential of 13 to 18 years of age. Some live even longer. But with advancing years come changes in the nature of disease. A wider range of age-related disorders are now being diagnosed in dogs than before — wear and tear, metabolic disorders, diseases that result from slow, steady accumulations of damage, such as cancers and heart disease. Senile dementia, akin in many ways to Alzheimer's disease in people, now occurs in dogs. My older Golden Retriever, at just under 15 years, has a variety of geriatric conditions; reduced hearing, muscle weakness, bowel sensitivity, and an inclination to bark for no reason while lying under the kitchen table.

Geriatric medicine is a new field in veterinary medicine, new, at least in part, because of the successes of disease control, owner responsibility, and good nourishment.

CHANGING TREATMENT

Just as the nature of diseases constantly change, so too does our approach to disease treatment. The veterinary medical establishment, aware that pet owners are concerned with drug side effects and expensive, unpleasant, or ineffective treatments, is showing increasing interest in complementary therapies. The American Veterinary Medical Association recognized these facts when it published new guidelines for alternative and complementary medicine in 1996. There is increasing integration of conventional and complementary systems in veterinary medicine.

CHECKLIST

- The nature of disease varies for many reasons.
- Economics determines the level of preventative medicine.
- Economics determines how early in a disease process a dog receives treatment.
- Age, sex, breed, and individual temperament affect disease.
- Geography affects incidence and natural resistance.
- We dominate the nature of disease through our influence in genetics and the environment.

NATURAL DEVELOPMENT

NATURAL TRAINING

NATURAL NUTRITION

NATURAL HEALTH CARE

HEALTH DISORDERS

THE DOG'S NATURAL DEFENSES

A DOG'S PHYSICAL WELL-BEING is directly related to how it is raised, fed, and cared for, first by its mother and then by you. Good health depends upon your dog's natural defenses and self-healing abilities, the methods that evolved to protect it from natural dangers. When diagnosing a medical condition, don't confuse your dog's defenses with the illness that has provoked those defensive responses.

CHECKLIST

Good natural defenses include:

- Cleanliness.

- Keeping natural barriers such as skin and the gut lining healthy.

- Avoidance of known pathogens.

If pathogens get through, good defenses will attack, poison, starve, and wall off the dangers.

ALWAYS ON GUARD

The concept of recruiting the body's self-healing capacities, amplifying recuperative processes and creating an environment conducive to well-being, has always been the premise of complementary veterinary medicine but has now become a part of conventional veterinary medicine. The emphasis on restoring good health rather than removing sickness is increasingly embraced by conventional vets.

Most animals are uniformly exposed to the causes of medical conditions. For example, all dogs in a household may be exposed to household fleas, but each dog responds in its own unique way. While one dog will not be bothered by flea bites, another may be driven to occasional

scratching, while a third may be intensely irritated and develop secondary bacteria infection or even a systemic disease. The competence and reactivity of a dog's immune system ultimately determines what illnesses that dog will get and how it copes with the illness, but there are other defenses too.

NATURAL BARRIERS

A pathogen is an organism or substance that causes disease. Any part of your dog that is easily accessible to pathogens has a superb ability to repair and regenerate itself. Your dog's first line of defense is its skin. Hair growing from the skin acts as an insulator but also offers physical protection. Skin acts as a barrier to pathogens and is a major organ in your dog's immune system.

The lining of the gut, and the liver, which is in open communication with the gut, has evolved equal powers of regeneration. The gut lining is the second largest organ in the immune system. Natural defensive actions take place throughout the gastrointestinal system. Pathogens are killed by saliva or stomach acid. Toxic substances are denatured in the stomach or intestines or detoxified by the liver. The system is sophisticated and highly effective. Places that are less accessible to pathogens, such as the brain and heart, have poor natural regenerative powers.

NATURAL MECHANICAL REACTIONS

Coughing, sneezing, vomiting, diarrhea, frequent urination, even scratching the skin, are all natural defensive maneuvers to rid the body of dangers. These are evolutionary methods used to expel pathogens from body surfaces. Coughing, for example, is a highly complex procedure involving coordination of the diaphragm, chest muscles, and voice box but when it is successful, foreign material that has entered the windpipe is either spat out or swallowed and destroyed by natural stomach acids. Grooming rids the body of parasites and potential pathogens. Limping rests an injured leg and creates the best circumstances for natural repair. Many dog

DEFENSIVE ABILITIES
Unwittingly, selective breeding has diminished natural defenses in some animals. Flat-coated Retrievers are more prone to long-bone cancer. Cavalier King Charles Spaniels are prone to develop heart disease. This Cocker Spaniel has a heightened risk of developing auto-immune hemolytic anemia.

owners see symptoms such as coughing and sneezing as the problem itself and take their dog to the vet to have these conditions – the dog's defenses – suppressed. Control, but do not necessarily eliminate. Suppressing the defense may create a greater problem.

DEFENSES TRIGGERED

When a pathogen tries to invade your dog's body, your pet may respond in other ways that may also be misinterpreted. Your dog's brain sets its thermostat at a higher level. A fever is a natural defense. Higher temperature is capable of killing certain pathogens but it has its costs. A moderate fever increases metabolic rate by about 20 percent. It may cause temporary male sterility. Not eating is another natural defense. Bacteria need iron in order to survive and multiply. Temporary fasting reduces iron available from the gut. During an infection, your dog releases a chemical called leucocyte endogenous mediator (LEM) that further inhibits iron absorption from the gut.

If a pathogen gets beyond the natural barriers of the skin, the lining of the gut, and the respiratory or urinary systems, and is not expelled mechanically, it is confronted by the second line of defense, white blood cells. The defensive capabilities of white blood cells are still being unraveled and the names of certain cells are aptly descriptive. Your dog's natural defenses depend upon not only macrophages, "big eaters," which

STRESS MANAGEMENT

Neuropeptides, the brain chemicals that can relieve pain, have powerful effects on a dog's health, level of energy, general constitution, and natural resistance to disease. These chemicals act like an invisible chemical nervous system that bridges the mind and body. When looking at canine disease, look at the state of a dog's psychological defenses as well as the dog's physical state, environment, and social relationships. Early learning about how to cope with stress enhances a dog's natural defenses.

DEFENSIVE ACTIONS
Your dog's skin is its first line of defense. Grooming keeps this barrier clean. Antiseptic in saliva kills germs on the skin, while licking removes some parasites. Pathogens such as tapeworms take advantage of natural grooming by depositing their eggs in fleas, which are likely to be swallowed.

wander the body searching for bacteria, dirt, even cancer cells to engulf, but also upon "natural killer cells" and "armed helper T-cells" (*see pages 114-115*). Every cell in your dog's body carries "photo identity" to prevent natural defenses from attacking it. The system is quite awe-inspiring. Only when this superb defensive system fails or is overwhelmed do invaders get through.

OLD AND NEW ENEMIES

Your dog's natural defenses evolved over the millennia to cope with the threats of its natural enemies. But in the last 100 years modern science has created enemies against which dogs have no defenses. Some man-made substances are harmful because dogs do not have natural ways to rid their bodies of these substances. Dangerous materials such as PCBs accumulate, sometimes to toxic levels. These toxic substances are never expelled from the body because there are no natural enzymes to attack and destroy them.

Your dog's defenses are most efficient during its prime of life. With time, they begin to falter. This is why auto-immune conditions (where the body attacks itself), cancers, infections, and metabolic failures increase in frequency with advancing years.

PATHOGENS FIGHT BACK

Pathogens have natural methods of defense and preservation too. Some actively attack your dog's white blood cells. Others, such as intestinal worms, consume your dog's natural nutrients. Some pathogens use other agents, such as fleas, to get into your dog. Some manipulate your dog's natural defenses and use mechanisms such as sneezing or diarrhea to spread themselves further. This is sometimes called the "co-evolutionary arms race."

PAIN

PAIN IS NOT A DISEASE, it is part of a dog's defenses, but because it plays an important role in so many health disorders I have separated it from other health problems. Acute pain is usually treated with painkillers. Chronic pain, lasting over six weeks, does not respond well to conventional therapies. Although chronic pain often has a specific cause, dogs also suffer from it for no detectable reason.

DON'T IGNORE YOUR DOG'S PAIN

Dogs are natural stoics. Just because they don't complain does not mean pain does not exist or is only mild. If you think your dog is experiencing pain, make sure it is examined by a veterinarian. Pain is a natural defense. It is also an early warning signal for many health disorders.

HOW PAIN AFFECTS DOGS

Pain is protective. Feeling pain causes a dog to stop a dangerous activity. Continued pain reduces use of damaged tissues, giving time for repair. Inactivity as a result of pain may assist the immune system's response to body damage. Pain has two separate dimensions – intensity and unpleasantness. The sensation of pain is not affected by a placebo but the unpleasantness of pain can be reduced by conditioning, and so is open to the placebo response. Your enthusiasm in treating your dog's pain may possibly help to control the unpleasantness of the experience.

ACUTE PAIN

Short-term pain ranges from benignly mild to so excruciatingly unpleasant it causes a dog to go into clinical shock. Experience of pain is the natural way in which a dog learns that it should avoid something or that something has gone wrong. Pain can have an obvious source. Nerve endings capable of receiving pain messages are everywhere but especially concentrated on the skin. Curiously, the amount of pain a dog feels is not related to the amount of damage sustained. Your dog's brain monitors the inflow of all information and sets a biological priority to a fraction of that information. Even if your dog suffers potentially painful, penetrating bite wounds from another dog, its response may be not to feel the pain but to bite back. Conscious, acute pain occurs only after other priorities have been met. The dog with deep puncture wounds from a dog fight may appear pain-free until its brain begins to register different priorities and pain sensation develops.

CHRONIC PAIN

Chronic pain is usually associated with degenerative disease, bone and joint conditions, and cancer. It is relentlessly uncomfortable, but most dogs suffering from chronic pain behave stoically. Owners often notice only changes in behavior, for example, a reluctance to play, or difficulty climbing stairs. The degree of pain that a dog feels varies enormously. There are breed differences, for example, most Bull Terriers appear to be less sensitive to pain than most small Spaniels. Some forms of chronic pain respond well to mild painkilling drugs, but other forms of chronic pain cannot be alleviated by conventional treatments.

HOW PAIN IS TRANSMITTED

Nerve receptors throughout the body, in muscles, joints, and especially in the skin, are stimulated by temperature, pressure, or natural chemicals called prostaglandins, which are released by damaged cells. Messages are relayed through nerves to the brain where they are interpreted as pain. Each dog interprets these signals in its own way, which is partly learned and partly inherited. Breeds differ in how they feel pain.

According to the "gate control" theory, information from nerve receptors traveling to the brain has to pass through "gates." A number of factors determine how wide open these gates become. Emotion certainly affects the size of the gate opening, probably by altering endorphins, the dog's natural painkillers. This is why, during the emotional intensity of a dog fight, dogs are resistant to pain and keep fighting despite serious injuries. An injection by the vet, on the other hand, may be registered as severe pain.

CONVENTIONAL TREATMENTS

Veterinarians will treat pain according to its cause. As well as a physical examination, vets use diagnostic tests such as blood and urine samples, x-rays, and ultrasound to pinpoint the source of pain. By monitoring a dog's resistance to or resentment of manipulation, he location and level of pain is assessed. Dogs wince or yelp only with severe pain.

To alleviate short-term pain, vets use a variety of medicines. Simple painkillers, such as aspirin and other non-steroid anti-inflammatories, work by inhibiting the production of inflammatory prostaglandins. Paracetamol blocks pain impulses in the brain itself. Narcotic painkillers, such as pethidine and morphine, mimic natural endorphins, blocking pain impulses at specific body sites. Narcotics are used for severe pain associated with trauma, major surgery, and some forms of cancer. Non-steroid anti-inflammatories are used to control mild to moderate pain. Steroids are sometimes used when pain is associated with intense inflammation.

PERCEPTION OF PAIN
There are no specific "pain receptors" in your dog's body. Rather, information received by the brain from nerve receptors throughout the body is interpreted as pain. The brain constantly gives information different levels of priority, which is why, during a fight, dogs don't feel pain.

COMPLEMENTARY TREATMENTS

ACUPUNCTURE The American Veterinary Medical Association and the World Health Organization both recognize acupuncture as a treatment for joint-related pain. Studies in humans show that acupuncture relieves joint pain, but studies in dogs are difficult to perform. Veterinary acupuncturists say that the more chronic the pain, the more treatments may be necessary before pain relief is observed. *See pages 72-73.*

TRIGGER POINT THERAPY Pressure on specific trigger points in muscles is claimed to relieve severe pain associated with nerve inflammation as well as muscle and joint pain. Dogs may initially resent pressure being applied but after therapy they have more mobility and fewer signs of discomfort. Trigger point therapy has been particularly effective in relieving neurological pain that is not responsive to conventional therapies. *See page 76.*

CHIROPRACTIC Correct manipulation of spinal joints and muscle tissues, especially in long-backed breeds such as the Dachshund, by chiropractors knowledgeable of canine musculature can help to ease acute pain. Chiropractic is less effective at easing chronic back and joint pain.
See page 78.

THERAPEUTIC MASSAGE Gentle, physical massage can alleviate muscle pain and tissue-injury pain. Active touch from its owner may have psychological effects that diminish a dog's pain sensation. *See pages 80-81.*

HYDROTHERAPY Ice packs can reduce pain caused by inflammation while cold compresses probably dull pain-sensing nerve receptors in the skin and underlying tissue. Swimming, especially in a heated pool, is one of the best forms of physical therapy and appears to reduce the severity of muscle and joint pain. *See page 82.*

OTHER PHYSICAL THERAPIES Transcutaneous electric nerve stimulation (TENS) and other physical therapies such as pulsating electromagnetic field (PEMF) therapy may be effective for reducing the intensity of chronic joint or soft-tissue pain. British studies on dogs suggest that electro-stimulation is as effective as some pharmaceutical painkillers. Laser therapy units have been tested in working sled dogs but the results are only available to people who buy laser systems. *See page 83.*

NUTRITIONAL THERAPIES High levels of omega-3 fatty acids, such as those found in cold-water fish including mackerel, appear

to have a natural anti-inflammatory effect. Supplements of fish oil are thought to reduce discomfort from chronic skin and joint inflammation. It is possible that fish-oil supplement may reduce pain associated with an irritable bowel. *See pages 86-87.*

BACH FLOWER REMEDIES Rescue Remedy is said to diminish pain but there are no scientific or even extended anecdotal studies to confirm this. *See page 95.*

RELAXATION THERAPY Conditioning your dog to relax may be an effective way to reduce post-surgical pain. Relaxation techniques are relatively simple to use. *See page 98.*

PHEROMONE AND AROMA THERAPY Natural pheromones, especially sex pheromones, work by distracting a dog from its pain. Eucalyptus and tea tree oil are said to stimulate the endorphin system when massaged on the human body but studies found the effect no greater than that of massage alone. *See page 100.*

MACKEREL

114

THE IMMUNE SYSTEM

THE IMMUNE SYSTEM RECOGNIZES and destroys anything foreign to the body, including renegade body cells. It can be activated by either physical or psychological causes, and should turn on and off as necessary. If the system doesn't turn on properly, a dog has a poor immune response and is "immuno-suppressed." If the system is over-sensitive, or doesn't turn off, allergy or auto-immune disease ensues.

production when a job has been completed. Appropriately named "natural killer cells" attack and destroy tumor cells and virus particles. Other white blood cells patrol the body, recognizing organisms they have met in the past, and mobilizing attack teams. Like sanitation workers, macrophages, the "big eaters," travel around the body cleaning up the battlefields.

INCREASING AUTO-IMMUNE DISORDERS?

Auto-immune disease can be triggered by bacteria and viruses, drugs, tumors, and, in rare circumstances, vaccines. Diseases such as systemic lupus erythematosis (SLE), auto-immune hemolytic anemia (AIHA), immune thromboctopenia (IT), and hypothyroidism, although all relatively rare, are certainly being diagnosed more frequently than ever before. Although it isn't known whether this is a result of increased incidence or better diagnostic abilities, many vets, including myself, feel that both incidence and diagnostic abilities have increased.

HOW THE SYSTEM WORKS
White blood cells are the "attack soldiers" of the immune system. Their function is to guard and protect the body, to maintain homeostasis. An efficient immune system recognizes and destroys internal dangers such as cancer cells and external pathogens such as viruses, mycoplasma, bacteria, and yeast. Bone marrow, the thymus gland, lymph nodes, and the spleen are the visible internal elements of the immune system, but in fact the skin and lining of the gut are the largest components. Some immune system cells produce antibodies to neutralize harmful microbes. Others turn off antibody

IMMUNITY AND IMMUNE DEFICIENCY
A natural balance exists within the system between "helper" and "suppressor" cells. Under certain conditions, suppressor cells become dominant and the immune system is weakened. The opposite is equally harmful: if helper cells dominate, the immune system becomes overactive and loses its ability to differentiate between normal cells in the body and real invaders. The immune system starts to attack its own body tissues. This produces an auto-immune disease. For example, most dogs with an underactive thyroid gland (*see pages 150-151*) are suffering from an auto-immune disease.

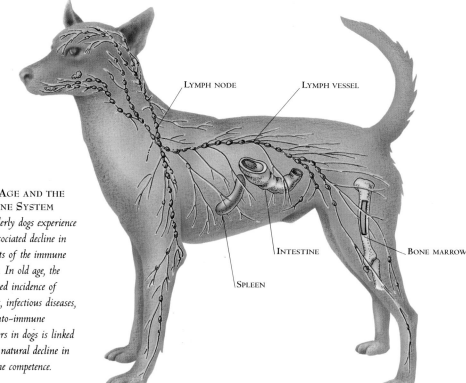

OLD AGE AND THE IMMUNE SYSTEM
All elderly dogs experience age-associated decline in elements of the immune system. In old age, the increased incidence of cancers, infectious diseases, and auto-immune disorders in dogs is linked to this natural decline in immune competence.

LYMPH NODE   LYMPH VESSEL

INTESTINE   BONE MARROW

SPLEEN

Their excess helper cells have attacked and damaged their own thyroid glands. Finally, the immune system may become over-sensitive, reacting to harmless substances such as flea saliva, dust-mite droppings, plant pollens, or foods. This is how allergic disorders develop (*see pages 116-117*).

CONVENTIONAL TREATMENTS

Conventional veterinary medicine has two ways in which it manipulates the immune system of a dog. Inoculation introduces dead or modified germs into the dog's body, which stimulates the immune system to produce antibodies, "immunizing" against the dangerous variety of that specific germ. Vets can also suppress the immune system when it becomes overactive, by dispensing corticosteroids and sometimes other more powerful immuno-suppressant drugs.

EXERCISE FOR IMMUNITY
In people, active exercise is known to increase total white blood cell numbers, natural killer cell numbers and activity, and levels of protective interferons. It is likely that mental and physical exercise are also beneficial for dogs.

COMPLEMENTARY TREATMENTS

Complementary practitioners claim that positive mental activity, a nutritious diet, and exercise support the immune system. Herbal remedies and judicious nutritional supplements may enhance the immune system's ability to respond. Feelings and emotions influence immune processes, so mind and emotion therapies may also help.

THERAPEUTIC MASSAGE Gentle touch and massage can reduce stress and induce relaxation. They may also strengthen the immune system. *See pages 80-81.*

NUTRITIONAL THERAPIES Studies in people show that substances that act as antioxidants improve the immune response. Antioxidants neutralize excess free radicals, which are chemicals that can damage cell membranes. Antioxidants include the minerals selenium (toxic in excess) and zinc, vitamins A (as beta-carotene), C, and E, and bioflavonoids. Beta-carotene improves skin and mucous membrane defenses and enhances antibody response. Vitamin C, which we must consume in our food but dogs have the ability to manufacture themselves, increases antibody

levels, while vitamin E protects body cells, tissues, and organs. Some nutritionists believe that vitamin D, the B-complex of vitamins, iron, calcium, magnesium, and manganese all have roles to play in an efficient immune system. When auto-immune conditions occur, a dog's diet should contain sufficient glutamine and fiber (to allow production of short-chain fatty acids), both of which fuel and nourish cells lining the small and large intestines. Essential fatty acid (EFA) supplements (fish oil, oil of evening primrose) are also said to enhance immune function. *See pages 86-87.*

HERBALISM Astragalus root, *Astragalus membranaceus*, a popular plant in Chinese medicine, is considered an immuno-stimulant herb. It is said to stimulate the development of cells in the immune system. The purple coneflower, *Echinacea purpurea*, one of the most popular of all herbs, is said to stimulate macrophages, especially in their action against yeast cells. According to research, both *Berberis* and *Aloe vera* stimulate an immune response. *See pages 88-91.*

RELAXATION THERAPY Stress is known to have deleterious effects on the immune system. Any therapy that reduces negative emotions may boost the immune system's ability to cope with threat. *See page 98.*

PHEROMONE THERAPY Practitioners claim that a feeling of euphoria enhances the immune system by stimulating the occupation of cell receptor sites with natural body chemicals and preventing viruses from using those receptor sites to gain access to the cell. *See page 100.*

ALOE VERA

NATURAL DEVELOPMENT

NATURAL TRAINING

NATURAL NUTRITION

NATURAL HEALTH CARE

HEALTH DISORDERS

ALLERGIES

ALLERGY IS AN EXAGGERATED and unnecessary response of the immune system to a harmless substance. Allergic reactions occur on a dog's skin, causing itchiness; on the lining of the air passages, causing difficult breathing; or to the lining of the gastrointestinal system, causing diarrhea or vomiting. Allergic reactions, especially to certain foods and chemicals, are a 20th-century phenomenon.

CHECKLIST

To determine whether your dog is allergic, ask these questions:

- Has the problem occurred before?
- Does the condition occur at a particular time or season?
- Does it occur in a particular environment?
- Do other members of the family have the same problem?
- Does the dog have external ear canal problems?
- What does the dog eat?
- Is there any possible exposure to fleas?

WHAT IS ALLERGY

The word "allergy" was coined only in 1906, by the Viennese pediatrician Baron Clemens von Pirquet. Allergies occur when the immune system overreacts to a harmless substance as if it were harmful. Chemicals in insect bites (as in flea saliva), certain foods, drugs, plants, dust mites, plant pollens, fungal spores, even the skin we shed (human dander) can set off an allergic reaction in your dog. A variety of canine disorders, including dermatitis, eczema, colitis, hay fever, coughing, asthma, diarrhea, and vomiting, can all have allergic origins.

ALLERGY IS INCREASING

Hay fever, the most common form of allergy, is a relatively new condition. It was not mentioned in medical literature until the early 1800s (by John Bostock at a lecture to the Royal Society in London). In 1950 it was still an uncommon condition. For example, less than one per cent of Japanese had hay fever then. Now over 10 percent of the population suffer from it. In Australia, over 30 percent of the human population have allergies. There has been a similar increase in allergies in dogs.

THE ALLERGIC RESPONSE

Pathogens, like viruses, normally stimulate the immune system to produce protective antibodies. Allergens such as dust-mite droppings, flea saliva, or human dander, when inhaled, swallowed, or in contact with the body, provoke the immune system, mistakenly, to produce an antibody called IgE (immunoglobin E). In an allergic dog, IgE binds to receptor sites on specialized immune cells called mast cells, which reside in the skin and the lining of the stomach, lungs, and upper airways. These cells are like primed mines, filled with chemicals waiting to explode. IgE makes mast cells release their chemicals, spreading inflammatory substances such as histamine and prostaglandins. The reaction takes about eight minutes.

CONVENTIONAL TREATMENTS

Conventional vets recommend avoidance as the best treatment for allergies. Through history taking, allergy testing using skin tests or blood samples, reducing dietary protein, elimination diets, and sometimes temporary

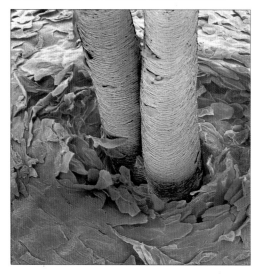

HUMAN ALLERGIES
Dogs produce the protein Can F-1 in flaking skin (right) and perhaps also in their saliva. Can F-1 makes allergic people sneeze and suffer watery eyes. Routine bathing and clipping reduces its concentration.

BREEDS PRONE TO ALLERGY

Just as allergy runs in human families, there is a predisposition in some dog breeds, such as Akitas and Shar Peis. Several breeds with predominantly white coats, such as West Highland White Terriers, Bull Terriers and English Setters are predisposed to produce excessive IgE and have a higher incidence of skin allergies. Golden Retrievers and Westies have a higher incidence of gastrointestinal allergies. Acquired sensitivities may develop later in life.

removal of a dog from its environment, they try to determine specific causes. For relief from allergy, veterinarians try to "turn off" the allergic reaction at its source.

Although many different chemicals are released when mast cells explode, only one of them, histamine, can be effectively controlled with an "anti-histamine." More recently an "anti" for another chemical, a leukotriene, has been licensed for use in people suffering from allergies and asthma.

Frequent shampooing is recommended for skin allergies. A Terrier's rough coat, for example, is ideal for capturing mold spores and pollen. Vets also increasingly recommend high-dose essential fatty acid (EFA) supplements. The EFAs are known to act at the cellular level, diminishing the intensity of mast-cell explosions.

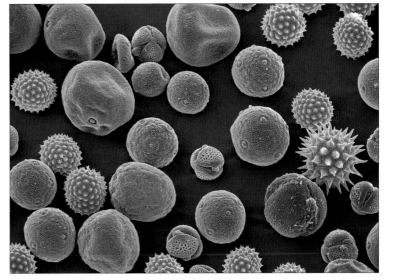

FALSE HAZARD
Microscopic pollen spores provoke an allergic dog's immune system to mistakenly produce an antibody that binds to its immune cells. The cells release inflammatory substances such as histamine. This allergic reaction takes about eight minutes.

COMPLEMENTARY TREATMENTS

Many holistic vets believe that problems in the gastrointestinal system are at the root of the increasing incidence of canine allergy. They argue that modern diets lead to "leaky guts." Healthy food and undisturbed gut flora are at the root of many complementary therapies.

ACUPUNCTURE Some reports suggest that acupuncture temporarily relieves asthma in people. There have been no studies with dogs. *See pages 72-73.*

HYDROTHERAPY Cold compresses or cooling baths may reduce skin itchiness and inflammation. *See page 82.*

NUTRITIONAL THERAPIES Holistic vets say that dogs probably consume over 100 synthetic chemicals in their food and water each day and that any of these may compromise a healthy immune system. They recommend filtering tap water, feeding antioxidant supplements, and avoiding commercial diets, even so-called hypoallergenic ones. Fresh diets, free from additives, wheat, dairy products, and gluten, and low in fish, beef, or chicken protein are often advised. Vitamin C and bioflavonoids

are used. Vitamin E is said to reduce histamine reactions. (People exposed to ozone and sulfur dioxide from car exhaust were less sensitive to these pollutants after being on a five-week course of vitamins E and C.) Oily fish and fish-oil supplements rich in omega-3 fatty acids are thought to have an anti-inflammatory effect. Asthmatic dogs may be deficient in vitamin B6 and niacin. *See pages 86-87.*

HERBALISM If the absorptive lining of the small intestines has been damaged and is "leaking," gentle herbs such as fennel seed, *Foeniculum vulgar,* and cumin root, *Cuminum cyminum,* are given. Turmeric root, *Curcuma longa,* is said to have anti-inflammatory properties and to aid digestion of protein. *Echinacea* before the allergy season may boost the immune system. Oil of peppermint, *Mentha x piperata,* is said to clear nasal congestion. The Ayurvedic herb *Coleus forskholii* is said to dilate the bronchi as powerfully as some prescribed drugs. *Ginkgo, Aloe vera* (which is said to have anti-inflammatory abilities), and khella, *Ammi visnaga,* are said to reduce bronchial constriction. *See pages 88-91.*

HOMEOPATHY Homeopaths treat like with like, at much lower levels than conventional vets do, by giving small but increasing doses of desensitizing injections. In homeopathic immunotherapy, extremely diluted preparations are made from the relevant antigen. This eliminates the risk of an allergic reaction to the homeopathic substance itself, although there is no clinical evidence that this form of therapy calms the immune system. The most common standard remedy for hay fever is *Allium 6c.* Other remedies that are recommended vary with the dog's personality and include *Euphrasia 6c, Nux vomica 6c, Natrum mur. 6c, Arsen. alb. 6c,* and *Kali iod. 6c. See pages 92-93.*

RELAXATION THERAPY
Helping a dog to relax may improve lung function. Reduced activity diminishes oxygen requirements. *See pages 98.*

NUX VOMICA

CANCER

CANCER CELLS ARE RENEGADES that avoid detection by your dog's defenses. They are "parasites," in conflict with your dog's body. Canine tumors occur most commonly in the skin, blood-related organs, mouth, and bones. Slow-growing benign tumors don't spread into surrounding tissue, but malignant tumors, called cancers, invade surrounding tissue and may spread through the body.

RISK BREED
According to Norwegian studies, the breed most at risk of cancer is the Boxer. Others with a greater than average incidence of cancers include the Flat-coated Retriever, English Cocker Spaniel, Giant Schnauzer, and Rottweiler. The breeds least at risk are the Dunker (Norwegian Hound), Elkhound, Papillon, Finnish Hound, and Collie.

WHAT IS CANCER?
Cancer is a common name given to a variety of unrelated diseases with different causes and effects but with a common, dangerous ability. Cancer cells escape detection by protective DNA policing enzymes (*see pages 58-59*). They also trick the natural killer cells of the immune system into regarding the cancer cells as "self," and not attacking and destroying them. Having eluded the body's natural defenses, cancer cells embark upon a program of producing countless generations of descendant cancer cells.

Cancers are technically malignant tumors. Malignant tumors are classified according to where they originate. Carcinomas arise from the tissues that line the internal and external surfaces of a dog's skin and organs, while sarcomas arise from within deep tissues such as muscles. Lymphomas develop from lymph tissue. Benign tumors are usually harmless and lipomas, fatty tumors under the skin,

are typically benign tumors in dogs that rarely cause harm. To differentiate between a benign and a malignant tumor, a vet may need to examine some of the tumor under a microscope.

HOW CANCERS SPREAD
Some injuries, and possibly infections, predispose to cancer, while conditions that provoke the need for tissue repair can lead to cancer. Radiation and excess sunshine can damage natural controls. Don't let your dog get fat — fat promotes certain cancers, including breast cancer. Social stress does not cause cancer but, certainly in cats and rats, it can increase the speed at which a cancer grows, especially cancers of the kind that are caused by viruses.

Hormonal factors are also related to cancer, which is why the most common cancers affect the reproductive systems and can be reduced by early neutering (*see pages 142-143*).

Some cancers evolved successful techniques that permit a wider spread throughout the body. These malignant tumors produce chemicals that actively suppress the dog's immune system.

CONVENTIONAL TREATMENTS
Conventional veterinary medicine uses common diagnostic procedures, including physical examination, blood samples, x-rays,

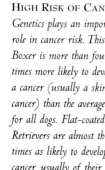

HIGH RISK OF CANCER
Genetics plays an important role in cancer risk. This Boxer is more than four times more likely to develop a cancer (usually a skin cancer) than the average for all dogs. Flat-coated Retrievers are almost three times as likely to develop cancer, usually of their long bones.

GUIDELINES FOR TREATING CANCER
Do not be panicked into a hasty decision about treatment. If a tumor can be surgically removed, it should be removed completely. Radiation therapy is painless and in dogs has no side effects. Chemotherapy is given at levels that do not cause side effects. Find out remission times for the type of cancer your dog has before deciding on treatment. Consider any therapy but be realistic. Be wary of "miracle" cures. Find out as much information as you can before starting your dog on any form of treatment. Do not unwittingly increase your dog's stress through therapy.

and ultrasound to make a diagnosis. Body scans are beneficial. Ultimately, a small sample of suspect tissue, a biopsy, is necessary for an accurate diagnosis. Once a specific name is given to the cancer, the vet discusses with the owner the pros and cons of three possible treatments: surgery, radiation therapy, and chemotherapy, either singly or in combination.

Surgery removes tumors, while x-rays and other forms of radiation therapy, and drug treatment, kill as many cancer cells as possible. Surgery is the most effective, while radiation and chemotherapy are not as successful. Because cancer is often an age-related problem, conventional vets often weigh the possible benefits and side effects

of treatment against life expectancy. No treatment, treatment restricted simply to pain control, or euthanasia are all additional, emotion-ladened options.

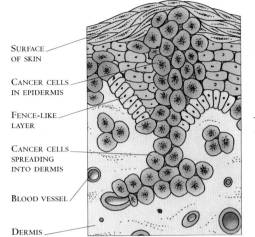

SURFACE OF SKIN

CANCER CELLS IN EPIDERMIS

FENCE-LIKE LAYER

CANCER CELLS SPREADING INTO DERMIS

BLOOD VESSEL

DERMIS

HOW CANCER SPREADS *Carcinomas develop in the epidermal cells of the skin and break through the fence-like layer at the base, gaining access to lymph or blood circulation for transport to other sites. When possible, early surgery is always the most effective way to combat a tumor. Be wary of "natural" cures.*

COMPLEMENTARY TREATMENTS

No complementary therapy is a cancer cure. Many may be beneficial in reducing the risk of cancers or in slowing their development once established. In some instances, dogs receiving complementary therapies go into "permanent remission." Cancers shrink and disappear. Like most vets, I've seen this happen in dogs and don't know why. Use any complementary therapy you like, as long as it does no harm and does not increase your dog's stress, or anxiety, all known to accelerate the growth of tumors.

THERAPEUTIC MASSAGE Gentle massage relaxes dogs, reducing anxiety and stress and diminishing stiffness and pain. In unknown ways this may slow down tumor growth. *See pages 80-81.*

NUTRITIONAL THERAPIES There is good evidence that you should avoid feeding your dog a high-carbohydrate diet. Carbohydrates (sugars) give cancer cells extra energy. High-protein diets, especially those enriched with glutamine and other amino acids, are more helpful. High-fat diets are excellent. Fat is palatable and energy-dense, which is ideal for a debilitated dog. Dr. Glenna Maudlin, Director of Nutritional Support Services at the Animal Medical Center in New York, says that, fed long-term, high-fat diets may "starve" cancer cells to death because they

are unable to use fats for energy. Feed a diet with 50 to 60 percent of the energy derived from fat. Dogs with cancer need more micronutrients. General vitamin and mineral supplements are excellent. A good balance of omega-3 and omega-6 fatty acids may reduce the severity of some cancers. Antioxidants may help to prevent cancers by keeping cells healthy, but their nourishing nature may also keep cancer cells healthy too. Vitamins A (as beta-carotene), C, and E, and the mineral selenium are antioxidants. Use with moderation in dogs with cancers. *See pages 86-87.*

HERBALISM Herbs that are claimed to have anti-cancer properties include lemon balm, *Melissa officinalis*, mistletoe leaf, *Viscum album*, barberry bark, *Berberis vulgaris*, Roman chamomile flower, *Chamaemelum nobile*, comfrey leaf, *Symphytum officinale*, Echinacea root, and fenugreek seed, *Trigonella foenum-graecum*. Recent research suggests that *Astragalus membranaceus* roots, *Ligustrum lucidum* seeds, and the TCM herbs *Oldenlandia diffusa* and *Scutellaria barbata* may be effective for preventing certain forms of human cancer. While the Chinese *Astragalus membranaceus* is non-toxic, other members of this genus are potentially dangerous. Only use herbs under supervision of a herbalist experienced with their use in dogs. *See pages 88-91.*

HOMEOPATHY Homeopaths use *Hydrastis* in early stages of cancer and *Echinacea* to boost the immune system. *Viscum alb.* is often used, while *Arsen alb.* is given to relieve pain in later stages of some cancers. Their value is unknown. *See pages 92-93.*

BACH FLOWER REMEDIES Hornbeam is given to strengthen a weakened dog, Mimulus for frightened individuals, and Olive to dogs that appear to have lost the will to live. Remember, do not harm. Do not give flower essences to the exclusion of more pragmatic ways of reducing your dog's stress. *See page 95.*

ROMAN CHAMOMILE

NATURAL DEVELOPMENT

NATURAL TRAINING

NATURAL NUTRITION

NATURAL HEALTH CARE

HEALTH DISORDERS

INFECTIOUS DISEASES

DOGS DEFEAT MANY INFECTIONS by forming antibodies when exposed to the infection. To hasten the process and extend the range of protection, we make vaccines, altering the microbes so that they are harmless; given to a dog, they stimulate the production of antibodies. This method of disease control has almost eliminated some diseases; but excessive vaccination may also create new problems.

CHANGING INFECTIONS

The infectious diseases that dogs suffer from, and their significance in dog care, have changed in recent decades. Distemper, a dog killer when I began veterinary practice, has diminished in importance in many countries, while another disease, canine parvovirus, unknown only 20 years ago, is now the most common infectious disease I diagnose in my clinic. We need to understand the dog's defenses and what can be done to enhance them, and we should know how to treat these diseases when the defenses are breached.

COMMON CANINE INFECTIONS

The infections below are those most commonly seen in veterinary practices around the world. Many of the diseases are relatively new and dogs have virtually no evolutionary protection against them.

INFECTION	PRIMARY AREA OF DAMAGE
Rabies	Brain
Distemper	Lungs, eyes, intestines, brain
Virus hepatitis (CAVI)	Eyes and liver
Parvovirus	Gastrointestinal tract and bone marrow
Leptospirosis	Liver and urinary system
Bordetella bronchiseptica (kennel cough)	Upper respiratory tract
Adenovirus 2 (CAV2)	Upper respiratory tract
Parainfluenza	Upper respiratory tract
Borrelia (Lyme disease)	Joints
Canine herpes virus (CHV)	Fading puppy syndrome

BREED SUSCEPTIBILITY TO VACCINES

There is evidence that some breeds are more at risk than others from adverse vaccine reactions. In 1996, Drs. David Duval and Urs Giger at the University of Pennsylvania's School of Veterinary Medicine reported a relationship between vaccination and cases of auto-immune hemolytic anemia (AIHA) in dogs. Cocker Spaniels have a higher incidence of this disease than other breeds and Professor Giger believes that 25 percent of the cases he sees may be vaccine-induced. Dr. Jean Dodds, a specialist in auto-immune diseases, says that Weimaraners, Akitas, and dogs with coat-color dilutions are more at risk than the rest of the dog population.

INNATE PROTECTION

The young are most at risk from infectious disease but evolution gives them "maternal protection." (The elderly are also at risk because of failing immune systems.) In the first milk that a pup receives from its mother it acquires temporary protection, in the form of "maternal antibodies," against the variety of infections to which its mother has been exposed. Puppies don't inherit the white blood cells that produce antibodies, just the antibodies themselves. These provide short-term protection, usually for eight to 12 weeks. A dog will produce further protection when its own cells learn the ability to produce antibodies. They do this when they are exposed to infectious agents such as viruses and bacteria.

PROTECTION BY VACCINATION

A vaccine stimulates an immune response that will protect a dog from the natural form of a disease. Rather than expose a dog to an infectious agent that causes unpleasant disease, vaccine manufacturers either kill microorganisms or modify living organisms so that they don't cause clinical illness. These modified microbes or parts of microbes are then introduced into the dog's system as "vaccines." Successful vaccination explains why distemper is no longer the killer it once was. Vaccination is a natural form of disease control. It induces the body to manufacture its own defenses. Great advances took place in vaccine research and manufacture in the 1990s. Today, vaccines are more effective than ever before. Old recommendations have been re-evaluated. Experts such as Professor Ronald Schultz from the University of Wisconsin's School of Veterinary Medicine now recommend three year-intervals between booster vaccinations against distemper and perhaps parvovirus. Research work done by Dr. Jean Dodds (*see box, left*) on polyvalent vaccinations has led me, in my practice, to recommend not vaccinating dogs within 30 days of estrus or during estrus, pregnancy, lactation, corticosteroid treatment, or if the animal is injured, ill, or otherwise stressed.

VACCINE CONTROVERSIES
While there is no doubt that vaccination is the safest and most effective protection against serious infectious diseases, there are valid questions about the efficacy, frequency of administration, range, and adverse side effects of some of the vaccines that are given to dogs.

VACCINATION
Never vaccinate pups before eight weeks of age. Vaccinate only against diseases that are a threat where you live. Polyvalent vaccines reduce white blood cell numbers and responsiveness in dogs. Studies with Hepatitis B vaccine in humans show that infants are protected by one fifth of a standard adult dose.

CONVENTIONAL TREATMENTS

Conventional vets routinely vaccinate against diseases that are prevalent in their localities. Because injections are unpleasant for dogs, vets prefer using "polyvalent" vaccines that protect against a variety of diseases through one inoculation. They use a yearly "booster" as an opportunity to give dogs annual check-ups. When infections occur, they are treated symptomatically. Suitable drugs are used to control symptoms, and often antibiotics are prescribed, even when infections are viral, to reduce risks of secondary infections.

COMPLEMENTARY TREATMENTS

Some complementary vets believe that over-frequent immunization with biological vaccines damages the immune system and is a cause of the increased incidence of auto-immune conditions, allergies, and even cancer in dogs. They advise careful thought before using multivalent vaccines, and tend to prefer "monovalent'" vaccines that induce protection against one disease only. This involves several different injections, at different times, for different diseases. When infection occurs, they use antibiotics for acute infection and a variety of other therapies for non-life-threatening infections.

NUTRITIONAL THERAPIES Ginger, cinnamon, cloves, and aloe vera are often recommended for their antimicrobial properties. Goldenseal and astragalus may enhance interferon production, while garlic may increase protective T-cell production.

Immune-suppressed dogs may benefit from supplements of vitamins A, B6, B12, E, and C, together with zinc and selenium. All of these may enhance the immune system. *See pages 86-87.*

HERBALISM Infusion of catnip , *Nepeta cataria*, is used for treating a fever, *Echinacea* to enhance the immune system, and thyme, *Thymus vulgaris*, to relax the windpipe and bronchial passages in respiratory infections. *See pages 88-91.*

HOMEOPATHY There is no evidence that homeopathic "nosodes" offer protection against infectious diseases. For respiratory infections, *Aconite 6c* is used in the early stages of a dry cough, while *Belladonna 6c* is given for repetitive coughing. *Drosera 6c* is used for coughing spasms and *Ipecac 6c* if coughing induces vomiting. *See pages 92-93.*

RELAXATION THERAPY The severity of any infection is potentially greater if a dog is stressed. Any therapy that reduces stress may be beneficial. Avoiding changes in a dog's routine will also minimize stress. *See page 98.*

AROMA THERAPY For upper respiratory tract infections, essential oil of lavender is recommended for its soothing effect, while essential oils of rosemary and eucalyptus are thought to fight infection. All are given as a few drops diffused by a vaporizer. *See page 100.*

GINGER

THE SKIN

THE DOG'S SKIN, together with its hair, form the first line of defense against injury and disease. Some skin cells play a key role in the immune system, coordinating defensive responses when injuries occur. The skin and hair form the dog's largest sensory organ; its functions include monitoring the environment, influencing body temperature and, through pain sensitivity, helping to avoid potential dangers.

WARNING

Tea tree oil has proven therapeutic value but is easily absorbed through the skin and is as toxic as turpentine. It can cause depression and weakness, uncoordination, behavior changes, and muscle tremors. Small animals have died of poisoning when concentrated oil has been applied directly to flea bites. Only use this and other herbal products under veterinary supervision.

WHAT SKIN DOES

A dog's skin protects its body from physical damage and microbial invasion. The fat beneath the skin offers insulation. Skin is durable, elastic, and capable of excellent repair when damaged. Skin consists of an outer layer (epidermis) of sheets of flat, scaly cells. These are shed through natural wear and tear. The epidermis derives its strength from the protein keratin, which also makes up the hair and claws.

Keratin-making cells do more than just make durable keratin. They also produce cytokines, which are chemical regulators that are important for a healthy inflammatory response when the skin is injured. Some of the surface cells produce a pigment, melanin, that gives color to the skin and hair. Skin sometimes thickens as a defensive response. Elbow calluses reduce the likelihood of skin breaking and pathogens getting through. In

SKIN FIRST-AID KIT

As well as the typical contents of gauze and adhesive bandages, a typical complementary first-aid kit for dogs may contain nettle cream for minor burns, calendula cream for speedy healing of minor wounds, arnica cream for relieving pain from skin damage, witch hazel for soothing stings and abrasions, echinacea capsules for helping ward off infection, garlic capsules to help fight infection, and Rescue Remedy to help overcome shock.

giant breeds, unnatural weight on the elbows while lying down can lead to callouses cracking and infection getting in.

WHAT HAIR DOES

Hair insulates the body and protects the skin. In wolves and certain breeds such as the German Shepherd, protective "guard" hair predominates. Finer "down" hair offers insulation. All dogs have a mixture of the two types, in proportions that are affected by breeding as well as environmental factors. Yorkshire Terriers have only about 900 hairs per in^2 (100 hairs per cm^2) of skin, compared to the 4,500 per in^2 (500 hairs per cm^2) of most Nordic breeds. Our intervention has left the Yorkie with less insulation and protection than it would naturally have.

Hair growth is affected by temperature, increasing or decreasing daylight, hormones, nutrition, and genetic factors. Dogs tend to shed their hair when they are stressed. The state of your dog's coat is a good reflection of its general health.

HOW SKIN IS DAMAGED

A dense coat is excellent protection for the skin. If my dogs run under barbed wire, tufts of hair remain on the barbs. Their skin is not touched. Fine-haired and short-coated individuals do not have this protection. Thick skin offers a second line of defense. Thin-skinned breeds such as Whippets are

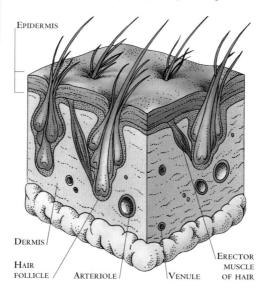

SKIN STRUCTURE
The outer layer of the skin (epidermis) consists of sheets of flat, scaly cells. The inner layer (dermis) consists of fibrous and elastic tissue that is infiltrated by blood vessels, hair follicles and associated sebaceous glands, and a varying density of nerves.

EPIDERMIS

DERMIS

HAIR FOLLICLE   ARTERIOLE   VENULE   ERECTOR MUSCLE OF HAIR more prone to skin tears. Punctures are the most common skin injuries, usually through bites from other animals. Skin has evolved an excellent way to repair this damage by forming an abscess and discharging foreign material (*see pages 124-125*). Skin may also be torn or abraded, and has natural ways of self-repair for these injuries.

How a Dog Cares for Its Skin

Dogs keep their hair and skin healthy by grooming, dry bathing, or by accidentally getting wet. Saliva contains natural antiseptics. Licking and scratching are normal activities that in moderation are beneficial. Licking removes debris, sloughing off skin and surface parasites. Only when carried out in excess does it cause damage (*see pages 124-125*). A dog also massages its skin by rolling and rubbing, activating its sebaceous glands and removing debris from parts of the body it cannot reach with its tongue or paws.

A primary function of the sebaceous glands is to secrete waterproofing for the skin and hair. The skin of dogs with well-lubricated coats of guard hair does not get wet when a dog is caught in rain, while the water naturally removes dirt and debris.

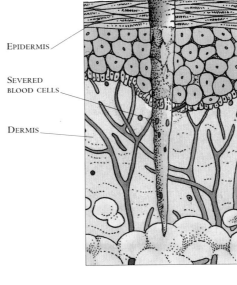

EPIDERMIS

SEVERED
BLOOD CELLS

DERMIS

PUNCTURE WOUNDS
Punctures heal quickly but the temporary breach in skin defenses allows bacteria to invade, causing an abscess to develop (see pages 124-125). Dogs are frequently bitten on the neck, legs, and flanks. Check for punctures by running your fingers through the fur, feeling for tiny blood-clot scabs.

Conventional Treatments

If a dog's skin defenses have been breached, which most commonly happens during a dog fight, conventional vets use antiseptics, painkillers, and sometimes antibiotics to assist repair. Skin tears are stitched when necessary, while serious skin injuries may be repaired surgically using a variety of skin grafting techniques. Protective Elizabethan collars, which are large cones that surround the dog's head, or padded neck braces are used to prevent the dog further damaging the skin through licking or chewing.

Complementary Treatments

Complementary vets are interested in the dog's ability to self-repair. They use conventional repair methods but also question a dog's diet and state of mind.

NUTRITIONAL THERAPIES A balanced diet, high in natural antioxidants such as selenium and vitamin E, is thought to promote good healing. A general vitamin and mineral supplement will often be recommended to provide new cells with micronutrients necessary for good cellular function. *See pages 86-87.*

HERBALISM Abraded skin is washed in warm, soapy water and any embedded material is gently scraped out. Warm, wet tea bags on wounds may help blood clots to form. Herbs with antibacterial and

antihemorrhagic properties are used. Tincture of pot marigold, *Calendula officinalis*, diluted in water may promote blood clotting. Tumeric root powder, *Curcuma longa*, can be effective but it causes intense, yellow staining to the skin and hair (and clothing and furniture!). Yarrow herb, *Achillea millefolium*, does not stain. It is applied topically until obvious healing begins. Yarrow may also be combined with peppermint, *Mentha x piperita*, or German chamomile flower, *Matricaria recutita*. To encourage epithelial growth from the edges of the abrasion, comfrey leaf, *Symphytum officinale*, may be used. Published studies say that new skin formation is faster when *Calendula* tincture is applied to a wound. *Hypericum* tincture by mouth is also said to accelerate wound healing. *See pages 88-91.*

HOMEOPATHY *Hypericum 6c* is used if a dog shows sensitivity when an abrasion is cleaned. *Arnica 6c* is recommended when there is bruising, and *Aconite 6c* if a dog is distressed. Homeopathic *Calendula* cream is often used for minor skin wounds. *See pages 92-93.*

AROMA THERAPY
Essential oil of tea tree can be toxic but it is a powerful antiseptic, antibacterial, and antifungal agent. Diluted in water, it may be beneficial for cleaning abrasions. *See page 100.*

TEA TREE OIL

NATURAL DEVELOPMENT

NATURAL TRAINING

NATURAL NUTRITION

NATURAL HEALTH CARE

HEALTH DISORDERS

SKIN DISORDERS

THERE ARE PROBABLY MORE DISORDERS of the dog's skin than of any other body system. Infections, tumors, and allergic reactions all occur within the skin while hormonal upsets and other internal disorders affect the health of skin and hair. Many of these conditions involve inflammation, with or without itchiness. Many complementary therapies have now become integrated into conventional treatments.

CHECKLIST

To help determine the cause of a skin condition, ask yourself these questions:

- When and where did the problem first occur?

- Does it occur indoors, outdoors, or both?

- Has it occurred before in the same season?

- Are there other pets in the home and are any affected?

- Has there been any contact with other animals?

WHAT IS SKIN INFLAMMATION?

Skin inflammation can be associated with infections, infestations (*see pages 126–127*), or allergic reactions. Inflammation is part of natural repair but if it is excessive it leads to further skin disorders. The skin contains specialized cells known as mast cells, which act as "gatekeepers," regulating the immune system's response to invading organisms. If mast cells multiply excessively they form a mast-cell tumor, a common skin tumor in young dogs. Skin also contains another form of defense, the "memory T-cells," which monitor the skin for microorganisms that they have met before. Many inflammatory skin conditions, even flea-bite inflammation, develop secondary microbial infections.

CAUSES OF ALLERGIES

A dog's environment today, like ours, is very different from that in which it evolved. In the United States, the majority of Americans spend 95 percent of their time indoors or in

transport. Houses are more airtight, with high humidity and temperature, conditions that are ideal for dust-mite breeding. The incidence of itchy skin allergies in dogs has increased as we and our dogs have increased the amount of time spent indoors. Cells involved in the immune system, in allergic response, can produce at least 12 known chemicals, many of which are irritating and cause itchiness if they are released. In allergy, eosinophils are stimulated by environmental factors and subverted from natural parasite targets to attacking the dog's own tissues. The damage caused often leads to cellular "chemical spillage," which causes itchiness.

SKIN INFECTIONS

Minor superficial bacterial and fungal infections are relatively harmless to dogs because skin is constantly being sloughed off from the top and replaced by new healthy skin from below. Licking helps sloughing. Dogs and cats are prone to a variety of infections, the most common of which is ringworm. An abscess is a deeper infection in a walled pocket of tissue just under the skin. Abscesses occur when bacteria are deposited by a tooth or claw that penetrates the skin. White blood cells attack the invaders while the body walls off the battlefield to prevent the skirmish from spreading elsewhere.

A hot spot is a local, superficial area of skin infection. Certain breeds, such as the Golden Retriever, are prone to hot spots. Malassesia is an increasingly common yeast infection causing itchy skin. *Staphylococcus intermedius*, a normally benign skin parasite, can sometimes produce an intense itch.

CONVENTIONAL TREATMENTS

Vets treat abscesses with warm salt-water poultices to draw toxins to the surface. They lance and drain superficial abscesses, flushing the empty cavities with hydrogen peroxide or antiseptic. Deep-seated abscesses that cannot easily be drained are treated with antibiotics. Sometimes surgical opening of deep abscesses is necessary. If a puncture

CANINE TUMORS
Skin tumors are benign or malignant. Mast-cell tumors and histiocytomas are common skin tumors in young dogs. Jack Russells, Boxers, Whippets, and pale-skinned dogs are more susceptible to skin cancer than other breeds.

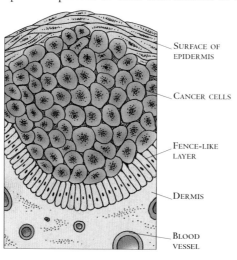

SURFACE OF EPIDERMIS

CANCER CELLS

FENCE-LIKE LAYER

DERMIS

BLOOD VESSEL

EFA SUPPLEMENTS

Omega-3 essential fatty acids (EFAs) reduce the intensity of the allergic response. Algae synthesize high amounts of omega-3 fatty acids, which find their way into the tissues of marine animals. Fish and algae, being natural sources of omega-3 fatty acids, offer good nutritional protection from allergic discomfort. Most land plants (and the meat of animals that feed on them) contain higher proportions of omega-6 fatty acids, which give less protection from allergic responses.

English Setters may suffer from gastrointestinal problems if given high-dose EFA supplements.

INFLAMMATION

PUSTULE

SEBACEOUS GLAND

FOLLICLE

INFECTED HAIR FOLLICLES

Selective breeding has reduced the protective hair covering on many breeds. Young short-haired dogs, such as Dobermanns and Great Danes, are prone to hair follicle infection (folliculitis) on the chin, caused by bacteria from food invading hair follicles.

enters a joint capsule, tendon sheath, spinal canal, abdomen or chest cavity, or touches bone, antibiotics are essential. Hot spots are treated by shaving the affected areas and cleansing them with topical antiseptics. Oral antibiotics are sometimes used, and a neck sleeve or protective Elizabethan collar may be used to prevent licking. Folliculitis (acne) is treated by cleaning the affected area with antiseptic cream. Some generic antibiotics, specifically erythromycin, clindamycin, and tetracycline, are thought to have useful anti-inflammatory properties as well as their better-known antibiotic abilities.

Ringworm is not common except in dogs that come into contact with cats or with livestock. Antifungal antibiotics are given orally, or less frequently as ointments or creams. Malassesia yeast, previously called Pityrosporum, is treated with antifungal shampoos that eradicate the microbes.

"The incidence of itchy skin allergies in dogs has increased as we and our dogs have increased the amount of time spent indoors."

If a dog has an allergic itch, a vet will advise avoiding all known allergens, and may also prescribe corticosteroids, antihistamines, anti-leukotrienes, or desensitizing injections.

COMPLEMENTARY TREATMENTS

Complementary vets advise dog owners to prevent problems when possible. Apply sun block (SPF 15 or higher) to the noses of dogs exposed to intense sunlight. Use zinc supplements in Nordic breeds prone to skin problems caused by zinc deficiency.

HYDROTHERAPY Either hot or cold compresses may be used to draw out pus. Epsom salts may be recommended to stimulate circulation. *See page 82.*

NUTRITIONAL THERAPIES Feeding less food starves bacteria of necessary carbohydrates. Add brewer's yeast to the diet as a vitamin supplement. Complementary vets believe canine acne is exacerbated by diet and feeding bowls. They may suggest using ceramic or stainless-steel bowls, avoiding plastic dishes and dairy products, and monitoring foods that contain natural hormone-like substances. When Malassesia yeast is present they recommend sound nutrition to restore natural defenses to the skin. *See pages 86-87.*

HERBALISM Marsh mallow, *Althaea officinalis*, and slippery elm, *Ulmus rubra*, ointment is applied to thin-walled abscesses. Open wounds are irrigated with peppermint tea, *Mentha x piperita*. Hot spots are shaved and cleaned with dilute cider vinegar. Aloe vera cream is then applied. Herbs said to have antifungal properties include tea tree oil, thyme, *Thymus vulgaris*, angelica root, *Angelica archangelica*, marigold flower, *Calendula officinalis*, and rosemary leaf, *Rosmarinus officinalis*. If the herbalist believes a skin infection occurs due to a hormonal imbalance, yam, *Dioscora*, may be given to correct hormone levels. *See pages 88-91.*

ROSEMARY

PARASITE CONTROL

THE VARIETY OF PARASITES that evolved to live on dogs is enormous. Many of these parasites, unpleasant themselves, are used by other infectious agents as vehicles to get into dogs. This is how common tapeworms, Lyme disease, and a variety of protozoal infections are transmitted to dogs. Parasite control is important. With few exceptions it is possible to win battles without using dangerous chemicals.

REASONS WHY TREATMENTS DON'T WORK

- Ineffective ingredients.
- Incorrectly applied.
- Wrong treatment times or intervals.
- Failure to treat all animals.
- Failure to treat the environment.
- Not all stages in life cycle destroyed.
- Reinfestation from open environment.

INTERRUPTING THE FLEA LIFE CYCLE
Fleas can be controlled before they reach adulthood and start feeding off dogs by intervening at different stages of their life cycle. Using growth regulators, flea "birth control" prevents eggs from hatching or larvae from maturing. If using a flea collar, make sure that it does not irritate your dog's neck.

WHAT ARE SKIN PARASITES?

Skin parasites are small creatures that live on or in a dog's skin. Some, such as demodex mange mites, commonly live in hair follicles (*see page 122*) without harmful effect; but if a dog's immune system is suppressed, then the demodex can multiply and cause clinical skin disease. Sarcoptic mange mites almost always cause itchiness because they burrow into the skin, damaging cells and releasing chemical irritants. *Cheyletiella* mites live on the surface of the skin; they are very contagious and often cause itchiness (sometimes not). Some people are very sensitive to them, getting an intense 24-hour rash just from coming into physical contact with an infested dog.

Fleas and ticks feed off dogs by injecting anticoagulants and sucking out body fluids. Most dogs can tolerate a few flea bites but some become hypersensitive to the injected chemicals and mount an intense, generalized allergic response. Biting and sucking lice tend to cause irritation as they lay their eggs on dog hair and feed off the skin.

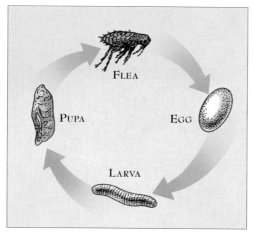

FLEA

EGG

LARVA

PUPA

ADAPTIVE ABILITY

Parasites and the microorganisms they carry have been successful in evolving methods of transmitting themselves to dogs. Ticks wait in the grass for a meal to arrive, being able to tell from vibrations, shadows, or changes in carbon dioxide level or temperature, when a dog (or a human) is passing nearby. Ticks may carry a variety of potentially dangerous diseases, among them tick paralysis, Lyme disease (*Borrelia burgdorferi*), and babesiosis, a blood disorder. Until recently Lyme disease was transmitted to dogs only by deer ticks, but now one deer tick species, *Rhipicephalus sanguineus*, common in northeastern North America, has evolved a totally new life-cycle that occurs indoors rather than out in the deer habitat, and in which its primary host is the dog and not the deer.

ITCHY SKIN

Parasites are not the only cause of skin irritation. Food sensitivities, some drugs, contact with irritants such as stinging nettles or poison ivy, internal disorders of the liver or kidneys, even emotional stress can cause skin itchiness. Conventional vets try to make an accurate diagnosis of the cause of itchiness and eliminate it. Itch is diminished with shampoos, antihistamines, corticosteroids and essential fatty acid (EFA) supplements.

CONVENTIONAL TREATMENTS

Vets say that prevention is as important as treatment. Having your carpets cleaned, on its own, will not get rid of fleas. However, professional carpet treatments with sodium polyborate, sodium tetraborate, or sodium borate are highly effective and usually come with guarantees for a year. Don't treat your carpets with laundry-grade borax; the National Animal Poison Control Center in the United States has reported increasing cases of serious eye, respiratory, and kidney problems in cats as well as small dogs when laundry-grade borax powder has been used. Only use powder that has been specifically altered for safe use with pets.

INSECT STINGS

Bee and ant stings are acidic. Irritated regions of the skin can be soothed with bicarbonate of soda solution. Wasp and hornet stings are alkaline, so lemon juice or vinegar neutralize their irritation. Jellyfish stings can be rinsed with vinegar, ammonia, or alcohol. Distilled witch hazel may soothe mosquito bites, while fresh aloe vera applied to areas irritated by insect bites is soothing and non-toxic. Some herbalists suggest applying half a raw onion to an insect sting, to deactivate the poison.

Insect-growth regulators like methoprene are used in the environment to target flea larvae, preventing them from maturing. Vets prefer insecticides that are selectively toxic to insects, rather than chemicals that are toxic to other animals. They use imidacloprid (Advantage) for dogs that don't swim, and fipronil (Frontline) which is not water soluble, for dogs that do. For dogs not allergic to flea saliva they use lufenuron (Program), an insect-growth regulator. Fleas consume it in the dog's blood. If pyrethrins are used to kill fleas, lice, or *Cheyletiella*, micro-encapsulated pyrethrins are considered better than natural ones: fewer adverse side effects are experienced with the modified form of the insecticide. To combat ticks, keep your lawns well-cut, and examine your dog every time it has been anywhere where other mammals are present; and give your dog a collar treated with Amitraz, which attacks the tick's nervous system. Vaccination against Lyme disease is available. Amitraz is also used to treat sarcoptic mange.

FLEA POISONS
What is toxic to a flea may also be dangerous to a dog. More dogs are accidentally poisoned by parasite-control treatments than by any other poison. Never use indoors a product designed for outdoor use.

COMPLEMENTARY TREATMENTS

ERADICATING PARASITES

While a variety of complementary therapies enhance immune defenses and promote well-being, herbal therapies and environmental enhancement are primarily used to control and eliminate parasites.

HERBALISM Cider vinegar is a repellent to some insects. Powdered garlic, *Allium sativum*, and goldenseal, *Hydrastis canadensis*, mixed in olive oil, are applied to areas of skin infested with demodex mange. Also for demodex, copious quantities of vegetable oil rubbed into the skin are said to starve demodex mites of oxygen. Because ear mites (*Otodectes cynotis*) are most active at night, treat infested ears just before your bedtime. Dilute nine drops of yellow dock tincture, *Rumex crispus*, in 15 ml water and instil in affected ears every three days for six weeks. Olive oil instilled alternate days for six weeks is also recommended. Six weeks are necessary because mite eggs hatch over this period.

For fleas, use a fine-toothed, metal flea comb. Place captured fleas in ammonia-laced water. Natural pyrethrin powder, especially from chrysanthemums grown in Kenya, is an effective natural insecticide. In India it is mixed with *Acorus calamus* and also used for ticks and lice. Flea control depends upon preventing or reducing reinfestations. Washing and vacuuming the environment reduces adult, larval, and egg stages of fleas. Always incinerate used vacuum-cleaner bags. Some herbalists advocate leaving eucalyptus leaves under furniture and rugs or rubbing fennel foliage into your dog's coat. Nematodes are bugs that eat fleas: these are commercially available and are introduced into the yard or garden. *See pages 88-91.*

PHEROMONE THERAPY

Sticky pads saturated in flea pheromone, placed under a light, are said to attract fleas to a sticky end. *See page 100.*

CONTROLLING ITCHING

Complementary vets try to avoid using drugs to reduce parasite-induced itchiness. They feel that conventional veterinarians' use of corticosteroids in particular will depress the immune system at a time when it should be bolstered in its fight against parasites. Massage, relaxation techniques, and pheromones are used to diminish sensitivity to itchiness.

HYDROTHERAPY Dogs with itchy skin may be bathed in warm water containing sodium bicarbonate or oatmeal. *See page 82.*

HERBALISM Corn starch, mixed with just enough boiled water to make a paste, may reduce itching when applied to irritated areas. Goldenseal, *Hydrastis canadensis*, and *Calendula* cream may also be useful. *Echinacea*, goldenseal, or *Pau d'arco* internally, may strengthen the immune system. Infusion of German chamomile flower, *Matricaria recutita*, is said to be soothing and cooling to irritated skin. Other herbs, such as burdock root, *Arctium lappa*, curled dock root, *Rumex crispus*, licorice root, *Glycyrrhiza glabra*, and southernwood herb, *Artemisia abrotanum*, may reduce itchiness. *See pages 88-91.*

HOMEOPATHY *Urtica 6c*, derived from stinging nettle, may be suggested to relieve intense itching. *See pages 92-93.*

FENNEL

BONES AND JOINTS

BONE IS LIVING TISSUE, two parts mineral and one part protein and cells, prone to injury and disease just like other parts of the body. If damaged, it has a considerable capacity to repair itself. Dogs have over 240 bones, about 40 more than we do. Bones support weight and facilitate movement, and are also a storage site for calcium, phosphorus, magnesium, and other minerals that the body needs.

FIRST AID FOR BONES

If your small dog breaks a bone, don't splint it. Confine it to a box while you take it to the vet. With larger dogs, take extreme care when you place a splint. If bone is visible, cover it with water-dampened, sterile gauze or a clean, wet cloth. Cover this with waterproofing. Remember, fractures are obvious but often only the visible results of trauma. There may be more serious injuries that need priority attention.

WHAT BONES AND JOINTS DO

Bone is as strong as steel and yet as light as aluminum. Despite appearing rigid and unchangeable, it is constantly remodeling and reforming itself. The protein in bone is supple collagen, the same as in nails. The skeleton, held together by tough ligaments, provides a superstructure for muscles and tendon attachments and articulates by means of different types of joints. Inside each joint is lubricating synovial fluid. Minerals stored in the bones are crucial to a dog's health. If reserves are depleted, serious illness ensues.

BONE AND JOINT INJURIES

Bones can break in many ways and repair depends upon the nature of the fracture and the weight and size of the dog. Fractures and dislocations are caused by trauma, primarily road-traffic accidents. Luxations occur when a bone slips from its normal position. Yorkshire Terriers' kneecaps are prone to luxating (this is painless, but the leg won't be able to bear weight). Infections are caused either by external injuries that penetrate to the joint (osteoarthritis) or bone (osteomyelitis), or by transmission via the bloodstream. Bone dies if its blood supply is cut off. Some breeds, such as Toy Poodles, are genetically predisposed to this happening to their hip joints.

METABOLIC DISORDERS

Metabolic disease of bones are, fortunately, uncommon. Osteoporosis, the thinning of bone, can be caused by an all-meat diet. Rickets, caused by a shortage of vitamin D,

STAGES OF OSTEOARTHRITIS

Osteoarthritis is common in older dogs, especially large individuals. Studies in people indicate that acupuncture, acupressure, shiatsu, and massage reduce forms of osteoarthritic pain. Needles or finger pressure are thought to stimulate release of natural endorphins.

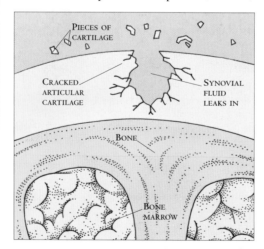

1 The cartilage surfaces of a joint may break down because of an inherited defect, injury, infection, or immune system disorder. Cracks form in the cartilage, synovial fluid leaks in, and pieces of cartilage break off, which leads to irritation of the joint lining.

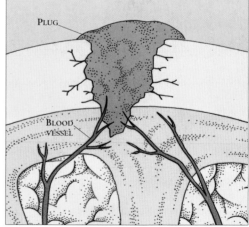

2 Damaged tissue releases prostaglandins, causing swelling, pain, and increased blood flow. Irritation reaches the bone, which builds a plug in the gap. The plug relieves pain but may be worn away, then rebuilt; inflammation is necessary for the building process.

now rare. Bone cancer may occur in
y dog, but is a considerable problem in
ottweilers and Flat-coated Retrievers.

ATURAL WEAR AND TEAR

Year and tear often affects the cartilaginous
scs that separate the vertebrae in the dog's
ine. The outer "capsule" of the disc may
urst, allowing the jelly-like contents to leak
t and create pressure on the spinal cord.
his is how a disc slips. Slight pressure from
slipped disc causes pain, and complete
ppage causes paralysis. Fluid-lubricated
ony joints are prone to wear and tear –
thritis. Golden Retrievers are prone to
thritis in their knee joints, caused when
cushion-like cartilage called the meniscus
ars. Hip and elbow dysplasia are forms
arthritis common in many breeds. These
sorders are partly inherited. In Sweden,
er half of all Bernese Mountain Dogs
d Rottweilers had elbow dysplasia until
eeders, using x-ray screening exams, started

selective breeding. The incidence of elbow
dysplasia dropped by 30 percent in 10 years.
Rheumatoid arthritis, an auto-immune
disease that develops when the body attacks
its own joints, relatively common in people,
is fortunately uncommon in dogs.

CONVENTIONAL TREATMENTS

The best preventions for bone and joint
problems are breeding for healthy-shaped
joints, good nutrition, and avoiding physical
injuries. Hip dysplasia (HD) is the most
frequently diagnosed orthopedic problem
in dogs. Over-rapid weight gain during
puppyhood increases the risk of developing
HD. Conventional treatment includes weight
reduction, moderate activity, and pain control
by means of anti-inflammatory drugs such
as carprofen, corticosteroids, or buffered
aspirin. Conditions such as a slipped disc,
diagnosed with x-rays, demand absolute rest.
Orthopedic surgery is often needed to repair
broken bones or remove slipped discs.

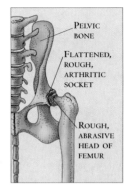

PELVIC
BONE

FLATTENED,
ROUGH,
ARTHRITIC
SOCKET

ROUGH,
ABRASIVE
HEAD OF
FEMUR

HIP DYSPLASIA
*Hip dysplasia is a typical
arthritis. Minor degrees are
common and painless in
many large or older dogs,
but occasionally damage
becomes painfully inflamed.*

NATURAL DEVELOPMENT

NATURAL TRAINING

NATURAL NUTRITION

NATURAL HEALTH CARE

HEALTH DISORDERS

COMPLEMENTARY TREATMENTS

The aim of most complementary therapies
is not to cure bone and joint problems, but
rather to alleviate the pain and immobility
associated with the various conditions, and
to promote self-healing. If antibiotics are
needed for bone infection, complementary
vets augment them with live yogurt or other
beneficial bacterial supplements to offset
unwanted side effects.

TRIGGER POINT THERAPY Australian
and Belgian vets report that trigger point
therapy may resolve bone and joint pain
that is not controlled by conventional
means. They believe that muscle trigger
points develop as a consequence of walking
abnormally after a bone or joint injury, or
surgery. *See page 76.*

CHIROPRACTIC Back problems caught
early, before discs rupture or vertebrae
rotate (as happens with Dobermanns), may
be treated with professional manipulation.
The therapist must understand the anatomy
of the animal he or she is treating. *See page 78.*

NUTRITIONAL THERAPIES Many holistic
vets believe that vitamin C is beneficial in
reducing viscosity of joint fluid. Antioxidants
are said to reduce damage in osteoarthritic
joints. A controlled-calorie diet reduces
weight, taking undue pressure off sensitive
joints. *See pages 86–87.*

HERBALISM Choose herb treatments
according to their recognized properties.
Use analgesics (*see pages 112-113*) or anti-
inflammatories such as angelica root,
Angelica archangelica, and greater celandine,
Chelidonium majus. Anti-rheumatics include
celery seed, *Apium graveolens,* and meadowsweet,
Filipendula ulmaria. Comfrey leaf, *Symphytum
officinale,* is thought to help heal synovial
membrane and joint cartilage. *See pages 88–91.*

HYDROTHERAPY Swimming strengthens
muscles while avoiding pressure on painful
joints. Hydrotherapy is ideal for most kinds
of bone and joint disease. In Japan, vets use
Hakone hot springs for hydrotherapy. Heat
is usually beneficial: a dog's bed can be

warmed with a covered hot water bottle or
microwavable heat retaining bedding made
especially for dogs. *See page 82.*

THERAPEUTIC MASSAGE Dogs with
slipped discs or similar injuries need
emotional support: frequent touch is ideal
therapy. For temporary paralysis, bicycling
the hind legs stimulates circulation and
relearning to use the legs. Towel walking
(supporting the hind quarters with a towel
slung under the abdomen) provides touch
and encouragement. *See pages 80–81.*

CHIROPRACTIC

MUSCLES, TENDONS, AND LIGAMENTS

MUSCLES, AND THEIR ASSOCIATED TENDONS, make up the bulk of a dog's body and account for about half of its weight. Voluntary muscles, the muscles used for active movement, are kept in tone by a steady flow of nerve impulses. If a muscle loses its nerve supply, it shrinks. Muscles tend to become injured rather than diseased and are immensely capable of self-repair.

TENSION INCREASES MUSCLE DAMAGE

Tension, anxiety, and stress all increase muscle damage. These emotional states stimulate production of pro-inflammatory chemicals. Relaxation turns off this chemical tap. Avoid treatments that may, even unwittingly, increase rather than decrease stress.

WHAT THE MUSCLES DO

A dog has over 500 individual muscles in its body. Some attach directly to bones. Others taper into elastic tendons for their attachment to the skeleton. Ligaments attach one bone to another – for example, the cruciate ligaments behind the knee hold the long bones of the leg in close proximity. Tendon and ligament fibers pass through the surface of bone and are embedded in the bone itself.

MUSCLE INJURIES

A muscle *strain* is a term used when there is moderate damage to muscle fibers with only slight bleeding and bruising. (Don't confuse this with a *sprain*, which is no muscle injury but an overstretched ligament – a common problem in racing Greyhounds.) A muscle *tear* occurs when large numbers of fibers are torn: there is extensive bleeding within the muscle, and rapid associated swelling.

Muscle cramp is an excruciatingly painful condition that occurs when muscle filaments, the components of muscle fibers, remain

permanently contracted. This happens most frequently in powerfully muscled dogs. Muscle, tendon, and ligament injuries are often caused by over-exertion or trauma. Active working dogs, especially sporting or racing individuals, are particularly prone to action injuries. Damage to a tendon may involve the tendon itself (tendinitis) or the tendon sheath (tenosynovitis). Because of their elasticity, tendons and ligaments tend not to repair well.

While humans can suffer from a variety of muscular dystrophies, these muscular disorders are rare in dogs. A hereditary muscular dystrophy has, however, been reported in Golden Retrievers.

NATURAL WEAR AND TEAR

With time, muscles naturally shrink and lo their power. Metabolic disorders elsewhere in the body may also affect muscle mass. I first knew that something was wrong with one of my Retrievers when she started havin difficulty jumping into the car. Her muscles were shrinking. She had no apparent pain but it transpired that she was developing a form of heart disease that was reducing the flow of nutrients, including oxygen, to her muscles. Improving her heart function soon increased her muscle mass. In the same way metabolic disorders of the urinary system, of the liver, or of the breathing, reduce the supply of nutrients to muscles, or produce toxins that damage muscle fiber. Inherited muscle disease is uncommon in dogs.

CONVENTIONAL TREATMENTS

Conventional veterinary medicine has been slow to accept that it is not only bones and joints, but muscles that can cause pain. Res and anti-inflammatory drugs are usually recommended. Specially buffered forms of aspirin and paracetamol, or more powerful anti-inflammatories such as carprofen, are used. In some circumstances, corticosteroid are prescribed. Tendon tears are repaired surgically when necessary. Ligament injuries are sometimes left to self-repair, although i

MUSCLE TEAR

The most common muscle and ligament injuries are caused by trauma rather than disease. Healing inflammation is associated with the release of pain-inducing natural chemicals. Pain tells the dog to rest the injured region. Excess pain should be controlled by suitable means.

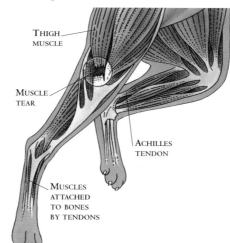

THIGH MUSCLE

MUSCLE TEAR

ACHILLES TENDON

MUSCLES ATTACHED TO BONES BY TENDONS

heavier dogs surgical repair is necessary. Muscle wasting is corrected by treating the metabolic disorder that lies at the root of the problem. New drugs that increase the ability of the lungs to pick up oxygen, and the ability of the circulation to transport it to muscles, are used, in older dogs, to increase muscle strength. Anabolic steroids, too, are used for this purpose in older dogs.

Tick paralysis of muscles is caused by a toxin in tick saliva. It is treated by removing the ticks and giving antiserum and practical, supportive care until the dog recovers.

VITAMINS MAY HELP

In people, vitamins B1, B6, B12, folic acid, and vitamin C are thought to be associated with myofascial pain. When treating muscular pain in dogs, consider whether vitamin insufficiencies have been caused by inadequate diet, increased metabolic requirements, or increased excretion. Pregnant, lactating, and older dogs may be most susceptible. So too are finicky feeders. In people, muscular irritability, tiredness, and depression have been related to low blood-folate levels.

COMPLEMENTARY TREATMENTS

Holistic vets advise prevention of muscle damage by avoiding sudden demands on muscles. Let your dog warm up and stretch first before going outdoors in cold weather. Practitioners advise against sudden exercise or over-exercising dogs. They believe that over-exercise builds up too much lactic acid in the muscles.

TRIGGER POINT THERAPY Research and clinical trials at Murdoch University's veterinary school in Perth, Australia, confirm that taut bands of muscle, felt as hard, twitchy nodules, can cause tension and pain in other parts of the body, especially around the lower spine. Unknotting trigger points is effective although this form of treatment can be uncomfortable for extra-sensitive dogs. *See page 76.*

OSTEOPATHY AND CHIROPRACTIC Manipulations that focus on stretching muscles rather than manipulating joints may achieve good results. Chiropractors believe that poor muscle function in one part of the body can lead to problems that will affect the entire system. *See pages 78-79.*

THERAPEUTIC MASSAGE Massage relaxes the dog's body while preventing the dog from overusing muscles that need to rest for effective self-repair. Massage stimulates blood flow and helps to eliminate the lactic acid that has built up from excess muscle use. *See pages 80-81.*

HYDROTHERAPY Ice packs or a packet of frozen peas applied immediately for 10 minutes to a strained or sprained area reduces excessive inflammation. *See page 82.*

OTHER PHYSICAL THERAPIES Patented equipment such as Transcutaneous Electrical Nerve Stimulation (TENS), Transcutaneous Spinal Electroanalgesia (TSE), and laser therapy are claimed to be effective treatments for overstretched muscles and joint pain. *See page 83.*

NUTRITIONAL THERAPIES A detoxifying diet is recommended. Muscle pain has been associated with the neurochemical serotonin. B vitamins, magnesium, and the amino acid tryptophan may be recommended because they help the body manufacture serotonin. Zinc and vitamin E supplements may be suggested too, as they are thought to reduce the intensity of muscle cramp. *See pages 86-87.*

HERBALISM Local treatments for sprains and muscle strains include liniments of yarrow herb, *Achillea millefolium,* hyssop, *Hyssopus officinalis,* or sweet pepper, *Capsicum annuum.* Bruising of muscles may be treated with lettuce leaf, *Lactuca virosa,* hop strobile, *Humulus lupulus,* German chamomile flower, *Matricaria recutita,* or rosemary leaf, *Rosmarinus officinalis.* Herbs that have been used to control muscle spasm include ginger root, *Zingiber officinale,* caraway seed, *Carum carvi,* and fennel seed, *Foeniculum vulgare.* *See pages 88-91.*

HOMEOPATHY *Apis mel. 6c* is used when joints suddenly swell. *Arnica 6c* may be helpful for muscle stiffness associated with joint pain. *Ruta grav. 6c* is also frequently recommended. *Rhus tox.* is a "classic" remedy for muscle and joint conditions that worsen in cold and damp. It is also used for persistent lameness following a strain or sprain. *See pages 92-93.*

PHEROMONE AND AROMA THERAPY Essential oils of lavender and rosemary, in a carrier oil, are said to enhance well-being and reduce pain sensation when diffused into the atmosphere. *See page 100.*

COOLING AN INFLAMMATION

THE TEETH AND MOUTH

TOOTH AND GUM PROBLEMS are overwhelmingly the dog's most common medical problems, so common that some owners consider offensive "dog breath" normal. It is not. About 85 percent of two-year-olds have some form of gum disease. It can be effectively prevented. The mouth is the first part of the digestive system, and a dog's health is reflected in the condition of its teeth and gums.

CHECKLIST

Warning signs of advanced gum disease:

- Bad breath.
- Yellow-brown tartar.
- Mouth ulcers.
- Teeth loose or missing.
- Dribbling saliva.
- Increased irritability.
- Swollen or bleeding gums.
- Dropping food on floor.
- Subdued nature.
- Eating on one side of mouth.
- Not playing with toys.
- Reluctance to eat.

NATURAL MOUTH CARE

In the wild, healthy teeth and gums are necessary for successfully capturing, killing, and consuming food. These activities keep the mouth "tidy," although chewing on bones sometimes cracks the large carnassial teeth, which leads to tooth infection and associated pain. Unlike us, dogs don't grind their food between their teeth, softening and adding digestive saliva before swallowing it. Because of the nature of the food we give our pet dogs, they tend to just crunch and swallow. Taste buds on the tongue register different sensations such as salty or acid flavors, and then the tongue pushes the food to the back of the mouth for passage to the stomach. The dog's teeth and gums get relatively little exercise.

ARE BONES GOOD OR BAD?

Chewing on skin and bones massages the gums, exercises jaw muscles, and keeps teeth clean, but whether to give your dog bones remains controversial. Raw bones are less likely to splinter than cooked bones but may harbor Salmonella bacteria. Hard-baked bones can fracture teeth. Swallowing bone is a common reason for painful intestinal blockages that often require surgery. If introduced to bones while still very young, many dogs learn to chew thoroughly. Introduced later in life they are more likely to cause problems.

THE ORIGINS OF GUM DISEASE

If teeth and gums are not regularly exercised, a deposit of plaque builds up on the surface of the tooth and lifts the gum margin away from the tooth. Plaque is a combination of bacteria (80 percent), food particles, and saliva. Some dogs appear to produce saliva that enhances plaque deposition. Diet and plaque formation are directly related; there is some suggestion that wet, sticky foods predispose to gum disease more than dry forms. Chewing (not swallowing) rawhide reduces plaque formation by 25 percent.

THE PROGRESSION OF GUM DISEASE

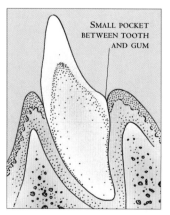

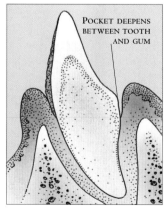

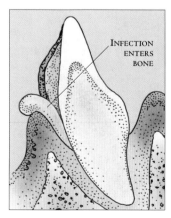

1 In healthy gums, the pocket between the tooth and gums is less than one millimeter. Healthy gums are maintained by natural activity or brushing.

2 If plaque builds up, the pocket deepens and the gum becomes inflamed, leading to gingivitis. Removing plaque and polishing the tooth prevents further damage.

3 Left unattended, peridontitis ensues. Infection enters the bone, loosening the tooth, and enters the bloodstream when the dog chews food, causing debility.

TEETH AND MOUTH PROBLEMS

When plaque builds up, it hardens into tartar, a visible deposit on the teeth. Tartar enlarges the pocket between the teeth and gums, creating a fertile environment for bacterial growth. Saliva cannot get past the tartar to flush the pockets, leaving bacteria to invade deeper. Left untreated, the gums will ulcerate, the supporting bone is affected, and eventually nothing remains to support the teeth. They loosen and fall out.

Abscesses, cavities, and tooth fractures, usually caused by chewing bones, all cause pain. Most of these problems are associated with bad breath. Ulcers may be caused by infection, injury, allergy, or nutrient deficiency.

CONVENTIONAL TREATMENTS

Fractures or erosion of tooth enamel are treated by tooth removal or root-canal surgery. Teeth scaling and polishing restores

CAVITIES ARE RARE

Because dogs have non-acidic saliva and low-carbohydrate diets, bacteria find it difficult to accumulate on the tooth enamel. Cavities are rare, but if they do occur, it usually means someone is sneaking sweets to the dog.

a healthy environment. Antibiotics are used to eliminate deep infection. Bad breath may be caused by gingivitis, digestive disorders, and sometimes by metabolic conditions such as kidney failure. The cause of bad breath is sought and appropriately treated. Mouth ulcers are also treated according to the cause. Treatment may include antiseptics, antibiotics, painkillers, and corticosteroids.

LEAD PAINT

There is evidence that if pregnant rats consume small quantities of lead, at levels higher than those given in health recommendations but below those that cause obvious lead poisoning, their offspring have weak teeth. This may apply to dogs too. Ensure that your dog does not chew on lead-based paintwork, once commonly used on fencing.

COMPLEMENTARY TREATMENTS

Complementary vets associate healthy digestive and immune systems with control of dental plaque, tartar formation, and gum problems. They may recommend digestive herbs and advise against overfeeding. Most complementary therapies aim to prevent mouth problems and, if they occur, to reduce inflammation and strengthen the body's natural defense, the immune system.

THERAPEUTIC MASSAGE Gum massage is the most effective form of care for your dog's mouth. Massaging its gums with your fingers will prepare it for the sensation of brushing. Gum massage through gentle brushing, using a soft-bristled brush and toothpaste formulated for dogs, eliminates plaque, which starts to reform six to eight hours after previous brushing. If your dog resents a toothbrush, massage its gums with a moist cotton swab. Anything is better than nothing. *See page 77.*

NUTRITIONAL THERAPIES If halitosis originates from the bowels, charcoal tablets are thought to help by absorbing waste products from deeper in the gastrointestinal system. Nutritional deficiencies are compensated for by ensuring adequate levels of B vitamins and other nutrients. Supplements with natural enzymes may be recommended to reduce gum inflammation. Enzymes are essential catalysts for all metabolic processes. Enzymes found in fruit and vegetables may act as antioxidants, protecting gums from damage by free radicals. A prepared supplement of beet fiber, flax seed, brewer's yeast, and microbially-produced enzymes may be recommended. Meat on the bone is fed to give teeth and gums natural activity. *See pages 86-87.*

HERBALISM Gentle herbs that may help the digestion include cardamom seed, *Elettaria cardamomum,* fennel seed, *Foeniculum vulgare,* and small amounts of ginger root, *Zingiber officinale,* and barberry bark, *Berberis vulgaris.* Marsh mallow root, *Althaea officinalis,* is said to help soothe soreness in the gums. Purple coneflower decoction, *Echinacea angustifolia,* may be recommended as a mouthwash both for oral health and for general condition. *See pages 88-91.*

HOMEOPATHY AND BIOCHEMIC TISSUE SALTS Pain associated with excessive salivation is treated with *Plantago 6c. Calc. Phos.* is recommended for early tooth and gum conditions, while *Calc. Fluor.* is said to strengthen the teeth. *See pages 92-94.*

AROMA THERAPY Oil of clove, diluted two drops in one teaspoon of carrier oil, is a traditional emergency measure to reduce tooth pain. It may be mixed into a paste with baking soda to use as a homemade toothpaste, applied with a soft toothbrush. Diluted tincture of myrrh is also recommended to relieve pain. *See page 100.*

MEAT ON THE BONE

NATURAL DEVELOPMENT

NATURAL TRAINING

NATURAL NUTRITION

NATURAL HEALTH CARE

HEALTH DISORDERS

DIGESTION – THE STOMACH

DIGESTION BEGINS IN THE MOUTH and continues with acid and enzyme activity in the stomach. Food passes into the small intestines, where digestive juices from the liver, pancreas, and gall bladder break it down into proteins, fats, and carbohydrates. Undigested matter passes into the colon and is excreted. Conditions inside and outside the gastrointestinal system can affect digestion.

NATURAL DEVELOPMENT

NATURAL TRAINING

NATURAL NUTRITION

NATURAL HEALTH CARE

HEALTH DISORDERS

REDUCING THE RISK OF BLOAT

Deep-chested dogs, but also Basset Hounds and Airedale Terriers, are prone to bloat. Feed dogs at risk three small meals daily and pre-mix dry food with water to avoid food expansion in the stomach. Avoid vigorous exercise for two hours before and after meals. Don't let your dog eat rapidly or drink large amounts of water before or after meals.

WHAT THE STOMACH DOES

A dog's stomach is more than just a holding tank. It is part of an active defense system that prevents dangerous microorganisms or poisons from upsetting homeostasis. Dog saliva kills some germs or exposes them to destruction by stomach acids and enzymes. Special receptors in the stomach detect poisons and signal a chemical recognition region (chemoreceptor trigger zone) in the brain. The brain responds with nausea, preventing further consumption of the poison. Toxic substances already in the stomach are removed by vomiting.

In the stomach, hydrochloric acid helps break down food for digestion. Mucus is secreted to prevent this acid from burning the stomach wall itself. (When dogs vomit back food that has been in the stomach for a short while, it may be enclosed in this protective mucus.) Bicarbonate is also secreted to neutralize acid. Stress diminishes

mucus and bicarbonate manufacture. If an anxious dog eats a meal when these defenses are low, a condition called "acid rebound" occurs and the dog vomits.

THE LIVER

Although vomiting is an efficient defense mechanism, poisons do get through and are absorbed into the body. When this occurs, the liver plays a defensive role. This is the dog's largest internal organ and a great chemical-processing factory, responsible for producing cholesterol and the digestive liquid called bile, both manufactured from old red blood cells that are worn out, and dietary fat. The liver is also responsible for removing toxic poisons that have evaded the gastrointestinal system's first lines of defense, or converting them to safer substances.

STOMACH PROBLEMS

Vomiting is a common reason for dogs to be brought to the vet. It has many causes and does not necessarily indicate a problem in the stomach itself. Inner-ear disturbances, head injuries, nervous tension, bladder infection, bowel upsets, a variety of medications, and, in females, the hormonal changes of oestrus, can cause nausea and vomiting. The exact cause should be known before any general treatment is undertaken.

Stomach ulcers are breaks in the stomach lining. They can be caused by conventional painkilling medicines or by corticosteroids. Gastritis (inflammation of the stomach wall) produces signs similar to ulcers – loss of appetite, weight loss, subdued behavior, occasional vomiting, and, if bleeding occurs, dark, tarry stools.

Deep, narrow-chested breeds, such as Great Danes and Irish Setters, are susceptible to stomach bloat, a potentially fatal condition in which the stomach twists and becomes distended. Less dangerous is belching, caused by eating too quickly and swallowing air.

Some dogs, especially young Dobermanns, develop a "depraved" appetite, eating stones and other articles. Many dogs also develop

STOMACH CELLS
Most cells that line the stomach secrete mucus, protecting the stomach lining from the acid produced by other cells for the purpose of breaking down food. Dogs have many lipase-secreting cells, which help them to break down fat.

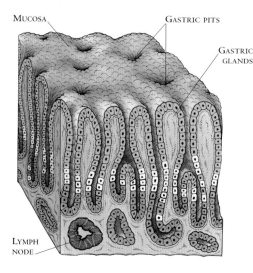

MUCOSA   GASTRIC PITS

GASTRIC GLANDS

LYMPH NODE

the more distressing habit of eating animal feces, and may, for example, treat the cat's litter box as a dessert plate.

CONVENTIONAL TREATMENTS

The body naturally wants to rid itself of potentially toxic chemicals. This is why dogs often vomit when they eat something unpleasant, but also why some drugs cause nausea and vomiting. Vets use potentially nausea-inducing drugs such as antibiotics to kill dangerous bacteria, and they may also prescribe other drugs that depress the sensitivity of the brain's chemoreceptor trigger zone. This allows the therapeutic drug to work unhindered. While nausea is controlled by influencing the brain, other drugs are given that reduce stomach-acid production, reducing clinical signs associated with gastritis and stomach ulcers.

Bloat is treated with emergency surgery and intensive shock therapy using large amounts of corticosteroids and intravenous fluids. With vigorous intervention, between 50 and 75 percent of bloated dogs are saved. Frequent small meals and antacids are

POISONS

Dogs are frequently poisoned as a result of their own curiosity, but just as often we unwittingly poison them by giving them human medicines. Never give your dog any medicine, conventional or complementary, without first checking with your vet. Apparently harmless foods can also be dangerous. A 4 oz (100 g) bar of dark chocolate may cause vomiting, muscle tremors, and heart abnormalities in a 22 lb (10 kg) dog. Ensure your dog has no access to your own food, to any "recreational" drugs, or to household and garden chemicals. Keep potentially poisonous plants, including philodendrons, hibiscus, and dieffenbachia out of reach. Standard antifreeze, ethylene glycol, tastes attractively sweet to animals and is potentially fatal if ingested: use less toxic propylene glycol.

used to control canine belching. A covered cat-litter box removes temptation from dogs that eat feces. If you want to be creative, drops of tabasco sauce on cat feces will train your dog to avoid the litter box in the future.

COMPLEMENTARY TREATMENTS

Complementary treatments emphasize the importance of a healthy gastrointestinal system. Interfering with vomiting can prevent the body from ridding itself of toxins. Therapies try, instead, to restore natural levels of acid and bicarbonate in the stomach. Relaxation therapies attempt to control the production of natural chemicals that in excess cause stomach inflammation.

ACUPRESSURE Repeated trials in people report that acupressure on the lower arm (acupoint Pericardium 6 in Traditional Chinese Medicine) relieves nausea associated with motion, anaesthetics, and chemotherapy. No similar trials have been conducted with dogs. See page 74.

NUTRITIONAL THERAPIES Avoid foods that irritate the lining of the stomach. Vitamin A may help prevent or treat

gastritis. Vitamin E may be protective and zinc may inhibit chemicals that weaken the stomach lining. Oily fish such as sardines contains fatty acids, beneficial to the immune system. Enzyme supplements may be beneficial for dogs that eat feces. See pages 86-87.

HERBALISM According to recent research work in Pakistan, extract of plums, *Prunus domestica*, is as effective as powerful drugs for inhibiting vomiting in dogs. Infusions of German chamomile, *Matricaria recutita*, fennel, *Foeniculum vulgare*, and peppermint, *Mentha x piperita*, are used to control nausea in dogs. Relaxants and tonics such as ginger, *Zingiber officinale*, may relieve nausea associated with anxiety. Ginger is said to improve digestion of proteins and control nausea in travel or motion sickness by strengthening the mucosal lining of the

stomach. It affects the production of prostaglandins and by doing so may be anti-inflammatory. For hepatitis, seeds of milk thistle, *Silybum marianum*, may inhibit liver damage and promote liver cell regeneration. See pages 88-91.

HOMEOPATHY *Nux vomica 6c, Ipecac 6c,* and *Phosphorus* are all suggested to control various forms of vomiting. See pages 92-93.

RELAXATION THERAPY Relaxation may alter the environment in the stomach, reducing stress chemicals associated with nausea and vomiting. See page 98.

SARDINES

DIGESTION – THE INTESTINES

WHEN DIGESTION IN THE INTESTINES is upset, the most common result is diarrhea. Small-intestine problems result in copious quantities of watery diarrhea, while colon, or large-bowel, upsets result in frequent, small stools often accompanied by mucus or blood. Blood from the small intestine is dark, and from the colon bright. Other large-bowel conditions lead to constipation.

CHECKLIST

Loss of appetite can be caused by:

- Fear.
- Diabetes.
- Constipation.
- Diarrhea.
- Colitis.
- Overactivity.
- Overweight.
- Heart disease.
- Urinary tract conditions.
- Arthritis.
- Metabolic disorders.

SCAVENGERS
Dogs naturally scavenge but this activity can lead to vomiting, abdominal pain, constipation, or varying forms of diarrhea.

WHAT THE INTESTINES DO

Digestion takes place in the small intestines, home to over 400 strains of beneficial bacteria. Diet changes may alter the balance of natural "digestive" bacteria. With careful dietary selection, it is possible to actively promote the growth of beneficial bacteria. Diets that do this are called "prebiotic," while diets containing good bacteria such as *Lactobacillus* are called "probiotic."

The pancreas produces enzymes, secreted into the small intestine, that break down protein, fat, and carbohydrate. Puppies have enough enzyme in their systems to digest 1½ oz (36 g) of lactose, the sugar in milk, daily. However this decreases in adulthood, when total lactose-digesting enzyme activity in the small intestine is sufficient to digest only about three grams of lactose per kg of body weight. This is why milk causes bowel upset and diarrhea in some dogs.

Peristaltic waves of muscle activity in the intestinal walls move food through the system. Further along, in the large intestine, or colon, excess fluid is removed. Water-soluble dietary fiber is fermented to short-chain fatty acids that protect the lining of the colon.

CAUTIONS

Don't give a dog an enema to relieve constipation. It is potentially damaging. Instead, with veterinary assistance, find the cause of the problem and then follow your vet's instructions. Avoid oral mineral oil (liquid paraffin) for constipation: it interferes with the intestines' ability to digest nutrients and, if aspirated (breathed) into the lungs, can cause lipid pneumonia. Take care with psyllium seeds;. in excess, they can cause intestinal blockage.

Unless a condition is caused by bacterial infection, avoid antibiotics. They kill good host bacteria and promote antibiotic resistance. Avoid high-fat diets. They stimulate the production of inflammation-promoting eicosanoids. Exclude all treats and feed a simple, bland diet.

INTESTINAL PROBLEMS

Gastroenteritis is an inflammation of the lining of the stomach and intestines, usually caused by (i) contaminated food, (ii) viruses or bacteria, or (iii) allergy or food intolerance. The dog's cecum, or appendix, seldom causes problems. This is where the small intestine joins the colon. Foreign bodies tend to block at this point and in pups, in particular, the small intestine can telescope into the colon, causing a life-threatening blockage.

Colitis is an inflammation of the colon and rectum, common in German Shepherds and Golden Retrievers, but also found in Collie breeds and in Terriers. Curiously, many of the breeds that are often affected with this disorder have rough or curly coats. For example, only long- and wire-haired Dachshunds tend to suffer from true, chronic colitis. Smooth-coated Dachshunds rarely suffer from this painful problem. There is a genetic predisposition to a variety of digestive disorders.

Constipation may be caused either by food or problems in peristalsis. Stress can trigger bowel problems in certain individuals and breeds, such as the German Shepherd. Irritable bowel syndrome sometimes develops after a long course of antibiotics.

CONVENTIONAL TREATMENTS

Some bowel conditions require detailed investigations with blood analysis, plain or barium x-rays, stool examinations, and endoscopic examination. Intravenous fluids restore fluid balance if a bowel condition has caused dehydration to occur.

Antibiotics and corticosteroids are usually prescribed to fight infection and to reduce uncomfortable inflammation in some forms of inflammatory bowel disease. Exclusion diets are recommended for many forms of colitis. Fiber enhances colon activity, binds with irritating products in the intestines, and increases absorption of fluids from the gut.

Vets recommend charcoal tablets for flatulence, and avoidance of gas-producing foods such as pulses. Constipation is common in scavenging dogs. The most common cause is eating bones. In constipation, delayed intestinal activity removes more water from the stools than normal. Eventually, the muscle wall of the colon degenerates and becomes permanently distended. Constipation can be helped in several ways. An undigestible sugar, lactulose, is given to soften stools. The drug cisapride stimulates movement in the intestines. It also inhibits bacteria that produce toxins, inhibits ammonia production, and acidifies the colon. Canned pumpkin is a popular bulk-forming dietary supplement that may help constipation.

Pancreatic inflammation is treated with painkillers, fluid therapy, and a fat-free, low-protein diet. For colitis, a variety of drugs are recommended, including corticosteroids.

WHAT DOES YOGURT DO?

Typical strains of *Lactobacillus* are acid-sensitive and do not survive passage through the stomach. Acid-resistant strains have been discovered and are used in some "therapeutic" yogurts. These friendly bacteria are believed to aid digestion in the stomach.

NATURAL DEVELOPMENT

NATURAL TRAINING

NATURAL NUTRITION

NATURAL HEALTH CARE

HEALTH DISORDERS

COMPLEMENTARY TREATMENTS

A short bout of diarrhea is considered the natural way in which the dog's body cleanses itself of harmful material. Complementary vets allow these short episodes to run their natural course. For longer episodes of diarrhea, relieving stress, restoring the balance of natural bacteria in the intestines, and feeding a balanced diet are integral parts of treatment. Historically, herbs used to be added to food to keep it safe because they kill bacteria. According to research at Cornell University in New York State, the best bacteria-killers of all are garlic, onion, allspice, and oregano, followed by thyme, cinnamon, tarragon, and cumin. These eight herbs kill 80 percent of consumed bacteria. Complementary vets try to avoid all drugs and treat gastrointestinal disease through dietary management.

ACUPUNCTURE Some veterinarians feel that acupuncture stimulates the pancreas and its secretion of digestive enzymes. *See pages 72-73.*

THERAPEUTIC MASSAGE Massaging the abdomen may help to stimulate bowel activity in constipated individuals (this applies chiefly to thin dogs). Increased physical activity reduces predisposition to constipation. *See pages 80-81.*

NUTRITIONAL THERAPIES Omega-3 fatty acids found in oily fish may ease the signs of some forms of colitis. Inflammatory bowel disease leads to excessive loss of essential nutrients. Supervised supplements may be needed. Acid-stable live yogurt is recommended to restore beneficial intestinal bacteria. Small-bowel disorders can lead to folic acid deficiency. Psyllium husks, oat bran, and wheat germ all help natural bowel elimination. Carrots and celery add bulk for regular bowel function. Linseed, senna, and cascara are natural laxatives, although the latter two make the colon more sluggish if used excessively. Lifelong dietary management is necessary to control colitis. For constipation, milk works wonders in lactose-intolerant dogs. *See pages 86-87.*

HERBALISM Various herbs are used to reduce bowel inflammation. Marsh mallow root, *Althaea officinalis*, and slippery elm, *Ulmus rubra*, soothe and protect tissues. *Echinacea* and goldenseal, *Hydrastis canadensis*, inhibit bacteria, while pokeroot, *Phytolacca americana* heals ulceration and comfrey, *Symphytum officinale*, eases inflammation. Arrowroot, *Peuraria lobata*, in water soothes the bowels. Dandelion, *Taraxacum officinale*, is a mild laxative and B vitamin source.

Peppermint oil, *Mentha x piperita*, supplied in capsules specially treated to survive the acid environment of the stomach, reduces intestinal contractions and associated pain and trapped gas. Other herbs said to have similar effects include German chamomile, *Matricaria recutita*, valerian, *Valerian officinalis*, rosemary *Rosemarinus officinalis*, and lemon balm, *Melissa officinalis*. Ayurvedic *triphala* powder may be suggested as a laxative, and light kaolin clay as a toxin absorbent and intestine protector. *See pages 88-91.*

HOMEOPATHY Homeopathic vets may recommend *Argent nit. 6c* for constipation, *Nux vomica 6c* for flatulence, *Colchicum 6c* for watery diarrhea, and *Arsen alb. 6c* for profuse, explosive diarrhea. *Ipecac 6c* is used for diarrhea caused by food intolerance. *See pages 92-93.*

PEPPERMINT OIL

INTESTINAL PARASITES

ONE OUT OF EVERY THREE DOGS harbors some form of intestinal parasite. Just because your dog does not show any obvious signs of infestation, it does not follow that it is not providing room and board to parasites. Most adult infestations have no clinical signs. Parasitized dogs spread their worms throughout the environment, infecting other dogs, and sometimes affecting us, too.

CHECKLIST

- Most parasites do not cause clinical disease.
- Some parasites are potential public health concerns.
- Worm your dog preventatively according to your vet's instructions.
- Repeat worming after corticosteroid therapy, false or real pregnancy, or stress.

NATURAL IMMUNITY TO PARASITES

A variety of parasites spend their adult lives in the comfort of a dog's intestines. Their objective is to do no harm to the dog, but heavy infestations early in life may cause intestinal bleeding and anemia. Some parasites consume so many nutrients from the intestines that the dog's health suffers. Sometimes, a heavy parasite infestation can be lethal.

As dogs mature, they probably develop a resistance to roundworms and hookworms, parasites with life-cycles that always involve migration through the dog's body. This is why roundworm infestations are common in pups but unusual in adults. Tapeworms don't migrate, so they don't stimulate an immune reaction. As a result, adult dogs are often reinfested with tapeworms.

Dormant roundworm larvae in a dog's body may be activated by corticosteroid treatment, or if a dog is stressed by trauma or disease. In pregnancy, dormant larvae are activated and appear in the mother's milk, or cross the placenta into the fetuses.

THE ROUNDWORM LIFE-CYCLE

Puppies can be infected via the placenta or from their mother's milk. Larvae migrate through the body, mature, and release eggs that are passed in feces. Over weeks or months, according to the temperature, these hatch into infectious larvae that can be accidentally swallowed by other dogs, or by children playing on grass.

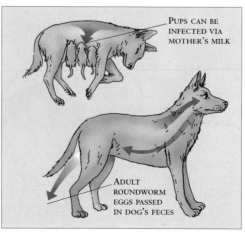

PUPS CAN BE INFECTED VIA MOTHER'S MILK

ADULT ROUNDWORM EGGS PASSED IN DOG'S FECES

TYPES OF PARASITES

When we think of parasites we usually think of worms: roundworms, *Toxocara canis*, hookworms, *Ancylostoma caninum*, and tapeworms, typically *Dipylidium caninum* from fleas but also the *Taenia* species contracted by eating infested raw meat. In addition, dogs can be infected by many single-celled organisms, including *Neospora*, *Coccidia*, and *Giardia*. All of these parasites are passed in feces and can survive in the environment for months. In recent years, *Giardia*, which affects most mammals, has spread worldwide, even to waters in previously uncontaminated regions such as New Zealand.

HUMAN HEALTH IMPLICATIONS

In theory, all canine internal parasites, with the exception of whipworms, can cause human health problems, but only one is a significant public health issue. Dog roundworms can cause health problems for people. Infected puppies, in particular, shed millions of roundworm eggs. Experts at the Royal Veterinary College in London estimated that 90 percent of the feces of heavily infected fox cubs can consist of roundworm eggs. The same statistic probably applies to puppies too. Children, with their hand-to-mouth habits, are most at risk. Once in the digestive system, roundworm eggs develop into larvae that may travel to various organs, including the eyes. They may over-stimulate a child's immune system and be associated with allergy and asthma. To prevent this condition, called *larva migrans*, worm the pups early and routinely (follow your vet's instructions). Remove dog feces before roundworm eggs can hatch into infectious larvae (*see caption, left*). The warmer the environment, the faster they incubate.

CONVENTIONAL TREATMENTS

Rather than restricting therapy to treatment of parasite infestations, prevention is recommended. No single drug kills all life stages of all worms. Vets use a variety of different drugs and regimens according to the local prevalence and seriousness of worm infestations. Worming should be undertaken after a dog has had immunosuppressive drugs or been "stressed." More frequent worming is necessary in warmer climates. (Conversely, Inuit dogs in northern Canada do not suffer from roundworm infestation because the environment does not allow the parasites a full life-cycle.) *Giardia* is treated with metronidazole. All animals that come into contact with the dog, and sometimes the owners too, are treated. Parasites are known to trigger a condition called eosinophilic colitis. Chemical by-products of defensive cells, cytokines and eicosanoids, cause damage to the colon, resulting in clinical disease.

COMPLEMENTARY TREATMENTS

Holistic vets agree that homeopathic and herbal methods of parasite control are not effective. They recommend using anthelmintics from veterinarians rather than over-the-counter products from pet shops or supermarkets. These drugs are highly effective and should be given under veterinary supervision.

"LEAKY GUT SYNDROME"

Holistic vets believe there is a relationship between parasitic infestations (and other conditions) that damage the lining of the gut, and the growing incidence of immune-related disease in dogs. The gastrointestinal system is a major line of defense against infection. If the gut lining becomes damaged, it becomes "leaky," allowing larger molecules of food than intended to leave the gut and enter the bloodstream. (The lining can be damaged by parasites, non-steroid anti-inflammatory drugs, corticosteroids, antibiotic therapy, infections, and other unknown factors.) The immune system is unfamiliar with these large molecules and produces antibodies against them. This needless attack leads to a profusion of antigen-antibody complex which may lead to immune-mediated asthma or arthritis.

This syndrome is not recognized by conventional veterinary medicine.

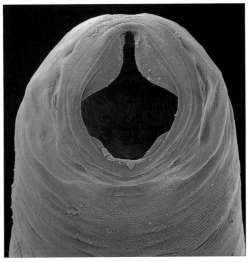

ANCYLOSTOMA CANINUM
Some intestinal parasites, such as this hookworm, voraciously suck plugs of intestine into their mouths, causing blood loss. Good hygiene reduces the risks of hookworm infestation.

TREATMENTS FOR "LEAKY GUT"

Holistic vets do four things simultaneously to control what they call "intestinal dysbiosis." They eliminate parasites, and small-intestine bacterial overgrowth, often with conventional anthelmintics, antimicrobials, and antifungals. Food antigens (allergens) are avoided. They add digestive enzymes, beneficial bacteria (probiotics), and food substances that support the growth of beneficial bacteria (prebiotics), such as fructo-oligosaccharides (FOS). Finally, they assist repair with antioxidants such as zinc, natural anti-inflammatories such as omega-3 fatty acids in fish oil, and a supplement of the amino acid L-glutamine, said to be beneficial for healing the gut wall.

Veterinary herbalists sometimes prescribe Oregon grape, *Berberis acquafolium*, because it is thought to be antiprotozoal and antifungal. *Artemesia annua* (*Qing hao*) is believed to be effective against the *Giardia* parasite, while Deglycyrrhizinated licorice is known to have anti-inflammatory properties in the gut. Garlic is said to be antiparasitic but in challenge trials has not been effective against intestinal parasites. Boswellia, *Boswellia serrata*, is said to be anti-inflammatory, while *Ginkgo biloba*, *Silybum marianum*, selenium, and vitamins A, E, and C act as antioxidants.

ANAL GLANDS

When a dog drags its backside on the ground it may have worms but it is just as likely that its scent-producing anal sacs are irritatingly full. In German Shepherds, intensive backside licking may be caused by parasites but also, because of its low tail carriage, by painful perianal fistulas, a condition called anal furunculosis.

GARLIC
Garlic acts as an anti-oxidant. It is said to be antiparasitic but in challenge trials has not been effective against intestinal parasites.

THE URINARY SYSTEM

THE KIDNEYS NOT ONLY TREAT and remove liquid waste, they help regulate blood pressure and reclaim essential substances such as minerals. Lower urinary tract disease (LUTD), involving the bladder and urethra, is quite common and usually controlled by altering the diet and the acidity of the urine. Kidney failure is most likely to occur simply as a result of advancing years.

URINATING WHEN EXCITED

There are some dogs, especially young or submissive individuals, that tend to urinate when excited. This is not incontinence, but rather a behavioral problem. This messy habit can be cured by training that will increase the dog's confidence. Avoid unwittingly acting in a dominant way when greeting a submissive dog. Initially, avoid eye contact. Do not reach down and pat its head. Rather, disregard your dog until it has calmed down. Then, get down to its level, still avoiding eye contact, and let it come to you. Raising your dog's self-confidence eliminates submissive urinating with a few short weeks.

NATURAL DEFENSES

Because the urethra connects directly to the outside world, natural defenses evolved to protect the urinary system from infection. Beneficial bacteria in the urethra prevent harmful bacteria from entering. In the bladder, mucus gathers together bacteria that get through. Antibodies are normally released into the urine while urea and natural urinary acidity make bacterial multiplication difficult. (Our more alkaline urine makes bacterial multiplication easier.) In the male, secretions from the prostate also act as barriers to infection. Because natural defenses are so good, bacterial infections are rare.

URINARY SYSTEM PROBLEMS

Because dogs now live so long, many will develop an age-related decline in kidney function, leading to chronic kidney failure.

Bladder conditions affect dogs of all ages Bacterial infection, mineral deposit, injuries, tumors, even stress can cause cystitis, an inflammation of the lining of the bladder, or urethritis, an inflammation of the urethra. These inflammations often occur together and are called lower urinary tract disease (LUTD). It is more often found in females than males because their urethra, connecting to the outside world, is shorter. Mineral crystals in the bladder or urethra are common. Three types of deposit can develop: struvite, calcium oxalate, and in the Dalmatian alone, urate crystals. More male than female dogs are affected by oxalate stones.

CONVENTIONAL TREATMENTS

Kidney failure is often treated with a low-protein diet, although there is no scientific reason for this. Uremia is managed by maintaining nitrogen balance, done by

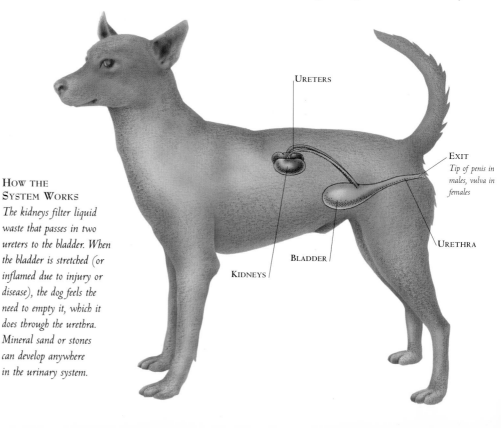

HOW THE SYSTEM WORKS
The kidneys filter liquid waste that passes in two ureters to the bladder. When the bladder is stretched (or inflamed due to injury or disease), the dog feels the need to empty it, which it does through the urethra. Mineral sand or stones can develop anywhere in the urinary system.

URETERS

EXIT
Tip of penis in males, vulva in females

URETHRA

BLADDER

KIDNEYS

NATURAL DEVELOPMENT

NATURAL TRAINING

NATURAL NUTRITION

NATURAL HEALTH CARE

HEALTH DISORDERS

STRESS AND CYSTITIS

Nerve cells send messages from cell to cell using chemicals called neurotransmitters. If these chemicals are not taken up by the next cell or degraded they build up and are "re-taken-up," creating stronger signals that last longer. Stress, somehow, causes this to happen. In cats, this can lead to emotion-induced cystitis. The same sequence of events may occur in dogs too. Drugs (re-uptake inhibitors) reduce this exaggerated neurotransmitter reaction. So do some complementary therapies.

JUVENILE RISK
Some Cocker Spaniels have a genetic predisposition toward juvenile kidney failure. Only selective breeding will eliminate this distressing and eventually fatal condition.

WHY ANTIBIOTICS SEEM TO WORK
LUTD is rarely caused by bacterial infection, yet dogs seem to get better on antibiotic treatment. Professor Tony Buffington suggests that some antibiotics have an antispasmodic action on the urethra, relieving discomfort. Spasm relief can also be achieved without using antibiotics.

reducing dietary phosphorus and feeding a medium-protein diet. The cornerstones of treatment for LUTD are reduction of the urine's specific gravity to approximately 1.020, and elimination of any urinary tract infection. Broad spectrum antibiotics are routinely used. To treat struvite crystals, potassium chloride capsules are given twice daily with meals. Blockages are flushed clear under general anaesthesia. Sediment collects just behind the os penis, the bone in the dog's penis, which is why blockages are more common in males. Large stones are surgically removed. Incontinence is controlled with drugs that improve the efficiency of the muscle at the bladder's exit.

COMPLEMENTARY TREATMENTS

Many complementary vets suggest feeding "wet" rather than dry food, and supplementing this with water. They pay particular attention to the digestive system, often recommending prebiotic or probiotic diets to reduce the risk of contamination of the urinary tract by bowel bacteria.

NUTRITIONAL THERAPIES Holistic vets suggest avoiding standard dry foods for dogs with LUTD. Supplement canned food with fresh cooked meat and a little cooked mashed vegetable. Always provide fresh water. To control calcium oxalate stones feed a diet with reduced protein, calcium, and sodium and that promotes an acid urine. Avoid excess vitamin D or ascorbic acid which predisposes to these uroliths. Avoid chocolate which contains oxalates. Asparagus contains asparagine which is said to break up oxalate crystals. *See pages 86-87.*

HERBALISM Herbs with a reputation for preventing urinary stones include stoneroot herb, *Collinsonia canadensis,* and horsetail herb, *Equisetum arvense.* Diuretic herbs that increase urine flow are sometimes used. These include dandelion leaf, *Taraxacum officinale,* and couch grass, *Elymus repens.* Cherry stalk extract, *Prunus avium,* reduces edema. Urinary antiseptics to treat bacterial cystitis include bearberry leaf, *Arctostaphylos uva-ursi,* and juniper berry, *Juniperus communis.*

Herbs that soothe the urinary tract, helping the passage of small stones, include peppermint herb, *Mentha x piperita,* fennel seed, *Foeniculum vulgare,* and marsh mallow root, *Althaea officinalis.*

For kidney impairment, a dog's general well-being may be improved when any of these herbs are appropriately used: cinnamon bark, *Cinnamomum zeylanicum,* comfrey leaf, *Symphytum officinale,* and celery seed, *Apium graveolens. See pages 88-91.*

HOMEOPATHY AND BIOCHEMIC TISSUE SALTS *Cantharis* and *Equisetum* are used as remedies for cystitis. *Causticum* is used to treat incontinence. *Calc. carb.* is employed for overweight dogs with uroliths. *Calc. phos.* is recommended for lean dogs with the same condition. *See pages 92-94.*

BACH FLOWER REMEDIES Rescue Remedy is recommended to relieve discomfort associated with acute cystitis. *See page 95.*

RELAXATION THERAPY Some dogs can develop an emotion-induced cystitis. Although the triggering events are unknown, gentle touch may be beneficial. *See page 98.*

RESCUE REMEDY

NATURAL DEVELOPMENT

NATURAL TRAINING

NATURAL NUTRITION

NATURAL HEALTH CARE

HEALTH DISORDERS

THE REPRODUCTIVE SYSTEM

MALE DOGS ARE LIFELONG sexual opportunists, while females ovulate and become interested in sex only two times per year. Reproductive tract infections are common in maiden bitches, while prostate conditions are frequent in older male dogs. Neutering may be considered unnatural but it is the most effective way to prevent the common medical problems that affect the reproductive system.

CHECKLIST

Take special precautions if your dog is pregnant:

- No vaccinations during the first four weeks.
- No drugs unless absolutely necessary.
- No insecticides, such as flea powders, unless absolutely necessary.
- No herbs unless proven safe in dogs during pregnancy.
- Worm only with anthelmintics known to be safe and effective during pregnancy.
- No excessive energy demands.

HOW THE SYSTEMS WORK

In females, usually twice yearly, the pituitary gland at the base of the brain produces follicle-stimulating hormone, which triggers estrogen production and causes eggs to form in the ovaries. When eggs are released, the vacant sites produce progesterone, the hormone of pregnancy, whether or not the dog has been mated. In males, year round, the pituitary produces leutenizing hormone, which triggers sperm and testosterone production in the testes. Sperm are manufactured in the testes and transported in a sugar-dense liquid made in the prostate gland. If the testes are removed, testosterone levels drop.

REPRODUCTIVE PROBLEMS

Natural dog reproduction involves frequent pregnancies, which somehow reduce the risk of genital tract infections and mammary gland problems later in life. Womb infections (metritis and endometritis, or pyometra), mammary gland infections (mastitis), and mammary cancers (which make up 40 percent of all dog tumors, half of which are malignant) are more common in older maiden bitches that have never been pregnant.

IS NEUTERING NATURAL?

No it isn't, but keeping a dog as a family pet isn't natural either. Think about reality when considering neutering your dog. Neutered dogs are healthier because of reduced medical risks. Neutered dogs are safer because they are more responsive to your commands. They are less likely to get injured in dog fights. They are less frustrated because they don't have to experience hormonal impulses that cannot be fulfilled because we won't let them. Neutered dogs reduce the surplus unwanted dog population, making life better for other dogs. Neutering does not change a dog's gender, only its production of hormones.

(This is similar to heightened risk in women for individuals who started their periods early and ended late without intervening pregnancies and milk production.) Early neutering reduces the risk of mammary tumors. By the time a bitch has had four heats she is about 300 times more likely to get mammary cancer than a bitch spayed before her first heat.

Older male dogs commonly suffer from enlarged or sometimes cancerous prostates. Castrating dogs does not prevent prostate cancer but does reduce risks of prostatic hyperplasia (and of course testicular tumors).

CONVENTIONAL TREATMENTS

Neutering is frequently performed, not only to prevent unwanted pups but also to reduce the risk of hormone-related disorders such as mammary tumors and womb infections in females, and testicular tumors and prostate disorders in males. Neutering as early as seven weeks of age has been shown to be safe long-term, but most veterinarians have personal reservations about neutering before physical maturity. To enhance fertility or suppress a phantom pregnancy, hormone-based treatments are used. Mastitis is treated with antibiotics and painkillers. Caesarean section is necessary if pups are too big to pass through the birth canal. During natural

GROWTH HORMONES
The female hormone estrogen promotes growth of long bones by acting directly on the bone and by increasing secretion of growth hormone. Very early neutering enhances estrogen effects and legs grow for a longer period than normal.

birth, pressure on the vaginal walls stimulates the release of the hormone oxytocin, needed for milk letdown. This appears to activate a brain mechanism that helps with bonding. Mothers are less likely to reject pups born by Caesarean if they are given oxytocin.

Excess demands for milk can reduce circulating calcium and may cause eclampsia. This is treated with intravenous calcium, sometimes corticosteroids, and milk substitute for the pups. A womb infection may be "flushed" by using powerful new drugs, but the most common treatment for pyometra is an emergency hysterectomy.

Lubricant production is normal in the dog's prepuce, but if the sheath becomes infected it is usually flushed with antiseptic or treated with antibiotics. An enlarged prostate is often treated by castration. Prostatic cysts require prolonged antibiotic therapy and sometimes extensive and difficult surgery. Retained testicles are often surgically removed as they are prone to cancer.

THE IMPORTANCE OF MOTHER
Studies have shown that if a baby rat is separated from its mother its growth-hormone level drops and growth slows. Swedish studies of dogs demonstrated that mothers that lick and touch their pups frequently are likely to produce pups that grow faster and are more healthy.

NEUTERING PROBLEMS

Problems associated with neutering include incontinence in individuals with a genetic predisposition, especially Bearded Collies and Dobermanns; small, "infantile" vulva and associated skin inflammation around the vulva; neutered male dogs becoming attractive to other male dogs; and weight gain because of excess energy uptake.

COMPLEMENTARY TREATMENTS

Holistic vets are divided over whether or not to neuter male dogs. Some feel that neutering reduces health problems, others feel we should learn to live with a male dog's behavior repertoire. Neutering does not significantly reduce the risk of medical problems because that risk is already low. Medical conditions are often treated with hormone-balancing and stress-control herbs. Optimum nutrition for breeding and pregnancy is maintained by ensuring appropriate natural nutrients in the diet.

NUTRITIONAL THERAPIES Food rich in magnesium, zinc, and vitamin B2 may help normalize hormone levels. Vitamin E and selenium enhance sperm motility. Zinc is necessary for testosterone production although it is also claimed that zinc deficiency is related to enlarged prostate problems. Sunflower oil and pumpkin are good sources of zinc. Vitamin A deficiency results in reduced testicle size. Foods derived from soybeans are rich in natural estrogens. *See pages 86–87.*

HERBALISM Sedative herbs such as Valerian root, *Valeriana officinalis*, lemon balm leaf, *Melissa officinalis*, hop strobile, *Humulus lupulus*, and lettuce leaf, *Lactuca virosa*, are used by veterinary herbalists to reduce stress or anxiety in bitches during mating. To enhance the performance of stud dogs they may recommend zinc supplement in the diet and any of ginseng root, *Panax ginseng*, celery seed, *Apium graveolens*, for one week prior to mating, or fenugreek seed, *Trigonella foenum-graecum*, for a longer period. Sage, *Salvia officinalis*, and motherwort, *Leonurus cardiaca*, are used as natural oestrogen supplements. The "female" herbs black cohosh, *Cimicifuga racemosa*, blue cohosh, *Caulophyllum thalictroides*, and wild yam, *Dioscorea villosa*, contain high levels of plant estrogens, and are recommended to control over-sexed male dogs. Dehydroepiandrosterone (DHEA), produced from wild yam, is recommended to improve sperm counts. It should be treated as a hormone, with caution. *See pages 88–91.*

HOMEOPATHY Homeopathic *Caulophyllum* is reported to reduce stillbirths in pigs. No equivalent studies have been carried out in dogs. *See pages 92–93.*

BACH FLOWER REMEDIES Rescue Remedy is given for a variety of male and female reproductive disorders. *See page 95.*

EXERCISE Good muscle tone and a lean body are ideal for breeding dogs. Overweight dogs appear to have reduced fertility. *See page 99.*

SAGE

THE CARDIOVASCULAR SYSTEM

THE HEART IS SYMBOLIC as well as functional. Physically, it controls the body's transport system – no cell in the body is more than five cells away from a blood vessel. In our minds, it is linked with emotions such as courage and love. Heart disease has a genetic component: it is rare in some breeds and common in others. There may be a link between chronic gum infection and valvular heart disease.

HEART ATTACKS

A heart attack occurs when a blood clot in a coronary artery cuts the blood supply to the heart muscle. Common in people, this is an uncommon condition in dogs. In people, high blood pressure is associated with excess dietary cholesterol or inhaling cigarette smoke. These are not causes of canine hypertension. Kidney disease is the most common cause of high blood pressure in dogs.

WHAT THE SYSTEM DOES

The heart's function is to pump blood around the body, through a network of blood vessels that, in an average-sized dog, is so extensive it would encircle the earth. The blood transports substances to and from all living cells. It contains three types of cells: red blood cells, which carry oxygen to all cells or take carbon dioxide away from them; white blood cells, always on the alert to co-ordinate defenses against potential threats; and platelets, the repair cells that start healing (clotting) after physical injuries.

Blood cells are formed in bone marrow and, to a lesser extent, the spleen. As well as the main circulation system (connected to the heart), white blood cells have their own private highway, the lymphatic system, which passes through the lymph nodes. Blood also contains glucose, minerals, hormones, and other compounds that maintain homeostasis.

If the heart is damaged, it has the capacity to increase in size to compensate for that damage. When blood vessels are damaged,

the body has the ability to enlarge others so as to repair the damage. There are millions of bifurcations as vessels become progressively smaller. These points of division are most vulnerable to injury. The whole system, including the bone marrow, is sophisticated and refined but can be affected by trauma, infection, infestation, poisoning, poor diet, and physical or emotional stress.

WHAT GOES WRONG

The most common medical condition that affects the dog's cardiovascular system is valvular heart disease. Valves separating the top chambers (atria) from the lower chambers (ventricles) become damaged and "leak." The heart compensates by enlarging itself, but as valve damage increases a limit is reached at which the heart can no longer cope. It is only then that a dog shows severe clinical signs of heart disease. Signs include pasty-colored gums, labored breathing, and severe coughing.

Other conditions affect the heart muscle: thinning it, causing dilated cardiomyopathy (DCM) or thickening it, causing hypertrophic cardiomyopathy (HCM).

Anemia is a reduction in oxygen-carrying red blood cells. Blood-cell parasites, injuries, infections, ulcers, poor diets, even fleas can cause life-threatening anemia. Sometimes the immune system attacks its own red blood cells, an affliction that is more common in Cocker Spaniels than other breeds.

CONVENTIONAL TREATMENTS

Valvular heart disease produces an audible murmur when the heart is examined with a stethoscope. Treatment is not recommended when a murmur is not associated with clinical signs of illness. When an individual develops reduced tolerance of exercise or a heart cough, treatment usually consists of a drug that relaxes muscle fibers and reduces arrhythmias, and a diuretic to reduce the volume of blood. These are not cures. Medication only slows down the natural progression of disease.

THE HEART
Blood flows from the body into the upper chambers of the heart, the atria, and through closable valves into the lower chambers, the ventricles. These contract, pumping blood to the lungs and back to the body. Healthy heart muscle and valves are necessary for cardiovascular efficiency.

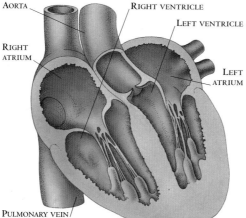

AORTA

RIGHT VENTRICLE

LEFT VENTRICLE

RIGHT ATRIUM

LEFT ATRIUM

PULMONARY VEIN

Anemia is treated by eliminating its cause and supplementing with iron, folic acid, and vitamins. Vitamin C and zinc help to absorb iron. Blood transfusions for anemia from disease or from trauma are given according to blood type. A newly developed alternative is an oxygen-carrying blood replacer fluid. Tufts University recommends marine fish oil supplementation for dogs with DCM (at a dosage of 40–50 mg/kg body weight of eicosapentaenoic acid (EPA) and 20–30 mg/kg of body weight of docosahexaenoic acid (DHA). It reduces dangerous cytokine production and increases appetite. Taurine is associated with DCM in cats but there is no known relationship in dogs. Corticosteroids are used to suppress an overactive immune system that attacks its own blood cells.

Many conventional vets feel that a low-sodium (salt) diet is useful for most forms of heart disease. Special low-sodium diets are produced by some dog food manufacturers. These have about half the salt content of standard brands of food. Palatability may be a problem with some dogs. Veterinary cardiologists often recommend low-sodium diets for dogs with clinical heart disease but not before clinical signs develop.

PREVENTING HEARTWORMS

Heartworms, *Dirofilaria immitis*, are transmitted by certain female mosquitoes when they dine on your dog's blood. The mosquito leaves parasitic larvae behind that migrate to the heart and grow into spaghetti-like worms. There are only two effective treatments, an arsenic-based drug, or surgery, and both are potentially dangerous. Some herbalists say that black walnut or hawthorn will prevent infestation. They do not. As much as you might want to avoid using conventional heartworm medicines, there are no truly effective holistic preventatives or treatments. If heartworms are a problem in the area where you live, use a licensed treatment that kills the larvae before they can start to cause problems.

COMPLEMENTARY TREATMENTS

Holistic vets say that the recent increase in the lifespan of dogs has occurred so quickly that their bodies do not naturally produce sufficient antioxidants for their old age. Consequently, they believe antioxidant supplements are beneficial for elderly dogs.

ACUPUNCTURE Scandinavian studies on people showed that acupuncture (at any points, not just TCM points) can increase the heart's working capacity. *See pages 72-73.*

THERAPEUTIC MASSAGE Slow, stroking massage releases muscle tension and temporarily reduces blood pressure. *See pages 80-81.*

HYDROTHERAPY Swimming is an excellent form of controlled, routine, moderate exercise that helps to maintain circulation. *See page 82.*

NUTRITIONAL THERAPIES Vitamin E and selenium are thought to be beneficial for efficient heart function. Vitamin B probably reduces levels of homocysteine, a substance that damages blood vessel cell walls. L-Carnitine is often recommended for all forms of cardiovascular disease, especially for Boxers and American Cocker Spaniels with dilated cardiomyopathy. Don't give D-Carnitine or D.L-Carnitine. These may worsen an existing heart condition. Magnesium supplementation is suggested for exaggerated arrhythmias. *See pages 86-87.*

HERBALISM Emblic myrobalan fruit, *Phyllanthus emblica*, angelica root, *Angelica archangelica*, Ashwagandha root, *Withania somnifera*, and rehmannia root, *Rehmannia glutinosa*, may help to regenerate blood cells in anemic dogs. German studies showed that bioflavonoids in hawthorn, *Crataegus laevigata*, dilate coronary arteries, improving the supply of oxygen to heart muscle. In a report in the Journal of Helminthology a purified extract of ginger, *Zingiber officinale*, when given in injections, partially destroyed adult heartworms and reduced microfilaria by up to 98 percent. *See pages 88-91.*

HOMEOPATHY AND BIOCHEMIC TISSUE SALTS *Adonis* and *Digitalis* are used for congestive heart failure. *Spongia tosta 6c* is given for ventricular hypertrophy. *Calc. sulf.* and *Nat. sulf.* are used when chronic damage has occurred. *See pages 92-94.*

RELAXATION THERAPY Training to relax leads to slower breathing and deep-muscle relaxation. This temporarily reduces both blood pressure and heart rate. *See page 98.*

MUSIC THERAPY It is possible that gentle music can relieve tension in animals. *See page 101.*

HYDROTHERAPY

THE RESPIRATORY SYSTEM

DOGS ARE LESS PRONE to respiratory disorders than other species such as cats or humans. However, our intervention in breeding has created new respiratory problems for dogs: nostrils that are too small for inhalation, windpipes that collapse, and soft palates that distend, swell, and block normal breathing. Any change in a dog's resting breathing rate or rhythm is a possible cause for concern.

THE REVERSE SNEEZE

Some dogs have spasms of "reverse sneezes." Usually (though not always) occurring when the dog is excited, these are not dangerous. Specially common in Yorkshire Terriers, they are caused by involuntary contractions of the diaphragm.

HOW THE SYSTEM WORKS

Breathing allows oxygen from the air to be absorbed into the bloodstream to provide fuel for the dog's body to function properly. Air is filtered in the nose, then passes through the windpipe and bronchial tubes to the lungs, and eventually into millions of thin-walled sacs where it is exchanged for waste carbon dioxide which is breathed out.

Mucus or debris and accompanying inflammation may occur anywhere in the system. Because the system is connected to the outside world, mechanisms evolved to protect it from dangers. Coughing, sneezing, and nasal discharge are all defensive actions used to expel unwanted material.

RESPIRATORY CONDITIONS

Rapid breathing may be caused by excitement or fear but is also a sign of possible pain, fever, heat prostration, and other conditions that demand immediate veterinary attention. Because dogs have a different distribution of inflammatory mast cells, unlike cats and us, they do not suffer from bronchial asthma but can experience allergic bronchitis. Elongated soft palates in breeds such as the Cavalier King Charles may interfere with breathing, as do abnormally small nostrils in some individual Shih Tzus, Pekes, and Pugs. Surgical corrections may be needed.

Coughing is associated with heart disease, kennel cough (tracheobronchitis), bronchitis, and pneumonia. Sneezing can be caused by acute infections, foreign bodies, and rarely, nasal polyps and tumors. Lung tumors can cause coughing or breathing problems in older dogs. Chest injuries, cancer, and heart and liver conditions can cause fluid to accumulate in the chest cavity. Lungworms (*Filaroides osleri* and *Capillaria aerophila*), heartworms (*Dirofilaria immitis*), migrating roundworm larvae (*Toxocara canis* and *Toxocara*

ACUTE TRACHEOBRONCHITIS

This highly contagious disease, also called kennel cough, is caused by a variety of different bacteria and viruses that attack the lining of the windpipe (trachea) and air passages in the lungs (bronchi). The most important and severe cause is the bacteria *Bordetella bronchiseptica*, which can evade the lung's natural clearing methods.

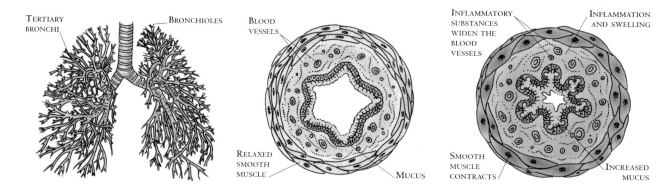

THE LUNG'S AIRWAYS
Air is breathed into the windpipe, down airways to the bronchioles. There, oxygen is exchanged for waste carbon dioxide, which is then breathed out.

NORMAL AIRWAY
A normal airway is wide and covered by a fine layer of mucus, necessary for protecting the lining of the airway from damaging external substances.

CONTRACTED AIRWAY
Under the influence of inflammatory chemicals, the smooth muscle of the airway contracts and excess mucus is produced, constricting breathing.

WHAT VACCINATION?

Distemper virus causes lung inflammation and predisposes to bacterial pneumonia. All pups should be immunized using an effective vaccine. In the absence of maternal antibodies, good distemper vaccine provides protection for many years. Vaccine is also available to control canine parvovirus and canine adenovirus type 2, known causes of chest problems. These are included in the annual polyvalent vaccination. Inoculation against the bacteria *Bordetella bronchiseptica*, the most important cause of kennel cough, is administered directly in the nose and offers short-term protection of several months. Vaccinate against kennel cough only if you know your dog is likely to be exposed to these respiratory infections.

leonina), or migrating hookworm larvae (*Ancylostoma* species and *Uncinaria stenocephala*), can all cause coughing.

CONVENTIONAL TREATMENTS

Distemper and kennel cough are the dog's most common respiratory infection; vaccination is usually recommended.

The fungus *Aspergillus* may cause inflammation of the nasal chamber, and is treated with antifungal drugs. Fungal agents may cause pneumonia. Conventional vets use antibiotics, broncho-dilators, and decongestants to relieve clinical signs, while expectorants help loosen phlegm. If allergy is involved, and allergic bronchitis ensues, vets often use antihistamines and corticosteroids. If fluid builds up in the chest, this is drained surgically and the dog is hospitalized while the condition is investigated. Routine worming controls parasitic lung conditions. Diagnostic techniques include physical examination, x-rays, respiratory tract swabs, blood sampling, and stool examinations for worm larvae or eggs.

FLAT FACE
Selective breeding for a flat face unfortunately also selects for thin nostrils. Some nostrils are so thin a dog has to breathe through the mouth. In turn, this irritates the soft palate, causing it to swell. This, in turn, makes breathing even harder and makes surgical repair become urgent.

COMPLEMENTARY TREATMENTS

Holistic veterinarians advise that dogs with respiratory problems are kept away from polluted environments. Installing a room ionizer reduces allergens; a humidifier keeps air moist. Ensure that surplus weight is lost. Overweight dogs have more difficulty coping with respiratory conditions.

OSTEOPATHY Soft-tissue techniques affecting chest muscles may improve the breathing capacity of dogs with chronic respiratory disorders. *See page 79.*

THERAPEUTIC MASSAGE Massaging the neck and chest and gentle tapping over the lungs may help a congested dog to cough up obstructing mucus. *See pages 80–81.*

HYDROTHERAPY Steam inhalation may loosen up phlegm and relieve bronchial congestion. Placing a well-insulated hot-

water bottle in the dog's bed to ensure the chest is warm may also loosen catarrh and ease congestion. *See page 82.*

HERBALISM A variety of herbs may be recommended to manage blocked sinuses and nasal congestion. These include hyssop herb, *Hyssopus officinalis*, cinnamon bark, *Cinnamomum zeylanicum*, celery seed, *Apium graveolens*, and elder flower, *Sambucus nigra*. Garlic, *Allium sativum*, and Echinacea may boost the immune system. *See pages 88–91.*

HOMEOPATHY *Kali bich.* is used for tenacious nasal discharge, while *Pulsatilla* is recommended for a looser catarrh. *Silicea* is used to treat sinusitis. *Arsen. alb.* is commonly used for a harsh cough, *Bryonia* for a dry cough, and *Ipecac* for coughing spasms accompanied by retching. If a cough is heart-related, *Spongia* may be

recommended. For Yorkshire Terriers and other small breeds with delicate windpipes, *Drosera* may be suggested. *See pages 92–93.*

AROMA THERAPY A holistic vet may recommend placing a vaporizer or diffuser in the room and using eucalyptus, tea tree, lemon, lavender, or cedarwood essential oils to relieve nasal, sinus, or windpipe congestion. *See page 100.*

ESSENTIAL OIL OF EUCALYPTUS

THE CENTRAL NERVOUS SYSTEM

THE BRAIN AND NERVOUS SYSTEM are evolution's most complex structure and require vast amounts of energy to function. The brain, for example, makes up only two percent of the dog's weight, yet at least 20 percent of the blood supply flows directly from the heart to the brain. Protected by the skeleton, this system has evolved little capacity for self-repair; any damage is often irreparable.

CHECKLIST

If your dog has a seizure do the following:

- Keep your hands away from the dog's mouth. Unintentionally, it might bite.

- Gently pull the dog by its scruff away from dangers such as stairways.

- Place something soft, like a cushion, under the dog's head.

- If the convulsion lasts more than six minutes, take your dog immediately to the vet.

- After the seizure, let your dog drink.

- Confine your dog if it seems disorientated.

- Comfort your dog if it is anxious. This is your turn to be the companion animal.

WHAT THE NERVOUS SYSTEM DOES

The brain's billions of cells communicate with every living cell in a dog's body through chemicals called neurotransmitters. The brain, through the spinal cord and nerves, coordinates all activities, thoughts, senses, feelings, movements, and body functions. As time progresses, nerve cells diminish in numbers, and in their connections to other nerve cells. There is no way to halt this loss of nerve cells, but experiments show that mental and physical stimulation increase the number of interconnections between remaining nerve cells. More connections mean improved physical and mental abilities.

WHAT CAN GO WRONG

Physical injuries, such as road-traffic accidents, are the most common cause of brain and nerve damage. Head injuries sometimes cause a facial nerve paralysis (neuropathy) with shrinkage of affected muscles. Selective breeding has enhanced the risk of spinal injury for dogs with elongated backs or short legs. Great Danes and Dobermanns are especially susceptible to spontaneous injury to the spinal cord in the neck.

SLIPPED DISK RISK

Selective breeding has left Dachshunds with a high risk of slipped disks, in turn leading to spinal-cord trauma.

WILD-ANIMAL BITES

If you think your dog has been exposed to rabies by a bite or scratch from a wild animal, contact your vet, who will know the local regulations. Any dog that is already vaccinated will probably be given a post-exposure rabies vaccination and be kept under confined observation for up to three months. A non-vaccinated dog may not be vaccinated and may be kept in quarantine for up to six months. After five months it is usually vaccinated. Whenever possible, health officials will try to catch any wild animal that bites a dog.

Infections such as cryptococcosis, rabies, distemper, and toxoplasmosis can attack the brain, causing convulsions, behavior change, or paralysis. Parasites such as roundworm larvae can also enter the brain and cause convulsions. Other parasites, such as female ticks, may transmit tick-borne paralysis, which deadens the brain's control over the body.

If body waste products accumulate in the blood, for example, when the liver fails to detoxify properly, a "hepatic encephalitis" develops. Treating the liver condition controls the neurological consequences.

Poisons can also enter the brain and cause damage to its tissues. Both natural and synthetic chemicals can be dangerous. The pyrethrins from *Chrysanthemum cinerariifolium*, used in some insecticides, can be toxic to the nervous system. A variety of disorders, some inherited, such as low blood sugar, others acquired, such as head injuries, can cause an animal to have seizures or convulsions. There are also cases in which, for unknown reasons, the nerves gradually degenerate. Chronic degenerative radiculomyelopathy (CDRM) is a degenerative disease of the fatty myelin sheath that surrounds nerves. This painless condition affects German Shepherd dogs in particular; insidiously they lose control of their hind legs. With the aid of MRI scans, vets now know that brain tumors are more common than was once appreciated. Strokes

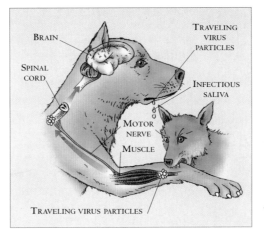

BRAIN

TRAVELING VIRUS PARTICLES

SPINAL CORD

INFECTIOUS SALIVA

MOTOR NERVE

MUSCLE

TRAVELING VIRUS PARTICLES

are uncommon in dogs, and they are usually associated with kidney deterioration or an overactive thyroid gland. Even with the best care, over time brain and nerve function diminishes. Most dogs over 16 years old experience forms of senile dementia in which brain cells progressively degenerate.

CONVENTIONAL TREATMENTS

Vets will recommend vaccination against rabies and distemper, worming to prevent parasites, and tick-control measures. Good leash control dramatically reduces the risk of road-traffic accidents. A slipped disc traumatizes the spinal cord. Depending upon the severity of the slippage, a vet will recommend absolute rest and treat with non-steroid anti-inflammatory painkillers, sometimes with corticosteroids. If the condition is severe, the vet may recommend surgery to remove the invading disc material.

A CLEVER INVADER
Evolution creates "clever" pathogens. A fox bite "injects" the rabies virus into the dog. The virus travels via nerves to the brain, stimulates the dog's rage center, paralyzes its throat, then congregates in saliva for transmission through bites to another animal.

For seizures, phenobarbitol and recently, but still rarely, potassium bromide, are used as anticonvulsants. With time the liver becomes more efficient at breaking down phenobarb, so increasing doses are often necessary. Dogs with CDRM are treated with routine exercise and drugs that increase muscle tone and mass. The drug capergoline is considered effective in delaying the ravages of senile dementia.

COMPLEMENTARY TREATMENTS

Holistic vets emphasize the mind-body relationship when treating brain and nerve disorders. They look at the diet to ensure that optimum levels of nutrients are available for necessary repairs. They may suggest physical or mental therapies that stimulate or relax the nervous system.

ACUPRESSURE Under a practitioner's guidance, acupressure at an appropriate site may diminish neural pain. *See page 74.*

TRIGGER POINT THERAPY A specialist can locate muscle trigger points that have developed as a result of an abnormal gait, which may have originally developed to protect the site of a nerve injury. *See page 76.*

CHIROPRACTIC AND OSTEOPATHY Manipulation can release a trapped nerve. These therapies may increase mobility after spinal injury by improving circulation in appropriate muscles. *See pages 78–79.*

THERAPEUTIC MASSAGE Touch is comforting to some dogs and reduces anxiety in individuals coping with the

sudden loss of motor function. Massage may be comforting to individuals recovering from seizures. It may also delay the onset of senile dementia. *See pages 80–81.*

HYDROTHERAPY A bag of frozen peas diminishes local nerve pain when applied for 10 minutes. This may be alternated with a hot-water bottle wrapped in a towel and applied for 10 minutes. For dogs with CDRM or recovering from neural damage, swimming is ideal exercise. *See page 82.*

NUTRITIONAL THERAPIES Vitamin C may play an important role in treating spinal pain, possibly because it improves the quality of connective tissue. Vitamin C is also required for the synthesis of the neurotransmitters serotonin and epinephrine and for the manufacture of the body's own anti-inflammatory, cortisol. The B vitamins are important for nerve-cell functioning. Sources include pork, liver, milk, and brewer's yeast. Antioxidant vitamins, minerals such as magnesium, and fish oil may aid recovery after a neurological accident involving cell destruction. *See pages 86–87.*

HERBALISM For senility, a veterinary herbalist may suggest ginseng root, *Panax ginseng*, or myrrh resin, *Commiphora myrrha*. *Ginkgo biloba* is thought to boost blood flow to the brain and may delay the development of senile dementia. St. John's wort, *Hypericum perforatum*, is thought to have painkilling properties. Yarrow infusion, *Achillea millefolium*, is thought to improve circulation and lower blood pressure. *See pages 88–91.*

HOMEOPATHY *Aconite 6c* and *Hypericum 6c* are considered for neurological pain. *See pages 92–93.*

PHEROMONE THERAPY Pheromones distract a dog from pain and stimulate neural activity. *See page 100.*

ST. JOHN'S WORT

THE ENDOCRINE SYSTEM

HORMONES ARE CHEMICAL MESSENGERS produced in endocrine glands throughout the body. When a hormone has done what it needs to do, it stimulates a chemical response that travels back to the hormone-producing gland with instructions to turn off. If hormone production does not turn on or off properly, a variety of medical conditions develop, from the subtle to the life-threatening.

MULTIPLE PROBLEMS

Sometimes endocrine disorders can involve several glands, for example a combination of an underactive thyroid and an underactive adrenal gland (Schmidt's syndrome). Breeds that may suffer from "polyglandular endocrinopathy" include the Leonberger, Portuguese Water Dog, Nova Scotia, Duck Tolling Retriever, Bearded Collie, Old English Sheepdog, and Standard Poodle.

WHAT THE SYSTEM DOES

Every cell in the body has receptor sites for one or more hormones, which orchestrate all body processes. The pituitary gland produces one hormone that instructs the kidneys how much to concentrate urine, another that controls growth, and others that instruct other glands, the thyroids, adrenals, ovaries, or testes in their own hormone production.

Thyroid hormones influence growth, and energy production and consumption. The parathyroid glands are responsible for calcium metabolism. Adrenal glands produce cortisol and adrenalin. On the surface of the pancreas, cells produce insulin for sugar metabolism.

ENDOCRINE DISRUPTERS

Recently scientists have discovered that a variety of natural and synthetic substances can affect hormones. These so called "endocrine disrupters" are chemicals that mimic, block, or jam normal endocrine processes. Environmental contaminants such as PCBs (polychlorinated biphenyls) and dioxins are known endocrine disrupters. Dr. Frederick vom Saal from the University of Missouri has shown how the smallest doses of a plasticizer called bisphenol A, an estrogen disrupter widely used in food packaging, may do as much damage as large doses, while low to moderate doses are not damaging at all. Vom Saal's discovery suggests that standard toxicology tests may need to be repeated, this time using very small exposures during critical periods such as early pregnancy.

WHAT CAN GO WRONG

Growth hormone deficiency may cause a rare skin disorder, treated by growth hormone supplementation. Lack of pituitary antidiuretic hormone (ADH) causes *Diabetes insipidus,*

5. MESSAGE CANCELLED
Pituitary gland receives adrenal hormone and cuts output of adrenal-stimulating hormone.

4. ADRENAL GLAND ACTS
Adrenal gland receives message and releases (i) hormones raising dog's state of alert and (ii) hormone that will return to pituitary gland acknowledging receipt of original message.

KIDNEY

1. DANGER
Unfamiliar object seen and reported to brain. Triggers activity in hypothalamus (region of brain in charge of pituitary gland).

THE "MASTER GLAND"
The brain and the endocrine system work together. Brain information is passed from the hypothalamus to the pituitary or "master" gland, which controls all other endocrine activity.

2. PITUITARY GLAND TAKES COMMAND
Pituitary gland is activated and releases adrenal-gland stimulating hormone.

3. HORMONE IN TRANSIT
Pituitary hormone is carried round the body by the bloodstream.

indicated by copious drinking and urinating. Cushing's Disease is an overactivity of the adrenal gland; an affected dog may drink and urinate excessively, and show skin and coat changes. Addison's Disease, an under-diagnosed condition, is an underactive adrenal gland.

A dog with sugar diabetes (*Diabetes mellitus*) may become thirsty and fatigued, lose weight, and have recurrent infections, and suffer from eye, and circulation problems. Sugar diabetes is caused by a lack of the hormone insulin (Type 1 diabetes) or an inability of cells to use insulin properly (Type 2). Some vets think that Type 1 diabetes, the most common in dogs, is caused either by the immune system destroying insulin-producing cells or by excessive cortisol production. Diabetes occurs most often in fat females. Under stress, cortisol acts on fat cells, making them less sensitive to insulin. The most common hormonal problem found in dogs is underactive thyroid glands, usually caused by the immune system destroying the thyroid.

THYROID DISORDER AND BEHAVIOR

Dogs with thyroid disease may show unexpected aggression, submissiveness, shyness, fearfulness, passivity, excitability, sensitivity to noise, anxiety, irritability, compulsiveness, chewing, moodiness, lethargy,

DISEASE AND HEREDITY
Some breeds of dogs seem to be more susceptible to illness than others. Boxers, Boston Terriers, and Dachsunds have a higher incidence of overactive adrenal glands (Cushing's disease) while the Leonberger (left) has a high incidence of both underactive adrenals (Addison's disease) and underactive thyroids.

or apparent depression. If your dog has had a recent mood change, always consider the possibility of an endocrine disorder.

CONVENTIONAL TREATMENTS

Overweight diabetic dogs are fed a high-fiber diet, and insulin is given by injection. Underweight diabetics are fed a high-calorie diet, then are switched to a high-fiber diet. Thyroid supplement is given to hypothyroid dogs, or thyroid-suppressing medication to those with overactive thyroid. Overactive adrenal glands are pharmaceutically suppressed while underactive gland activity is supplemented with corticosteroid medications. Synthetic ADH controls the symptoms associated with *Diabetes insipidus*.

COMPLEMENTARY TREATMENTS

Complementary therapies often approach endocrine problems obliquely. Rather than stimulating or suppressing endocrine glands directly, they aim to encourage the immune system to react normally and stabilize hormonal function through diet, lifestyle changes, gentle exercise, and supplements.

HYDROTHERAPY Routine swimming or other daily controlled physical activities reduce insulin requirements and limit weight in diabetic dogs. *See page 82.*

NUTRITIONAL THERAPIES Vitamin B6 is important in the synthesis of most hormones. Naturopaths recommend kelp, rich in iodine, for hypothyroid dogs. Susan Wynn, a holistic veterinarian working at

Emory University's medical school, says that feeding kelp to dogs with thyroid disease may stimulate an already overstimulated immune system, making the condition worse. Thiamine may potentiate the effectiveness of thyroid hormone and is beneficial for dogs with underactive thyroids. Iron and zinc are important in regulating thyroid metabolism. So too is selenium. Holistic vets may recommend chromium supplementation (in brewer's yeast) for diabetic dogs. Recommended diets may include high-fiber, wholegrain, complex carbohydrates found in wholemeal bread, rice, pasta, oatmeal, and bran. Do not feed any foods containing sugar. Feed a variety of vegetables, including soybeans, garlic, and Brussels sprouts. *See pages 86-87.*

HERBALISM Veterinary herbalists suggest following orthodox therapy for diabetes, including diet management and insulin injections, but may recommend herbs said to reduce blood sugar. These include marsh mallow root, *Althaea officinalis*, coriander seed, *Coriandrum sativum*, and nettle, *Urtica dioica*. *See pages 90-91.*

MARSH MALLOW

EMOTIONS AND BEHAVIOR

ANXIETY ITSELF IS NOT A DISEASE. A dog may from time to time have what we think of as unpleasant emotions — anxiety, worry, or stress. These are a natural part of the body's defenses. They evolved to protect dogs from threats and dangers by influencing them towards more safety-oriented behavior. Chronic anxiety, however, is harmful to a dog's health and can lead to behavioral disorders.

CHECKLIST

If your dog develops stereotyped behavior in any of the following ways it may be suffering from a physical or an emotional disorder.

- Tail chasing (especially Bull Terriers).
- Flank sucking (especially Dobermanns).
- Self-mutilation.
- Circling.
- "Invisible fly" catching.
- Eating inedible objects such as pebbles.
- Pacing.
- Vacant staring.
- Rhythmic howling or whining.
- Air biting.

THE VALUE OF EMOTIONS

Anxiety is like a chemical first-aid kit. The cortex of the dog's brain thinks there is a stress, communicates through the limbic system with the rest of the brain, and triggers a cascade of chemical changes that affect the entire body. These short-acting chemical changes are vital for survival. The chemicals themselves are dissipated through activity, such as escaping from danger. In conditions of chronic stress, chemical changes are not broken down.

THE ROLE OF THE LIMBIC SYSTEM

The American neurologist Robert Sapolsky says, "People with chronic depressions are those whose cortex habitually whispers sad things to the rest of the brain." In people and dogs, the whispering takes place through neurotransmitter chemicals in the limbic system, the primitive area of the dog's brain

DO DOGS GRIEVE?

Of course they do. The level of anxiety a dog experiences when people or other animals they are close to die, or simply move away, varies with the individual dog's personality. When an animal death occurs, whenever possible let the survivor see and scent the body of the recently deceased animal. In the following weeks, give the survivor greater attention. Increased activity with others is almost always beneficial. In rare circumstances, sedative herbs may be required.

that orchestrates instincts and emotions. Serotonin is a neurotransmitter linked with mood enhancement. Decreased serotonin in people leads to depression. Some research with dogs suggests that serotonin is also related to confidence. Dogs that are pack leaders are likely to have good levels of serotonin while "underdogs" may produce less of this vital neurotransmitter.

In people, drugs can be used to affect brain chemicals such as serotonin, but non-physical therapies such as counseling affect them too. This is also true for dogs. Training, desensitizing, counter-conditioning, relaxation, and exercise can affect levels of neurotransmitters, behavior, and emotions.

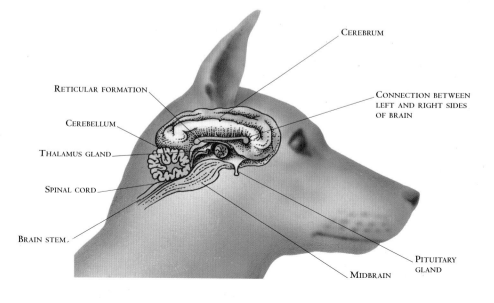

THE DOG'S BRAIN
While there are discrete regions of the brain, such as the cerebral cortex and cerebellum, all areas are connected by the amorphous "limbic system." Limbic function may vary slightly between breeds.

CEREBRUM

CONNECTION BETWEEN
LEFT AND RIGHT SIDES
OF BRAIN

RETICULAR FORMATION

CEREBELLUM

THALAMUS GLAND

SPINAL CORD

BRAIN STEM

PITUITARY
GLAND

MIDBRAIN

BEHAVIORAL PROBLEMS

Dogs develop rational fears, of veterinary clinics for example, but also irrational fears of non-threatening sights or sounds. Anxiety, part of natural "fight or flight," is normal in many circumstances but may become irrational, as when a dog becomes anxious if its owner leaves the room. This may lead to panic attacks or compulsive behavior in which a dog ritually performs a certain activity, such as pacing back and forth or licking itself. An inability to relax is an extreme form of canine anxiety. Depression is difficult to diagnose in dogs. It may manifest itself in lost appetite, clinging behavior, irritability, or lethargy.

CONVENTIONAL TREATMENTS

Fears, phobias, depression, and grieving have not been treated by conventional vets until recently. Sedatives such as acepromazine are often used to tranquilize anxious dogs, as are anti-anxiety drugs such as diazepam.

TAIL CHASING
Tail chasing may be caused by anal irritation. It may on the other hand be a form of compulsive disorder, most common in Bull Terriers and German Shepherds. There is a strong genetic component in this behavior problem, which responds moderately well to counter-conditioning training.

Increasingly, vets are treating these disorders with combinations of environment changes and desensitization or counter-conditioning treatment. Drugs affect such neurochemicals as serotonin: a typical drug may raise a dog's serotonin levels. This can have a profound and not always anticipated effect on the dog's behavior. Behavioral therapy is vital: drugs alone do not cure emotional problems.

COMPLEMENTARY TREATMENTS

Holistic vets consider diet to be central to treating emotional disorders. They recommend natural sources of the amino acid tryptophan, needed for the manufacture of serotonin and thought to help relieve depression. Mind-body therapies are commonly used, together with herbal and other treatments that reduce anxiety or increase concentration. Desensitizing a dog to its emotional problems, increased play, and improved relationships are integral to all complementary therapies.

THERAPEUTIC MASSAGE Massage, mental activity, and physical exercise are beneficial for reducing anxiety in dogs. Physical activity, in particular, has a "tranquilizing" effect on anxiety, reducing muscle tension and releasing mood-enhancing endorphins. *See pages 80-81.*

NUTRITIONAL THERAPIES Foods such as fish, chicken, and turkey are good sources of the amino acid tryptophan. Tryptophan is necessary for serotonin production. For

hyperactive dogs, avoid any food (or drugs) with the colorant tartrazine (E102), especially suspect for enhancing nervous hyperactivity. Ensure adequate levels of B vitamins and zinc to control nervousness. Some holistic vets believe there is a relationship between high-carbohydrate diets and nervous aggression. *See pages 86-87.*

HERBALISM For anxiety, herbal veterinarians may suggest sedative herbs such as valerian root, *Valeriana officinalis*, guelder rose bark, *Viburnum opulus*, lemon balm, *Melissa officinalis*, Roman chamomile flower, *Chamaemelum nobile*, and lettuce leaf, *Lactuca virosa*. Hops, *Humulus lupulus*, may also have a sedative effect, calming nervous individuals. St. John's wort, *Hypericum perforatum*, is three times better than placebo for treating mild depression in people according to a report in the British Medical Journal in 1996. It is used with increasing frequency as "background therapy" for anxious dogs undergoing desensitization training. *See pages 88-91.*

HOMEOPATHY *Ignatia* may be recommended for dogs that are pining for their owners or grieving. *Pulsatilla* may be given for dogs that, for emotional reasons, have become reclusive, while *Belladonna* is suggested for excitable individuals. *Nux vomica* is added for anxious dogs that suffer from car sickness. *See pages 92-93.*

BACH FLOWER REMEDIES Rescue Remedy is frequently recommended to reduce anxiety while visiting the vet's. *See page 95.*

AROMA THERAPY Citronella collars are used as an "aversion therapy" to stop dogs from barking excessively. Citronella is triggered and released from the collar when the dog barks. *See page 100.*

HOP STROBILE

EYE AND NOSE DISORDERS

NATURAL DEVELOPMENT

NATURAL TRAINING

NATURAL NUTRITION

NATURAL HEALTH CARE

HEALTH DISORDERS

THE DOG'S SENSES, which transfer information about the environment to the brain, are well maintained. The eyes are constantly washed clean with tears laden with defensive chemicals. The nose is flushed with a natural bacteria-killing discharge. If either of these intricate structures is harmed, whether by infection, foreign bodies, or metabolic disease, the resulting medical problems can be complex.

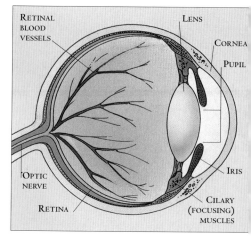

THE EYE
The cornea is prone to physical injuries, especially in flat-faced breeds like the Pekingese. Inflammation of the iris and ciliary body (uveitis) is common in most internal eye problems. Cataracts can form in the lens.

TASTE BUDS
When dissolved in saliva, food chemicals enter taste pores where they interact with tiny taste hairs that send taste messages to the brain. Dogs have far fewer taste buds on their tongues than we do, which is why they are not as selective as humans about what they eat.

HOW THE EYES WORK
The tough, transparent cornea protects the eye but allows light to pass through the pupil onto the lens, which focuses light onto the retina at the back. The amount of light entering is controlled by contracting or dilating muscles in the colored iris. The nictitating membrane acts as a windshield wiper, removing debris. This, and the rest of the conjunctival membrane lining the eyelids, is constantly bathed in a protective film of tears that ensures clear vision, prevents drying, and controls infection.

EYE PROBLEMS
Conjunctivitis is an inflammation of the eye's protective mucous membrane. It may involve redness, swelling, and a watery or mucoid discharge. If infected, the discharge becomes yellow-green. Allergic conjunctivitis and sneezing appears to be increasing in dogs. Corneal injuries may be caused by trauma or a lack of tears. A cataract develops when the transparent proteins

in the lens become cloudy. This may be hereditary or caused by diabetes, injury, or overuse of corticosteroids. The development of a cataract is irreversible. Glaucoma is a build-up of pressure inside the eye and may be a consequence of internal damage, such as inflammation of the muscles supporting the iris. Drainage channels are blocked.

Progressive retinal atrophy (PRA) is a hereditary deterioration of vision, leading to blindness, in which the blood vessels to the retina shrivel. Anatomical faults around the eyes are not uncommon in some breeds. A tear overflow occurs in flat-faced breeds such as the Pug. The natural drainage of tears into the nose becomes blocked because of the angle of the nasolacrimal duct in breeds such as small Poodles. Eye problems may also be a sign of metabolic disease.

HOW SMELL AND TASTE WORK
Smell is the least understood of the dog's senses. Scent chemicals activate at least eight different types of chemoreceptors in the nose, mouth, and throat, most with direct access to the brain's limbic system. The vomeronasal organ in the roof of the mouth "scents" sex-related pheromones. To get to

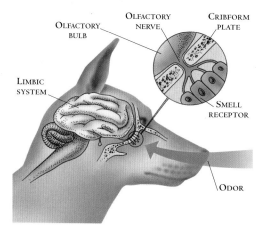

THE SENSE OF SMELL
Scent-sensitive cells lining the nasal cavity connect directly to the brain. These cells pick up scent chemicals, convert them to information, and feed this to the limbic system of the brain. Such behavioral responses as aggression, or euphoria, may be triggered.

the vomeronasal organ, these scents must be pumped up from the mouth to the scenting organ. Dogs do this so quickly it can only be seen on high-speed film. Scent is produced by body glands and is placed on objects and people. Unwittingly, by stroking our pets we anoint them with our own scent.

SCENTING AND TASTING PROBLEMS

A flat face reduces the nasal-lining surface area for scenting. Small nostrils impede natural scenting ability. Nasal infections or foreign bodies, such as inhaled grass seeds, cause inflammation and associated loss of scenting ability. Tumors or polyps can develop in the nasal chambers.

Some oral cavity infections, or eating hot food, can damage the dog's tongue and taste sensation. Tumors occasionally develop on the tongue. Smell may also be impaired in hypothyroidism and diabetes.

CONVENTIONAL TREATMENTS

Conjunctivitis is often treated with antibiotic, anti-inflammatory, or antihistamine drops, ointments, and lotions. Many eye conditions are hereditary. Registers exist in many countries to monitor these conditions and advise on the suitability of breeding. In

PRA RISK
Genetic testing is now used with Toy Poodles to see if breeding individuals are carriers of the recessive gene that causes progressive retinal atrophy (PRA).

Sweden, for example, all Cocker Spaniel, Labrador, Poodle, and Tibetan Spaniel breeding stock have their eyes examined for PRA. New genetic "fingerprint" tests have been developed for Toy and Miniature Poodles to see if breeding individuals are carriers of the recessive gene that causes PRA. If cataracts develop, always investigate for undiagnosed diabetes. When cataracts cause blindness and the retina still works, the defective lenses are surgically removed. In some circumstances it is possible to replace the faulty lens with a plastic one (this is less practical than in people.) Nasal infections are treated with oral antibiotics. When possible, foreign bodies, tumors, and polyps are surgically removed.

CHECKLIST

- Sight gradually deteriorates with age.

- Distance vision remains acute for longer than near vision.

- Age-related hardening or "sclerosis" of the lenses occurs in dogs over 10 years old.

- The naturally developing cloudiness of sclerosis is often mistaken for a cataract.

- The dog's most highly refined sense is that of smell.

- Metabolic diseases, as well as upper respiratory tract infections, interfere with scenting.

COMPLEMENTARY TREATMENTS

Many eye and nose problems are associated with allergy. Holistic vets will investigate diet and environment to determine causes of problems. They often recommend large quantities of natural antioxidants in the diet to assist both sight and scent. Some feel that systemic antibiotics may interfere with bacterial fermentation in scent glands that produce natural odors. This could lead to problems in recognition, leading to increased fighting.

NUTRITIONAL THERAPIES Naturopaths believe that cataracts result from free-radical damage and may recommend dietary supplementation with vitamin E and selenium to slow the development. Vitamin C and zinc are also suggested to slow

cataract formation. Antioxidants may be recommended to slow the development of PRA. Vitamin A is considered important for strengthening the layer of lutein and zeaxanthin in the retina. *See pages 86-87.*

HERBALISM To soothe sore, inflamed, "allergic" eyes or sore nostrils, a herbal vet may suggest bathing the eyes with a lightly boiled decoction of any of fennel seed, *Foeniculum vulgare*, eyebright, *Euphrasia officinalis*, or elder flower, *Sambucus nigra*. To control bacterial eye infections, decoctions of either fennel seed or Roman chamomile flower, *Chamaemelum nobile*, are used. Greater celandine, *Chelidonium majus*, infusions may also be used to bathe sore eyes. Codliver oil may be applied as a lubricant for dogs with

a crusty nose. Infusion of mullein, *Verbascum thapsis*, may be suggested to help clear blocked sinuses. **Warning:** don't smear decongestants on a dog's fur. Some may be toxic if swallowed. *See pages 88-91.*

HOMEOPATHY *Apis mel.* may be used to bathe sore eyelids, while *Arsen alb.* is used for watery, inflamed eyes. *Arnica* is recommended if there is any bruising around the eyes or nose. *See pages 92-93.*

ARNICA FLOWER

NATURAL DEVELOPMENT

NATURAL TRAINING

NATURAL NUTRITION

NATURAL HEALTH CARE

HEALTH DISORDERS

THE EARS

A DOG'S LONG EAR CANALS amplify sound. Their length, however, makes them prone to problems when foreign bodies such as grass seeds get in. The ears are lubricated by bacteria-killing wax that prevents infection within the external ear. If the balance of protective microorganisms in the ear is upset, infection by bacteria, yeasts, or other fungi may develop. The ears are prone to allergic sensitivity.

CHECKLIST
While congenital deafness occurs most frequently in white-coated dogs, it has also been reported in these breeds:

- Akita.
- Australian Heeler.
- Beagle.
- Border Collie.
- Boston Terrier.
- Cocker Spaniel.
- Dalmatian.
- Doberman.
- English Bulldog.
- Fox Terrier.
- Great Dane.
- Pyrenean Mountain Dog.
- Miniature Poodle.
- Old English Sheepdog.
- Papillon.
- Pointer.
- Rhodesian Ridgeback.
- Scottish Terrier.
- Sealyham.
- Shetland Sheepdog.
- West Highland White Terrier.

HOW THE EARS WORK
The ears are responsible for hearing and balance. The ear flaps and outer ear canals capture and convey sound to the middle and inner ears. Airwaves, striking the ear drums, trigger movements in tiny bones (ossicles), which in turn affect fluid-filled chambers in the inner ears. This stimulates nerve impulses that travel directly to the brain, where they are perceived as sounds. The Eustachian tubes, from the middle ears down to the throat, prevent too much pressure from building up in the middle ears. Deep within the ear are the organs of balance.

EAR PROBLEMS
Ear flaps are prone to frostbite in winter and sunburn in summer. They are also tasty targets for biting insects such as mosquitoes. Trauma to ear flaps is relatively common, usually as a result of fighting. If the ear bleeds inside, a blood blister or "hematoma"

THE IMPORTANCE OF TOUCH
The dog's fifth sense, touch, has receptors throughout the skin, even in the joints but especially in the paws. Some touch receptors are sensitive to pressure, others to vibration while still others are sensitive to temperature. Receptors in the joints respond to rotational movements. Each hair shaft has sensory fibers sensitive to slight movement. A dog's paws are less sensitive to cold than our hands or feet. This is why dogs can walk on ice and snow without unduly suffering. Even so, excessive exposure to extreme cold can lead to frostbite in your dog's feet.

develops. The external ear canal is like a warm, moist incubator. Infections caused by bacteria, yeast, or fungi are perhaps the most common of all canine problems. The affected ear may be red, uncomfortable, and often sensitive to touch. Depending upon the causes, there may be a brown, yellow, white, or even green discharge.

Infestations with ear mites are frequent, especially in young pups. Ear mites stimulate an over-production of defensive ear wax. Hair that grows down the ear canal, a condition that is common in breeds such as Schnauzers and West Highland White

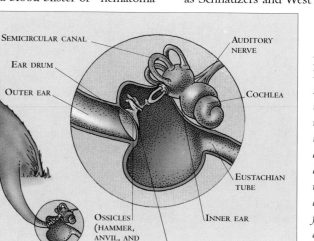

SEMICIRCULAR CANAL
AUDITORY NERVE
EAR FLAP
EAR DRUM
OUTER EAR
COCHLEA
OSSICLES (HAMMER, ANVIL, AND STIRRUP)
INNER EAR
MIDDLE EAR
EUSTACHIAN TUBE

HEARING AND BALANCE
Long ear canals protect the important structures of the middle and inner ear from injury, but are prone to accumulations of wax and debris. This changes the micro-environment, and creates ideal circumstances for infection. Infection can also reach the middle ear from the throat, via the Eustachian tube.

Terriers, accentuates problems. Middle- and inner-ear concerns are usually caused by spread of infection, either from the external ear, or up the Eustachian tube from the back of the throat. An affected dog shakes its head and may vomit, have a loss of balance, or appear uncoordinated.

Tumors and polyps may develop on the wall of a chronically inflamed ear canal. Deafness may be hereditary or acquired. Some drugs are known to damage hearing.

CONVENTIONAL TREATMENTS
Veterinarians generously use antibiotic, anti-inflammatory, and anti-parasitic ear drops and lotions to control external ear infections. Middle-ear infections are usually treated with oral antibiotics or decongestants. When balance is affected, anti-emetic drugs are used. Because of the ear's great depth, severe or chronic external ear disease may be treated by syringing the ear under sedation or general anaesthesia. Surgically opening the ear canal to remove one side of the funnel is a common treatment for chronic ear infections that lead to constricted canals. Hematomas, caused by excessive head shaking or injury, are surgically drained.

Deafness may be caused by nerve damage or problems in conduction of sound. Nerve deafness is hereditary in many breeds. Conductive deafness can be caused by age-related hardening of the bones in the middle ear (otosclerosis, not uncommon in elderly Retrievers), inflammation, foreign objects such as grass seeds, or copious wax. Vets often use Elizabethan collars to prevent a dog from scratching at an ear undergoing treatment or recovering from surgery.

A condition that affects a dog's balance on one side, called vestibular syndrome, is commonly mistaken for a stroke. Dogs that develop vestibular syndrome, usually elderly individuals, are treated with anti-nausea medication. They frequently recover their sense of balance over a period of weeks.

DO DOGS HAVE A SIXTH SENSE?
How do dogs seem to know you are about to come through the door? Do they have a homing instinct? Just as, inexplicably, some dogs recover from presumed fatal diseases, there are many unanswered mysteries in their behavior. Knowing you are about to come home can be explained by the circadian rhythm, the dog's genetically controlled biological clock. But how a dog finds its way home over territory it has never seen still remains a mystery.

NATURAL DEVELOPMENT
NATURAL TRAINING
NATURAL NUTRITION
NATURAL HEALTH CARE
HEALTH DISORDERS

COMPLEMENTARY TREATMENTS

Holistic vets emphasize the importance of preventative action. They recommend "non-allergenic" diets and good ear ventilation for lop-eared dog breeds. This may involve shaving the hair off the inside of the ear, and also placing balls of cotton in the ears before bathing to prevent moisture from entering the ears. After any hair has been removed from the ear, they may suggest instilling a mixture of vinegar and water into the ear in order to prevent bacteria from taking hold.

ACUPUNCTURE The nausea that is associated with vestibular syndrome and other conditions affecting balance, as well as car sickness, may be treated with appropriate acupuncture. *See pages 72-73.*

NUTRITIONAL THERAPIES Naturopathic vets feel that many ear problems are the result of immune disorders. They will ask about your dog's diet, checking for possible food intolerance. Vitamin D is often suggested as a supplement for dogs going deaf. Vitamin A is said to help the cochlea to function and may be recommended together with vitamin E. *See pages 86-87.*

HERBALISM Olive or almond oil may help to clear residual wax after an ear infection or infestation. Damage to the ear flap may be cleaned with witch hazel. For white dogs, prone to sunburn to their ear tips, aloe vera may be soothing. Marigold, *Calendula officinalis,* is used for cleaning inflamed ear canals. Ginger, *Zingiber officinale,* and *Ginkgo biloba* are said by some to reduce

deafness by improving circulation to the ear. Commercially produced herbal gels are available for controlling external ear canal conditions and infestations. *See pages 88-91.*

HOMEOPATHY *Arnica* is used when there is bruising to the ear flap. *Kali mur.* is used to alleviate pressure in the middle or inner ear. *Aconite 6c* and *Belladonna 6c* are both used for ear infections. *See pages 92-93.*

BACH FLOWER REMEDIES Rescue Remedy may calm dogs frightened by ear pain. *See page 95.*

ACONITE LEAF

INDEX

ACKNOWLEDGMENTS

Author's Acknowledgments

Researching and writing about evolutionary or "natural" veterinary care has been fascinating. And practical. It's satisfying to be able to incorporate new ideas into veterinary practice. Veterinary colleagues around the world, at universities, and in private practice contributed their observations and experience in using methods other than licensed pharmaceuticals or surgical interventions to prevent or contain a variety of medical conditions. My grateful thanks go to:

In Australia, Liz Frank and Clive Eger, Murdoch University, and Kersti Seksel; in Canada, Brenda Bonnett and Wendy Parker, University of Guelph; in England, Richard Allport, Ted Chandler, Christopher Day, Jill Hewson, Susanna Penman, Onno Wieringa, and the nutritionists Ivan Berger and Amanda Hawthorne; in France, Patrick Pageat; in Japan, Kiyoshi Kawase; in Norway, Jorunn Grondalen, Osqlo University; in Scotland, John Rohrbach, (who contributed his 30 years' clinical experience in herbal veterinary medicine); in the United States, Tony Buffington, Ohio State University, Karen Overall, University of Pennsylvania, Elizabeth Lund, University of Minnesota, Lisa Freeman, Tufts University, Neils Pedersen and Benjamin Hart, University of California, James Richards, Cornell University Feline Health Center, and Jean Dodds.

Thanks too, for their creativity and flair to the Dorling Kindersley group, all of whom I've worked with before and look forward to working with again: Tracie Lee Davis, Anna Benjamin, Edward Bunting, and Sonia Charbonnier, and to Tracy Morgan for her usual photographic excellence. Finally, I really appreciate how the staff at my veterinary clinic made sure I didn't feel guilty when I took time off to write. Special thanks to everyone at the clinic: Manda Hackett, Hester Small, Tina Leake, Ashley McManus, Jenny Berry, Bas Hagreis, Grant Petrie, and Simon Tai.

Bibliography

Canine and Feline Nutrition, Linda Case, Daniel P. Carey, & Diane A. Hirakawa, Mosby, St. Louis, 1995

The Encyclopedia of Complementary Medicine, Anne Woodham & Dr. David Peters, Dorling Kindersley, London, 1998

Evolution and Healing, The New Science of Darwinian Medicine, Randolph M. Nesse & George C. Williams, Weidenfeld & Nicolson, London, 199

The Handbook of Alternative and Complementary Medicine, Stephen Fulder, Oxford University Press, Oxford, 1996

The Handbook of Human Stress and Immunity, Editors, Ronald Glaser & Janice Kiecolt-Glaser, Academic Press, London, 1994

The Homeopathic Treatment of Small Animals, Christopher Day, C.W. Daniel Co. Ltd., Saffron Walden, 1992

Kirk's Current Veterinary Therapy, Editor, John D. Bonagura, W.B. Saunders, Philadelphia, USA, 1995

Molecules of Emotion, Why You Feel The Way You Feel, Candace Pert, Simon & Schuster, London, 1998

Myofascial Pain and Dysfunction, Janet Travell & David Simons, Williams & Wilkins, Baltimore, 1986

Textbook of Complementary and Alternative Veterinary Medicine, Editors, Alan Schoen & Susan Wynn, Mosby, London, 1998

Good general websites and starting points to other sites are:

Algy's Herb Page; AltVetMed; Animal Chiropractic and Holistic Healt Forum; Herbs Research Foundation; Martindale's Health Science Guide Virtual Library Animal Health; Virtual Library Veterinary Medicine.

Publisher's Acknowledgments

Photography: Tracy Morgan, Steve Gorton

Additional photography: Jane Burton, Peter Chadwick, Tim Ridley, David Ward

Artwork: Janos Marffy

Index: Margaret McCormack

Editorial assistance: Edward Bunting, Sharon Lucas

Thanks to the following practitioners: Margie Craib BSc BHSI MC MIPC; Tracy Crook MCSP SRP, Chartered Physiotherapist; Onno Wieringa BA Vet MB MRCVS lic Ac

Thanks to the following owners and their dogs: Debbie Anstead – *Keno*; Adele Bolkonsky – *Nigel and Oscar*; Brenda Bowgen – *Scindo and Flicka*; Judy Cooper – *Bruno and Misty*; Tracy Crook – *Sam*; Linda Marcham – *Culray Amberfine of Chapledown and Cinmarsh Chadley of Chapledown*; Onno Wieringa – *Belinda*

Picture Credits

The publisher would like to thank the following for their kind permission to reproduce their photographs:

a=above, c=center, b=below, l=left, r=right, t=top

Animal Photography: Sally-Anne Thompson 82 b, 100 bl; **Ardea London Ltd:** 17 b, 111 tr, Chris Martin Bahr 119 bl, J M Lambat 143 t, John Daniels 1 c, 2-3, 22-23, 24 bl; **Barnaby's Picture Library:** 11 tr, 85 bl; **BBC Natural History Unit:** Dietmar Nill 66 bl; **Bridgem Art Library:** London/New York *Men caring for hunting dogs* by Gaston Phebus, *Livre de la Chasse* (early 15th century), British Library, London, UK, 84 b; **British Chiropractic Association:** 78 tr; **Bruce Coleman Lt** Adriano Bacchella 104-105, 115 tr, Jane Burton 38-9, 55 tr, 133 t, Andrew J. Purcell 101 cr, Fritz Prenzel 118 b, Hans Reinhard 46 t, Jor and Petra Wegner 142 b; **Environmental Images:** John Morrison 40 b; **Frank Lane Picture Agency:** Mark Newman 4 r, 145 b; **Natural History Photographic Agency:** Gerard Lacz 97 bl, 113 tr, Yves Lancea 8-9, 86b, 160 b; **Oxford Scientific Films:** Deni Brown 143 b, Donald Specker 115 bl; **RSPCA:** Angela Hampton 36 tl, 99 br, E.A. Janes 109 t, Ken McKay 7-8, Colin Sedon 103 t **Science Photo Library:** Dr Kari Lounatma 87 tl, David Scharf 116 b, 117 t, 139 t; **Spectrum Colour Library:** G. Carlisle 61 t **The Stock Market:** D. Stoecklein 43 br; **Tony Stone Images:** Jim Simmen 70 b; **Telegraph Colour Library:** G. Randall 96 **TTeam & TTouch Training:** Mike Brinson br; Jack Parsons 77 b; **Warren Photograph** Jane Burton 12, 42 tr, 121 t, 157 t

-03)'97

3

x-9/10
P

06/14
35x-11/12
OP